COMMUNAL SOCIETIES IN AMERICA
AN AMS REPRINT SERIES

HISTORICAL SKETCHES OF WESTERN NEW YORK

.

AMS PRESS

NEW YORK

Yours truly
E D Vanderhoof

HISTORICAL SKETCHES OF WESTERN NEW YORK

THE SENECA INDIANS

PHELPS AND GORHAM PURCHASE

MORRIS RESERVE AND HOLLAND PURCHASE

MARY JEMISON

JEMIMA WILKINSON

JOSEPH SMITH, JR., AND MORMONISM

MORGAN AND ANTIMASONRY

THE FOX SISTERS AND ROCHESTER KNOCKINGS

BY

E. W. VANDERHOOF

I have here only made a collection of culled facts, and have brought nothing of my own but the thread that ties them together.

— MONTAIGNE.

MCMVII

PRINTED FOR PRIVATE DISTRIBUTION BY
THE MATTHEWS-NORTHRUP WORKS
BUFFALO, NEW YORK

The Library of Congress Cataloged the AMS Printing of this Title as Follows:

Vanderhoof, Elisha Woodward, 1832-
    Historical sketches of western New York. [1st. AMS ed.] New York, AMS Press [1972]
        viii, 232 p. illus. 22 cm.
        Reprint of the 1907 ed.
        CONTENTS.—The Seneca Indians.—Phelps and Gorham purchase.—Mary Jemison.—Jemima Wilkinson.—Joseph Smith, Jr., and Mormonism.—Morgan and Antimasonry.—The Fox sisters and Rochester knockings.

    1. Genesee region, N.Y. 2. Mormons and Mormonism. I. Title
    F127 G2 V18   1972
    ISBN 0-404-08476-1   71-134434

Reprinted from the edition of 1907, Buffalo
First AMS edition published in 1972
Manufactured in the United States of America

AMS PRESS INC.
NEW YORK, N.Y. 10003

CONTENTS

PREFACE

(Written in 1887)

I ONCE asked an old friend, whose income was ten times greater than any personal use to which he could devote it, why he speculated in stocks? His reply was that he did so in order to keep his mind active. Upon reflection, I saw there was sound philosophy as well as Yankee shrewdness in the old gentleman's answer. He did not wish the world to go by him, but was determined, so long as he lived in it, to be of it, to keep abreast of the times and in the swim, and he knew the best way to accomplish this was to dabble a little in Wall Street, for the stock exchanges of the world are mirrors which reflect every light and shadow upon their surfaces. He might have set down and hugged and reinvested his income, might have grown into a moldy nuisance, as most men do who have money only, and whose only resource is to talk about it; but he wisely preferred to take a hand in the enterprises going forward around him, and wear out rather than rust out.

Having given up business some years ago on account of ill health, and determining upon my recovery not again to take an active hand in the dizzy games that are played on the stock exchange and the board of trade, yet at the same time wishing, like my old friend, to keep my mind active, I determined to look into the early history of that section of the State where I was born and jot down such things as might be of interest to myself and possibly to others resident in the Genesee Country.

Although my memory goes back to the tales of my grandfathers, who were pioneers of the eighteenth century, I found myself lamentably ignorant of many important and prominent facts connected with our early history. Phelps and Gorham I had indeed heard of, but did not know that their purchase was made from the State of Massachusetts, and not from New York. Robert Morris was a familiar name in connection with Revolutionary history, but I was unaware that he had ever owned a rood of ground in this section.* The London Associates, Sir William Pulteney, William Hornby, and Patrick Colquhoun, I had never heard mentioned in connection with pioneer affairs. " The Holland Purchase " had a familiar sound in my ears, but of the details of that important transaction I knew nothing. Now, the fact that I was ignorant of local history would be of no consequence, and discreditable to me only provided means of ready information on the subject were at hand, and that a fair proportion of those around me possessed such information. But they do not, for the simple reason that no comprehensive history of Western New York is now in existence. Turner's volumes never had a general circulation and have long been out of print. It is doubtful whether one in five hundred of the present residents on the Massachusetts Pre-emption ever saw them. They are becoming rare books. Occasional copies are advertised for sale at three to five times their original cost. A dealer had my order more than three months before he was able to procure for me a copy of the " History of the Holland Purchase." " The Phelps and Gorham Purchase " is equally scarce.

Big and bad as those volumes are, devoted as they are to almost every subject except the one announced on the title-page, if they were in free circulation this history would not have been undertaken. For no one knows better than I that I do not possess a literary faculty or a good " style," and am not well equipped either by nature, study, or practice for the task I have set myself. But something needed to be done, and done promptly. Our early annals were fast slipping away from the minds and memories of men. The pioneer is no longer here to recount the story of struggle and privation. The ring of his axe and the crack of his rifle died away as the twilight began to gather round the declining years of the nineteenth century. Not one remains whose farm was " articled " to him by Phelps and Gorham, and probably none who remembers when William and James Wadsworth settled in the Genesee Valley. I found that the young men and women growing up about me, the generation that has come upon the stage since the outbreak of the Civil War, were, like myself, sadly deficient in their knowledge of our early history. They seemed to think that handsome, commodious farm houses, substantial, gaily-painted out-buildings, thriving towns, and busy, populous cities had always existed here. To correct

* Written at Clifton Springs.

such impressions, to tell the younger generation of Western New Yorkers that there may be now living a few men and women who were born before any white habitations existed west of Seneca Lake, that a century has hardly elapsed since this highly cultivated and populous region was an unbroken wilderness through which the Seneca Indians roamed at will, and to give them some notion of the resolute purpose, the patient toil, and the cheerfully-endured privations which, after the lapse of a century, have made that wilderness to blossom like the rose, is the object of this compilation. And now a word or two regarding it.

In the preface to his translation of the Iliad, Pope tells us that " Homer is universally allowed to have had the greatest Invention of any writer whatever. The praise of Judgment Virgil has justly contested with him, but his Invention remains yet unrivaled. Nor is it a wonder if he has ever been acknowledged the greatest of poets who most excelled in that which is the very foundation of poetry. It is the Invention that in different degrees distinguishes all great geniuses — the utmost stretch of human study, learning, and industry, which masters everything besides, can never attain to this. It furnishes Art with all her materials, and without it Judgment itself can at best but steal wisely, for Art is only like a prudent steward that lives on managing the riches of nature."

History affords little room for the exercise of Homer's wonderful faculty. It deals with a world of events and facts, and ceases to be valuable when it ceases to be veritable. Its dignity, its philosophy, and its lessons are worthless if not drawn from its truth. Invention has no place in its framework. Unless it be contemporaneous, it must to a great extent be based on preexisting records. The ratiocinations of the author, his comments, inferences, and conclusions may or may not be of value. A good narrator may be narrow, unfair, and partisan as a commentator. It is generally conceded that the most eloquent historian of our time was a prejudiced man.*

In this volume I have invented nothing. Those who read it must decide whether I have had the Judgment " to steal wisely."

The *Spectator* says: " A great book is a great evil. Were all books reduced to their quintessence many a bulky author would make his appearance in a penny paper." Bearing this in mind, I determined from the outset that my work must be limited to

---
* Macaulay.

giving an outline of the principal events in our pioneer annals. To have gone into details, to have attempted even a meagre sketch of the early history of localities and of the lives of those pioneers whose prominence might entitle them to mention, would have taken half a score of volumes rather than one. It is better to be incomplete than tedious, to set forth a few prominent facts which may fix themselves in the reader's mind, rather than present a vast mass of detail which he rejects at sight. The history of an adjoining county was carried on through two volumes of more than four hundred pages each, and left in an unfinished state on account of the ill health of its author. By shunning his voluminous error I hope to escape its consequences.

It has been my endeavor herein to avoid tediousness, elegant writing, and impersonal dignity. My work is too frank and amateurish for the editorial " we," hence it is composed in the first person. " We " is falling into desuetude even in newspaper work.

My compilation is put forth in the hope that it may be of value to my neighbors of the present and future generations, and while I do not expect from it either fame, profit, or applause, may I not comfort myself with the reflection that though

" The letters Cadmus gave "

have not been employed with literary skill, they have not been devoted to an unworthy purpose?

E. W. V.

Clifton Springs, New York, 1889.

RED JACKET

INTRODUCTION

THE SENECA INDIANS

As monumental bronze unchanged his look;
A soul that pity touched but never shook;
Trained from his tree-rocked cradle to his bier,
The fierce extremes of good and ill to brook
Impassive — fearing but the shame of fear —
A stoic of the woods — a man without a tear.
— CAMPBELL.

THE predecessors of the white man in the Genesee Country were the Seneca Indians. They were the most intelligent, numerous, and powerful of the six tribes which at the date of the Massachusetts cession (1786) formed the League of the Iroquois. These tribes or nations were the Mohawks, Oneidas, Onondagas, Cayugas, Senecas, and Tuscaroras, and occupied the central portion of the State of New York from the Hudson to Lake Erie, in the order indicated by their names. Originally the League consisted of but five nations; the Tuscaroras, a kindred and fugitive tribe from North Carolina, having been admitted as a sixth nation about 1715. They were to some extent wards of the original five, and were without sachems, or voice in league government. These tribes or nations were found in possession of the country indicated at the period of the earliest Dutch settlement (1609), beyond which we have only their traditions to guide us as to the locality of their previous occupation, or their origin.

The project of a league originated with the Onondagas, and tradition assigns the northern shore of Onondaga Lake as the place where the Iroquois sachems assembled to agree upon the terms of the compact by which they were to act as one people on all questions concerning their common welfare. The form of government adopted was based upon the family relation. The Indian name of the league, Ho-de-no-sau-nee, signifies a long house, and conveys the idea that its occupants live in one cabin and form one great family. The Senecas being more numerous

1

than any other two tribes combined were the hereditary door-keepers of the Long House, and were known as the first fire, the Mohawks, who kept the eastern door, being known as the fifth. Being the central fire, and for reasons of locality and conveni-ence, meetings of the league were held among the Onondagas, but the sachems and warriors of all the tribes were of equal rank, dignity, and voice in conducting the affairs of the confederacy. Their form of government was oligarchical — the rule of the few — and up to the time of the Revolutionary War unanimous consent of all the tribes was necessary before entering upon any enterprises not merely local in their nature. War, peace, league legislation, and the government of conquered and subject tribes required unanimity. In 1776, the Oneidas refused to join the other tribes in making war upon the Colonies, and remained true to a treaty in which all had joined, promising a strict neutrality between King George and his rebellious subjects.

Their laws were few and simple, and are perhaps a good illus-tration of the saying that the best government is that which governs least. Living in the hunter state they had no individual possessions — one Indian was as rich as another — and for this reason nine-tenths of the statutes that encumber the law books of civilized and enlightened nations were useless to these simple-minded, straightforward people.

The league was interwoven into one political family by a law which forbade the young warriors and maidens of the same tribe to intermarry. A Mohawk warrior might marry an Oneida maiden, and a Cayuga maiden might become the wife of a Seneca or Mohawk warrior, but young people of the same tribe were forbidden to enter the marriage state. By this simple means the tribes became consolidated into one great family, and the warriors and women of one tribe regarded all other tribes of the league as brothers and sisters, as much so as though they had been children of the same parents. The children followed the condition of the mother. If she was a Seneca or Onondaga woman they were Senecas or Onondagas. These unschooled bar-barians were wise enough to know that parentage on one side is indisputable. All titles and rights of property were con-fined to the female line; as the mothers of the warriors, the squaws were held to be the rightful custodians and owners of the homes of the tribes. It was a knowledge of this fact that enabled Mr. Thomas Morris, at the Treaty of Big Tree (Geneseo) in 1797, to reopen the council fires, and obtain from the women a cession which the eloquence of Red Jacket had persuaded the assembled sachems, chiefs, and warriors of the Seneca Nation to refuse to grant.

The Iroquois can hardly be said to have had a criminal code. Witchcraft, in which they believed, was punishable with death. Any person could take the life of another when discovered in the act of witchcraft. Adultery was punished by whipping, but women only were presumed to be offenders. To the honor of the Indian, it must be said, that he was loyal and true in his domestic relations. The murderer was given over to the private vengeance of the friends and relatives of the victim. They could take his life whenever they found him, even after a lapse of years. The crime, however, might be condoned, and strenuous efforts were often made to that end. A belt of white wampum sent by the offender to the family of the slain was the usual mode of effecting a condonation. If not sent in due time, or if the family of the deceased refused to receive it, and remained implacable, their vengeance was permitted to take its course. To the credit of the North American natives, it may be said that previous to the introduction of ardent spirits among them crimes of any sort were of very rare occurrence.

The women of the Iroquois arranged all marriages, the father never troubling himself about such matters. To have done so would have been to interfere with female rights, and these he respected as inflexibly as he guarded his own. Marriages of affection were unknown. The warrior and maiden, who, perhaps met for the first time at their betrothal, accepted one another as gifts from their respective mothers. There was little sociability between the sexes. The men went forth together on the war path, the chase, or for amusement, leaving the women to the companionship of their own sex. Sociability between male and female as it is understood in polite society had no existence amongst the Iroquois. The Indian was an aboriginal aristocrat. He was a sportsman, a warrior, and an hereditary legislator. Beyond the fashioning of his implements for hunting, fishing, and warfare, no labor soiled his hands. When not upon the war-path or beside the council fire, " he loved to lie a-basking in the sun," and did it. The squaws did all the drudgery out of doors and in.

Strictly speaking, the Iroquois had no religious faith. They believed in the Great and Evil Spirits, who, according to their legend, were of finite origin, being brothers born at the same birth, and destined to an endless existence. They ascribed to each creative power, believing that the Great Spirit created them, and everything that was good, useful, and beautiful; while the Evil Spirit originated monsters, reptiles, and noxious plants. Unlike some other tribes, the Iroquois did not believe heaven to be a " happy hunting ground." In their future abode they deemed subsistence to be no longer a necessity, and held that the spontaneous luxuries existing around them there were for the gratification of taste and not for the support of life. One of the most beautiful of all their simple beliefs was that there is a road from heaven to every man's door. But if the plain, honest truth must be told, it compels the statement that nearly all attempts to civilize and Christianize the red men have been failures. " He asks no angels' wing, no seraphs' fire." He is almost absolutely without hope, fear, or affection. Hatred and revenge are his only prominent passions. The warrior who would caress his wife or children would be thought unfit for the sterner duties of life. The Indian is, and will forever be, " The Stoic of the woods, the man without a tear."

Contact between white and red men has always been fatal to the latter. The Iroquois reached the summit of their power nearly two centuries ago. Previous to that period, their confederacy was feared from the Hudson to the Mississippi. They gave laws to the conquered nations from the ice-bound region of Canada to the Carolinas. Their war whoop echoed along the great lakes of the North, and struck terror to the hearts of their dusky enemies on the banks of the Ohio, the Tennessee, and the Roanoke. They dominated numerous subjugated tribes, some of whom they denationalized and deprived of tribal relations, and others they practically extirpated. They were alternately courted by the French, the Dutch, and the English, who recognized and feared their prowess and power. The pale faces, however, introduced among them two potent agents of destruction, ardent spirits and firearms, and at the period of the Genesee Settlement their decadence had already made marked progress. But they were still numerous and powerful enough to be dangerous neighbors. Told, as they constantly were by British emissaries from Canada, that the King of England and not General Washington was their Great Father, that the war would soon be resumed and rebellious subjects brought under subjection and punishment, that their only safety lay in loyalty and adhesion to the good King, and that duty and safety alike should prompt them to aid him in regaining dominion over his colonies, it is little wonder that the pioneer regarded his tawny neighbors with suspicion and dread, and felt that he took his life in his hand in making his home in a region over which they had so long held sway, and to which they sincerely believed they had a prescriptive and inalienable right. Fortunately for the colonists, the distinguished, eloquent, and sagacious sachem of the Senecas — Red Jacket — was a man of peace, and was not easily misled or cajoled by the mendacious tales of Canadian emissaries and their Indian confederates, amongst the latter of whom Joseph Brandt was active and conspicuous. To the firm but conciliatory hand of Governor George Clinton; to the wise, prudent, and patient counsels of the Indian Commissioners — Colonel Timothy Pickering and General Israel Chapin; and to the thorough knowledge of the native character possessed by Captain Parrish and Horatio Jones, who acted as Indian agents and interpreters, as well as to the pacific disposition of the leading sachems of the Seneca Nation, must be ascribed the fact that the pioneers and their red brethren lived upon terms of amity, and that the scenes of Cherry Valley and Wyoming were not re-enacted in the Genesee Country a century ago.

PHELPS AND GORHAM PURCHASE.

ONE hundred years ago that portion of the State of New York, lying west of Seneca Lake, known to eastern people as the " Genesee Country," was an unbroken wilderness.* Smoke from the cabin of no white settler arose in that vast region, now the garden of the State. Red Jacket, Cornplanter, and Farmer's Brother reigned supreme. Let it not be understood that no white man had set foot there. More than two centuries ago — away back in the days of Champlain and Jacques Cartier — two French Jesuit fathers, Brebauf and Chauminot, crossed Lake Ontario and came upon the Niagara River near Lewiston. With the proselyting zeal so characteristic of their faith, they came as the bearers of good tidings to the Neuter Nation and surrounding tribes. The fathers found the stoics of the woods indifferent to their teachings, but though unable to convert the heathen of the western world they were not converted by them, as happened in later times to Lord Bishop Colenso in the eastern hemsiphere. Occasional Indian traders had camped for a time upon the Niagara and Genesee rivers, but they were itinerants, who came and went, and had no permanent abiding place.

The expedition of De Nonville in 1687, consisting of French regular troops and allies from a number of tribes of western Indians, penetrated as far as the present village of Victor, Ontario County, where an indecisive battle was fought with the Senecas. The French retired to Niagara, establishing a fort there. Their Indian allies were greatly incensed at this move and at the barren results of an expedition from which so much had been expected. They had " come with banner, brand, and bow," hoping to assist in the extermination of their implacable enemies, the Iroquois, and spoke in contemptuous terms of the retrograde move of the French commander.

The little army of Sullivan had destroyed the cornfields and burnt the villages of the hostile natives in this region during

---

* Written in 1887.

the war of the Revolution, but having accomplished this, it returned to the white settlements from whence it came.

The title to the lands of the Genesee Country had long been in dispute. Possessed of little knowledge of the geography of the newly discovered world, English, French, and Dutch kings had given conflicting grants to various parties, had granted the same lands to different colonists, had granted lands they never possessed, and the extent of which they little dreamed. James I., in 1620, gave to Massachusetts all the lands within certain north and south lines extending from the Atlantic to the Pacific oceans. He probably had as little notion of the number of miles between the two coasts as he had of the distance to the dog-star, perhaps not so much. New York claimed under both Dutch and English grants. The expulsion of the French from Canada had obliterated any title from that source, and as Massachusetts had the prior lien she got the Genesee Country. By a treaty ratified in 1786, New York State ceded to her the pre-emption right or fee to all the lands west of a certain line running north and south between the northern boundary of the State of Pennsylvania and Lake Ontario. It was agreed that the starting point of this line should be on the Pennsylvania boundary, eighty-two miles west of the northeasterly corner of that State. Running thence due north to Lake Ontario, its course was very nearly through the middle of Seneca Lake.

Soon after Massachusetts became possessed by deed of cession from New York of the pre-emption right to these lands, certain adventurous spirits, who had made a little money by assisting the Colonies during the Revolutionary struggle as commissaries and quartermasters, began negotiations for their purchase of this region. In saying this there is no thought of casting the slightest shadow upon the fair fame of the men who nobly risked their means in order that the continental army might be kept in the field. They staked not their money only, but their lives; and at best their profits were in continental currency, or the scrip of the different Colonies whose troops they helped to feed and clothe. That we succeeded in the struggle inaugurated at Lexington and Concord was largely due to the patriotic merchant and banker of Philadelphia, Robert Morris, and to his coadjutors, amongst whom may be mentioned Oliver Phelps, Jeremiah Wadsworth, and John B. Church. But for the cheering words and more cheering assistance of Mr. Morris the army of Washington

could not have been moved south to undertake the seige of York-
town.   His money and credit furnished shoes, clothing, and
subsistence — the indomitable will was never lacking — and the
patriot army moved on to the final victory of the war.

Amongst those who early foresaw the inducements which the
Genesee Country held out to enterprise was Oliver Phelps.   Mr.
Phelps was a native of Windsor, Connecticut, but had removed
to Massachusetts about the time that resistance to king and
parliament began in that colony.   With nothing to recommend
him but ardent patriotism and uncommon energy of character,
he was — though but a youth — enrolled as a member of the
famous Committee of Safety, and was among the men of New
England who assembled at Lexington.   When the troops of his
native State were organized and sent into the field, he accepted
an appointment in the commissary department, the duties of
which he continued to discharge until the close of the war.
He then became a resident of Suffield, Mass., and held in succession the offices of member of assembly, senator, and member of
the governor's council.   Business relations brought Mr. Phelps
and Mr. Morris often together, and the latter confirmed the
former in the favorable opinion he had formed of the fertility
and value of the lands in Western New York.   Major Adam
Hoops, of Philadelphia, who had been the aid of Gen. Sullivan in
his expedition to that region, was an acquaintance of Mr. Morris
and had given that gentleman a glowing account of its beauty and
adaptability to every purpose of agricultural and manufacturing
enterprise.   It needed but these confirmatory opinions to induce
Mr. Phelps to become interested in the purchase from Massachusetts of its pre-emption title or fee of these lands.   Applying to
the Legislature for that purpose, on behalf of himself and several
of his friends in Berkshire, he found that they had been anticipated by Nathaniel Gorham, a merchant of Boston, residing in
Charlestown.   To prevent a conflict of interests, Mr. Phelps
had a conference with Mr. Gorham, at which they agreed that
the latter should join the former and his associates, and that the
proposal of purchase by Mr. Gorham should be considered as
made for their common interest.   Nothing, however, was
accomplished at the session of 1787.

Before the Legislature convened in 1788 a new syndicate had
been formed, which included all who desired to become interested,
of which Messrs. Phelps and Gorham were constituted the repre-

sentatives. They made proposals for all the lands embraced in the cession to Massachusetts, which were accepted; the stipulated consideration being £300,000 Massachusetts currency, or £290,000 of said currency and £2,000 in specie. It will be seen that the paper was worth in coin about twenty per cent. of its face value. The public obligations of the State, then much depressed, were also made receivable at par in payment. As there were more than 6,000,000 acres conveyed, the purchase price was about five cents per acre. Imagine the corner lots of Rochester and Buffalo being sold at such a figure, and that within the memory of a few people still living!

Mr. Phelps knew very well that it would be impossible to induce emigration to the new country if the Indians were hostile, so his next step was to placate them, and by purchase and treaty to extinguish their title. He accordingly met them in July, 1788, at a council fire which they had lighted at Buffalo Creek. A full delegation of Seneca chiefs was present, but they had come determined on making the Genesee River the western boundary of their cession, and stoutly resisted any attempt to secure the whole of their hunting grounds. They, however, generously granted to Mr. Phelps a mill lot west of the river, twelve miles by twenty-four in extent. One hundred acres of this tract were given to Ebenezer Allen upon condition that he would erect a grist and sawmill thereon. It is said that the red man, when he saw the mills, was rather astonished that they should require so large a lot. The best business portion of the city of Rochester stands on the hundred acres given to Allen. The whole Indian cession constituted what is known as the Phelps and Gorham purchase, and was bounded as follows: " Beginning on the northern line of Pennsylvania due south of the point of land made by the confluence of the Genesee River and Canaseraga Creek; thence north on said line to the said point or confluence; thence northwardly along the waters of the Genesee River to a point two miles north of Canawagus Village; thence running due west twelve miles; thence running northwardly so as to be twelve miles distant from the western boundary of said river to the shores of Lake Ontario." It will be seen that these bounds include the celebrated " mill lot." The eastern boundary of the purchase was the pre-emption line before described.* The con-

* The territory in this tract now comprises the counties of Ontario, Steuben, Yates, and Livingston; a part of Wayne, most of Monroe, a small part of Genesee, and about one half of Allegany.

sideration paid to the Indians was $5,000 in silver and an annuity of $500 forever. A dispute as to the cash payment subsequently arose; Red Jacket and Farmer's Brother claiming that it was to be ten instead of five thousand dollars. Butler, Brant, and Lee, as referees, and the Rev. Mr. Kirkland and others who were present at the treaty, sustained Mr. Phelps, and made depositions that the Indians were mistaken as to the amount of the purchase money. A new pecuniary difficulty was soon after encountered by the purchasers. They had stipulated to make payment in the public paper of Massachusetts, issued during the Revolution, which they expected to obtain at about fifty per cent. of its face value. The meeting of the Constitutional Convention in Philadelphia in 1787, and the prospect of success in forming a federal union which would take over the debts of the States, had caused an advance in this paper to nearly par. Being unable to extinguish the Indian title over the whole of their purchase, they petitioned the Legislature to be released from that portion of it which the Indians refused to cede. Their petition was granted ; the more readily, perhaps, as a purchaser for the remaining lands came forward in the person of Mr. Robert Morris.

Being now ready to give title, Messrs. Phelps and Gorham and their associates bent their energies toward promoting settlement. Pamphlets and handbills descriptive of their lands were scattered throughout the older settled States, and offers to exchange them for improved property at the East were attractively presented. A house and lot in an eastern village would be taken on even terms for hundreds of acres in the new region, enabling men of narrow means and growing families, but possessed of energy and enterprise, to provide homes in the future for themselves and their descendants. Who was the first white settler, who sowed the first wheat, who erected the first frame house, or the first grist mill, are moot questions. There is a conflict of statement on these points, a correct settlement of which would be of little value could it be reached.

The early settlers came largely from New England. Better material could nowhere have been found. General Micah Brooks thus speaks of them: " I saw the scattered pioneers in their lonely cabins, cheered by the hope and promise of a generous reward for the privations they then suffered. I found in most localities that three-fourths of the heads of families had been soldiers of the Revolution. These pioneers inherited the principles and firmness of their fathers. They subdued the forest, built houses and temples for worship, and were well skilled in all the practical duties of life. In seven or eight years from the first entrance of a settler, a number of towns in Ontario County were furnished with well-chosen public libraries."

It required much energy and force of character to undertake the journey to the Genesee Country a hundred years ago. West of Fort Stanwix there was only an Indian trail. Blazed trees, the stars of heaven, and the courses of the rivers and creeks guided the settlers to their new homes. On sleds in winter, and in bateaux and canoes in summer; on foot and on horseback, at all seasons, the toilsome journey was made. Shelter at night was found under tents, if the emigrants were fortunate enough to be provided with them; if not, their boats and carts and the trees of the forest were their only protection. There was not a human habitation, except an occasional wigwam, between Fort Stanwix and Kanandasaga, now the handsome and flourishing town of Geneva. It may here be stated that the Genesee Country was settled before the central part of the State, and that Ontario was the first county west of Montgomery a hundred years ago. It was also, until 1796, the only county in the State west of Seneca Lake.* Conflict of title prevented settlement on the " Military Tract " until about the beginning of the century. This tract included the present counties of Onondaga, Cayuga, Seneca, Cortland, and Tompkins.

A mere sketch of the journey from the East of two pioneers will suffice to show the difficulties of the way, and may be taken as the common experience of all emigrants previous to the year 1800. William and James Wadsworth were natives of Durham, Connecticut; the sons of John N. Wadsworth, whose possessions made him what was called in those days " well to do."   James was graduated from Yale College in 1787, and passed the two succeeding winters in Montreal, teaching school. While yet undetermined as to his career, he paid a visit to his kinsman, Colonel Jeremiah Wadsworth, of Hartford, for the purpose of seeking advice of the older man as to his pursuits in life. Colonel Wadsworth, as has been stated, was active in aiding with his means to keep the army of Washington in the field, and, in connection with John B.

---

* Counties were formed from Ontario as follows : Steuben, 1796; Genesee, 1802; Allegany, 1806; Niagara, 1808; Chautauqua, 1808; Cattaraugus, 1808; Monroe, 1821; Erie, 1821; Livingston, 1821; Wayne, 1823; Yates, 1823; Orleans, 1824; Wyoming, 1841; Schuyler, 1854.

Church, had charge of the subsistence of the French fleet under Rochambeau. He had early made the acquaintance of Washington, who paid frequent visits to his hospitable mansion to consult with its owner and other prominent men of the Revolution as to the means of carrying on the war. Mrs. Sigourney thus describes these meetings:

" Round thy plenteous board have met,
　　Rochambeau and La Fayette,
　　With Columbia's mightier son,
　　Great and glorious Washington;
　　Here, with kindred minds, they plann'd
　　Rescue for an infant land."

Having been intimately associated with Robert Morris and Oliver Phelps in business and financial measures connected with the prosecution of the war, and being possessed of ample means, it was natural that Colonel Wadsworth should become interested with those gentlemen in the land speculations that followed the establishment of peace and independence. It is probable that he was an original member of the syndicate acting through Messrs. Phelps and Gorham — it is certain that he became a very large owner of lands on the Genesee River previous to 1790. The result of Mr. James Wadsworth's visit to Hartford was a proposal on the part of his kinsman to sell to him on advantageous terms a portion of his tract at Big Tree (Geneseo), and the offer of an agency that would embrace the care and sale of his remaining lands. James was then but twenty-two years old, and pioneer life had probably never been included in any horoscope of the future he had cast for himself. His brother William was six years his senior. He was a man of splendid physique, of boundless energy and force of character, and was every way fitted to encounter and overcome the perils and hardships of frontier life. In later years, his superb courage was shown upon the battlefield of Queenston, where he dared every danger in seconding the operations of General Scott; repeatedly interposing to shield the person of the general, whose tall form attracted unwelcome attention from the enemy's marksmen. Upon consultation, the brothers jointly accepted the proposition made them, and in the spring of 1790 began preparations for their migration to the then far-off wilderness. James started by way of the Sound and the Hudson, and continued up the Mohawk and the Oswego and Clyde rivers to the head of navigation on Canandaigua outlet. William, the practical working partner, started across country with an ox team and cart, two or three hired men, and a colored woman, a favorite servant of the family. Before reaching Utica he had added a small stock of cattle bought along the Mohawk, thus early giving evidence of taste for a pursuit which continues to the present time to be a favorite one with the family — the breeding and rearing of cattle. His progress was slow. Logs had to be cut and moved out of his track, and small streams and sloughs had to be rudely spanned and causewayed. There was no ferry at Cayuga Lake, but Indian canoes were lashed together, a deck was made of poles, and the party succeeded in crossing. The average progress between Fort Stanwix and Canandaigua was about twelve miles per day. Arrived at Big Tree, the question of shelter was soon settled, Mr. William Wadsworth hewing logs by daylight and by torchlight with so much energy that in a few days a rude cabin lifted its humble roof-tree in the wilderness — the first abode of a family well and widely known from that day to this.

If such was the pioneer experience of men of energy and culture, with ample means at command, what must have been the toil and privation of the poorer class, which constituted the great majority of settlers in the new region ? It has been stated by one of these, that not one in ten of his fellow pioneers could have paid in cash for a hundred acres of land, even at twenty-five cents per acre. A new comer with five hundred dollars in money was a much rarer bird then than millionaires are to-day in the Genesee Country.

Fortunately, it did not take money to buy land, else settlement would have been very tardy. It could be readily obtained on long credit and easy terms, and there was little else for sale. Merchandise, even in the way of articles of utility and necessity, was as scarce as coin. One or two instances will illustrate this: As late as 1805, Peleg Redfield — father of Hon. Heman J. Redfield, and of Lewis Redfield, the pioneer printer of Syracuse — wishing to erect a frame dwelling on his farm near Clifton Springs, put fifty bushels of wheat on an ox sled and drove with it to Utica for the purpose of exchanging it for builders' hardware. He sold his wheat for $1.68 per bushel, and bought window glass, putty, nails, and other material, of a merchant by the name of Watts Sherman. The bill was made out and receipted by Henry B. Gibson, who was a clerk for Mr. Sherman.

It is hardly necessary to state that Watts Sherman, Esq., of the banking firm of Duncan, Sherman & Co., was a son of the Utica merchant, and that Henry B. Gibson became the well-known railroad man and banker of Canandaigua. If articles of utility and necessity were thus difficult to get, luxuries were still more difficult to obtain. In the recollections of Ebenezer Spear, of Palmyra, he says: " The wife of Webb Harwood, our predecessor in the wilderness, being in delicate health, her indulgent husband determined to procure some wine for her, as a tonic. At his request, I went to Canandaigua but found none, to Geneva and found none, to Utica and was equally unsuccessful, and continuing to Schenectady procured six quarts of Charles Kane. I was fourteen days making the journey on foot, carried my provisions in a knapsack, and slept under a roof but four out of thirteen nights." If the wine was as good as the act of procuring it was neighborly, it certainly " needed no bush." The frontiersman often carried his grist more than thirty miles to mill upon his back, and frequently walked the same distance to procure the use of a grindstone. Bread to strengthen his arm, and a sharp axe to clear up a portion of " the continuous woods," were among the prime necessities of his existence. His table would have been scanty had not " Nature, a mother kind alike to all," come bounteously to his succor. Game abounded. The woods were full of it. The larger streams swarmed with salmon, and the smaller ones with trout. Next to his axe, his rod and gun were the most important articles of a pioneer's outfit. Skill in their use was a part of his birth and training. If he did not have venison, partridge, or a mess of trout for supper, it was the fault of demand, not that of supply. His life was hard enough even with these now-a-day luxuries to furnish forth his meal.

Let us look for a moment at the pioneer and his surroundings after he had arrived at the spot selected for his future home. The perils and privations of the journey are past and civilization is behind him. Alone, it may be, or perhaps assisted by one or more stout-hearted, ruddy boys, he swings the axe which clears away the space, and furnishes the material for an humble dwelling. The logs, cut and notched, but not hewed, are at last ready to be laid one upon another until a height sufficient for the roof poles to begin is reached. A kind-hearted, helpful neighbor or two, coming perhaps for miles through the forest, assist at

the raising. If it is too late for the bark to peel, a roof of pine
and hemlock boughs has to suffice until another spring, when
bark can be obtained. Such things as boards, shingles, nails,
and window-glass are not within any possible reach. Openings
are, of course, left for doors and windows, and blankets are
hung at these until something more substantial can be substituted. If a bank of clay is within reasonable distance it
is mixed with water, and the crevices between the logs are plas-
tered with it. A rude chimney built of sticks and laid up with
similar mortar is, perhaps, constructed — if not, a hole in the
roof at one end of the cabin permits the ingress of light and the
egress of smoke and heat. Questions of ventilation and plumb-
ing are not discussed, but in many of these humble structures
men and women lived in health and vigor a score of years beyond the scriptural allotment. The furniture, brought from the
East, is primitive and scanty, and only in rare instances included
such smart articles as a clock or bureau. But necessity, the
grandmother of genius, and mother of invention (Pope and Gold-
smith both tell us that invention is the parent of genius), im-
provised a mechanic out of a rude farmer, who, without tools except an axe and a jackknife, soon fills the house with shelves,
bunks, benches, tables, brooms, and other useful, though not
ornamental, articles of furniture. This sort of work was performed at night or on rainy days. From early dawn to twilight
the axe of the pioneer rang through the surrounding forest,
until a space had been cleared upon which to make a vegetable
garden, plant corn, and sow wheat. Black bass, trout, and
salmon are very nice articles of food, and so are partridges,
woodcock, venison, and squirrel, but man cannot live by these
alone, any more than he can by bread; but by a judicious blending
of these edibles ought to, and in the case of many of the pioneers
did, suffice for daily food until beef, mutton, pork, chickens,
eggs, and the more ordinary vegetables could be added to the
daily fare. Wheat and corn, when obtained, were pounded in a
stump mill, and, unsifted and unbolted, were made into homely
loaves by the pioneer mother. The stump mill was made by
cutting down a maple, hickory, or other hardwood tree, and hol-
lowing out the top of the stump until it would contain a small
quantity of grain, which was pounded with a stone until it was
sufficiently soft to be made into cakes or loaves. But having
always the same thing would make appetite revolt at Big-

non, Voisin, or Delmonico's; and so it is small wonder that the pioneer has been, as before stated, known to carry his grist upon his back thirty miles to mill in order to get bolted flour. While land was cheap and abundant, labor was scarce and dear. For one day's work a laboring man could buy two acres of as good land as ever the sun shone upon. Fifty cents per acre was the current price of the soil, but to clear that acre, log and burn it, and fit it for the plow, from fifteen to twenty dollars was the going rate. And when the descendant of the pioneer asks why his great-grandfather did not buy more land at the extremely low figures asked for it, the cost of fitting it for production will be a sufficient answer.

Food and shelter being provided, the next prime necessity of the early settler was clothing. Flax could be raised in abundance, but it was almost impossible to keep sheep, on account of those howling marauders, the wolves. So ravenous were they that they would enter the settler's dwelling in the day time and seize any fresh meat within their reach. A loaded rifle was usually kept in readiness for their reception. The pioneer mother was the Sartor Resartus of her time. By shifting and turning, by patch upon patch, she managed to make the stock of clothing brought in by her family last them until further supplies could be obtained from the East, or sufficient wool could be raised to meet the home demand. Let us glance for a moment at some of the duties performed by the good woman at the head of the pioneer's home. She did all the labors indoors, and was often the gardener, as well as cook, washer, ironer, and baker. She carded, spun, wove, dyed, cut, and made the entire clothing of her family, both male and female. She was tailoress, milliner, dressmaker, chambermaid, and waitress. Her woolens and linens for bedding and the table were made by her own hand. She pickled, preserved, and dried the fruits and vegetables of the season for the family table. And, in addition to all this, she bore to her husband a numerous household of vigorous, healthful children, whom she reared in honor and obedience without assistance, until the elders had attained a sufficient age to share in the care of their younger brothers and sisters. This seems to the present generation to have been a hard life, and so it was, but many of the pioneer mothers lived to receive the love and homage of their great-great-grandchildren.

" Who can find a virtuous woman! for her price is far above

rubies. She seeketh wool, and flax, and worketh willingly with her hands. She riseth while it is yet night, and giveth meat to her household, and a portion to her maidens. Her children arise up and call her blessed, her husband also, and he praiseth her. Many daughters have done virtuously, but thou excellest them all." The wise man seems to have had the pioneer mothers in his mind when he wrote his inspired description. From homes presided over by such mothers men went forth to attain distinction in every line of human endeavor. The Genesee Country furnished to the Government six of its cabinet officers — four of whom were residents of Canandaigua — and a President in the person of the Hon. Millard Fillmore. It furnished to the bench and bar the names of Geo. P. Barker, James Mullett, Henry Wells, Vincent Matthews, John Young, George Hosmer, Wm. M. Hawley, Jno. C. Spencer, Herman J. Redfield, Evert Vanburen, Dudley Marvin, Albert H. Tracy, Daniel Conger, Samuel Fitzhugh, Mark H. Sibley, Alvah Worden, Jared Wilson, Solomon K. Haven, Wm. G. Angel, Martin Grover, Washington Hunt, and Charles James Folger. A much longer list of representatives of the other learned professions might be named, and then the half would not be told.

Messrs. Phelps and Gorham and their associates dealt in principalities larger than half those in the old world, upon the business principle of "a nimble sixpence." They had hardly completed the survey of their domain into townships and ranges, when they sold it to Mr. Robert Morris. A considerable part of it had already found owners, and this, in addition to reservations made, constituted more than one-half of the original tract. The amount conveyed to Mr. Morris was about one million, two hundred thousand acres. The price paid was thirty thousand pounds, New York currency. The associates had thus cleared a handsome sum in cash, and more than a million acres of land on their purchase from Massachusetts — a fair profit on a business transaction in those days. When the pre-emption line as originally run was corrected by transit instruments, the land bought by Mr. Morris overran about one hundred and twenty thousand acres; but as the deed read "more or less," no account was taken of this trifle, which is worth to-day, at the moderate price of fifty dollars per acre, nearly six millions of dollars.

The conveyance to Mr. Morris had hardly been completed

when he placed his lands on sale in London through William Temple Franklin, a kinsman of Dr. Benjamin Franklin, offering them at a handsome advance. They were quickly sold for seventy-five thousand pounds sterling to the "London Associates," who, so far as is known, comprised but three gentlemen, Sir William Pulteney, William Hornby, and Patrick Colquhoun. It has been thought that Sir William Pitt, who was intimate with these gentlemen and encouraged their enterprise, had an interest with them, but there is no evidence upon which to base the surmise. The associates were men of distinction and ability.

The original Pulteney was a statesman and plutocrat of the reigns of George I. and George II., who in the early part of his career was a member of Sir Robert Walpole's government, and one of that minister's most powerful coadjutors, but having quarreled with his chief he became as strenuous in opposition as he had been in support. Macaulay says: "Walpole might have averted the tremendous conflict in which he passed the latter years of his administration, and in which he was at length vanquished. The opposition which overthrew him was an opposition created by his own policy, by his own insatiable love of power.

"In the very act of forming his ministry he turned one of the ablest and most attached of his supporters into a deadly enemy. Pulteney had strong public and private claims to a high situation in the new arrangement. His fortune was immense. His private character was respectable. He had acquired official experience in an important post, and was a distinguished speaker. He had been — through all changes of fortune — a consistent Whig. When his party was split into two sections, Pulteney had resigned a valuable place and had followed the fortunes of Walpole. Yet when Walpole returned to power Pulteney was not invited to take office.

"An angry discussion took place between the friends. The minister offered a peerage. It was impossible for Pulteney not to discern the motive of such an offer. He indignantly refused to accept it. For some time he continued to brood over his wrongs and to watch for an opportunity of revenge. As soon as a favorable conjuncture arrived he joined the minority, and became the greatest leader of Opposition that the House of Commons had ever seen." *

---

* Review of Thackeray's Life of Chatham.

In another Review,* Macaulay tells us what Akenside expected from the fall of the tyrant Walpole and the elevation of Pulteney:

"See private life by wisest arts reclaimed,
    See ardent youth to noblest manners fram'd."

"It was to be Pulteney's business to abolish faro and masquerades, to stint the young Duke of Marlborough to a bottle of brandy a day; and to prevail on Lady Vane to be content with three lovers at a time." Researches in English history do not enable us to say whether Pulteney succeeded in these laudable undertakings or not. The great rivals were at length "kicked up-stairs into obscurity;" Walpole as the Earl of Orford and Pulteney as the Earl of Bath. When they met in the upper house Walpole extended his hand to his old opponent, saying: "Here we are, my lord; the two most insignificant fellows in England." **

The Earl of Bath left no heirs of his body, and his fortune succeeded to his first cousin, Frances, only daughter of Daniel Pulteney, who became the wife of Sir William Johnstone, who thus acquired the great Pulteney property. With her estates he took her name, becoming known as Sir William Pulteney. He died in 1805, one of the richest subjects in the British Empire, leaving his immense fortune, including his American property, to his only child and heiress, Henrietta Laura Pulteney, who was created Countess of Bath. The town of Bath in Steuben County was named for her. A town in Monroe County bears her first name, Henrietta.

Lady Bath died in 1808, leaving no children and no will of real estate. Her lands in America descended to her cousin and heir-at-law, Sir John Lowther Johnstone. Dying in 1811, the latter left his American estate to trustees for the benefit of his eldest son and heir, George Frederick Johnstone, who was born in 1810, married in 1840, and died in May, 1841, leaving his widow enciente. She gave birth to twin sons, Frederick and George Kemper Johnstone. Coming into the world a few minutes before his younger brother, the title and estates devolved upon Sir Frederick. He is the well-known sporting baronet, whose colt, Friars Balsam, was first favorite for the Two Thou-

---

* Walpole's letters to Horace Mann.

** Chesterfield says that Pulteney "shrunk into insignificancy and an earldom."

sand Guineas and Derby in 1888, and whose defeat and the cause which led to it are among the turf sensations of that period.   Upon examination, after being beaten for the Guineas, it was found that the horse's jaw was ulcerated, the result of a fracture.   No explanation of this remarkable state of affairs could be given by anyone connected with the stable.   It is supposed that Sir Frederick won " a pot of money " over Hermit's Derby, when the Marquis of Hastings was ruined.   He was the only outsider who had the tip from Mr. Chaplin and Captain Machell.

William Hornby had been Governor of Bombay in the days of Warren Hastings, and had returned to London with the fortune of a nabob.   Patrick Colquhoun was eminent as a statesman and philanthropist, had been Sheriff of Middlesex, and representative in Parliament of the aristocratic Westminster district.*   A marble tablet erected to his memory by William Wood, Esq., recording a few of the principal events of his useful life, occupied for many years a niche in the front wall of the Congregational Church in Canandaigua; but iconoclastic hands have defaced it, and substituted another inscription on the same stone.   A trustee of the church said of this, that there seemed to be no impropriety in removing it, as Mr. Colquhoun had never been a member of their organization, and, so far as he knew, had never been in Canandaigua or in any way interested in that section. Yet he was associated with all the Whig statesmen who advocated in Parliament the cause of the Colonies, and denounced the coercive measures of the king and his ministers.   Burke, Fox, Pitt, and Sheridan were among his intimates.   The trustee was not bound to know these facts, but being an old resident he might have known that Mr. Colquhoun was one of three men who at one time owned a million and a quarter acres of land surrounding in every direction the church which for a time bore a tablet to his memory.   The interest of each of the associates in the purchase was as follows: Sir William Pulteney nine-twelfths, William Hornby two-twelfths, and Patrick Colquhoun one-twelfth.

The associates promptly appointed Charles Williamson their attorney and agent to promote settlement and sale, open roads, and make other improvements upon their property.   To facili-

* Mr. Colquhoun was the author of a work on statistics, and " The Police of the Metropolis."

tate business Mr. Williamson become a naturalized citizen, and title was taken in his name. He was the friend and associate of his principals, a man whose intelligence and culture had been rounded by travel, and was possessed of signal ability and force of character. He was, however, dashing and impulsive, and was imbued with the singular error that commercial towns and villages can be built up in advance of a rural population to sustain them. But for the hundreds of thousands of farmers in the Northwest, there would be no Chicago; and New York would be an unimportant town were it not the main tributary through which the production and consumption of more than sixty millions of people flow.

Mr. Williamson also seemed to be unaware of the fact that a large city generally grows up near the mouth of some navigable stream draining a fertile country; hence he ignored Rochester and its water power, and bent his energies toward establishing a commercial emporium on Sodus Bay. But though the location reminded him of the Bay of Naples, the town and the commerce failed to materialize. His travels, however, enabled him to give names to the handsome villages of Geneva and Lyons. The first was changed from Kanadasaga because Seneca Lake reminded him of Lake Leman, and the second took its name because the confluence of Ganargwa Creek and the Canandaigua outlet recalled to his mind the Rhone and the Saone. But leaving moods and sentiment aside, there is little doubt that his energy and dash, seconded by the abundant means of his London principals, forwarded settlement on their purchase by more than half a score of years. In 1800 his account stood as follows: Receipts, $147,-974.83; payments, $1,374,470.10. To make this look better there was on hand an immense tract of unsold land, mills, hotels, and other town property, and a very large amount outstanding against lands sold. Credit is to some extent due him for the enhanced value of the estate under his administration. His principals had bought it for about thirty-five cents per acre; he left it when selling at from $1.50 to $4.

Although Mr. Williamson was a citizen and a taxpayer, and twice represented Ontario County in the Legislature, he was never thoroughly Americanized, and returned to Scotland in 1803. He had early retained Aaron Burr as counsel, and during his attendance upon legislative duties in Albany, business and social relations made them close companions; and in whatever project

Burr had at the South, Williamson would probably have taken a conspicuous part had the scheme not been so promptly nipped in the bud.

Mr. Williamson reconveyed the property to his principals as follows: To William Hornby and Patrick Colquhoun by deed bearing date December 13, 1800, and to Sir William Pulteney by deed dated March 5, 1801. The London Associates also owned lands on the military tract, and in the counties of Albany, Montgomery, and Herkimer. There is no doubt that the extravagant management of Mr. Williamson greatly disappointed his principals, and there is the best authority for saying that Sir William Pulteney seriously contemplated abandoning his interests in the Genesee Country, but was dissuaded from doing so by Williamson's successor in the agency, Colonel Robert Troup. The estate was divided at this period, the affairs of Messrs. Hornby and Colquhoun passing into the hands of John Johnstone, Esq., while Colonel Troup, as already stated, assumed the management of the Pulteney property. Colonel Troup's successor was Joseph Fellows, of Geneva. The clerks in the Geneva office were successively Thomas Goundry, George Goundry, William Van Wort, David H. Vance, Wm. Young, and Jno. Wride. Agents at Bath have been James Reese, Samuel L. Haight, Dugald Cameron, William McKay, and Benj. F. Young, the latter gentleman being in charge at the present time.

Upon the death of Mr. Johnstone in 1806, Mr. John Greig succeeded to the agency of the Hornby and Colquhoun estate, a position which he held for more than half a century. Few men were better or more favorably known in Western New York than Mr. Greig. A native of Scotland, he came to Canandaigua in 1800, and was among the foremost of a conspicuous galaxy of names that made the handsome town famous during the first sixty years of its history.

Mr. Greig was succeeded by his chief clerk, William Jeffrey. Upon the decease of the latter, the management of the estate passed into the hands of Walter Heard, long an associate clerk under Mr. Greig's agency. The affairs of the estate, so far as realty was concerned, were closed by Mr. Heard about fifteen years ago, but the heirs of Messrs. Hornby and Colquhoun still have investments here in personalty. As early as 1850, Mr. Greig began to invest a part of the surplus receipts of his principals in the railroads that now form the New York Central, and the estates of Messrs. Hornby and Colquhoun were considerable holders of that stock when it was doubled by Commodore Vanderbilt.

In 1791, soon after completing his sale to the London Associates, Mr. Morris bought from Massachusetts her remaining lands in Western New York, which included all that portion of the State west of the Genesee River except the mill lot. This was the tract Messrs. Phelps and Gorham were released from taking in consequence of being unable to extinguish the native title, and contained more than 4,000,000 acres. Reserving 700,000 acres lying along the westerly bank of the Genesee, he sold the remainder in 1792 or 1793 to Herman LeRoy, William Bayard, Gerrit Boon, John Linklaen, and Matthew Clarkson; acting as agents for an association of Amsterdam merchants and bankers, known as the Holland Company. Possibly a few New Yorkers are still living who remember the famous mercantile house of LeRoy, Bayard & McEvers. In his terms of sale Mr. Morris guaranteed the extinguishment of the native title. This was a thing easy to stipulate but hard to accomplish, and it was not until 1797 that he succeeded in bringing the Indians to terms. In that year a council fire was lighted at Big Tree, which was attended by commissioners on the part of the United States, the State of Massachusetts, and the Holland Company. Thomas Morris and Charles Williamson represented Robert Morris. The then unfinished residence of William and James Wadsworth was used for the accommodation of those directly connected with the negotiations. The proceedings were tedious, and at one time threatened to become abortive; but, by much skill, patience, and diplomacy on the part of Mr. Thomas Morris, a successful conclusion was reached, and what is known as the Morris Treaty became an accomplished fact.

The money consideration paid to the Indians was one hundred thousand dollars. President Adams directed that it should be invested in the stock of the United States Bank. This fund has not been traced beyond its original disposition, but it is likely that the red man's money went with the white man's, in the crash that caused the suspension of the bank. The Indians made numerous reservations of land, twelve in all, amounting to about three hundred and fifty square miles. The largest of these were at Buffalo Creek, Tonawanda Creek, Cattaraugus Creek, and Allegheny River.

As soon as surveys were made, the lands of the Holland Company were opened for settlement; but little progress was made previous to 1800.

Real estate speculation has not been confined to any country or age. Its existence antedates Los Angeles and Kansas City. Probably at no time has it been conducted upon a more gigantic scale, so far as area is concerned, than during a number of years succeeding the close of the Revolutionary struggle. The inevitable collapse came and carried with it Mr. Robert Morris. The half million acres which he had reserved along the banks of the Genesee, representing a part of his profit on the Massachusetts purchase, and fondly looked upon as a princely domain for himself and his descendants, was parcelled out to preferred creditors, among whom was John B. Church. This gentleman was of English birth, but while yet a young man had emigrated to Boston, where he conducted for a number of years, and with great success, the business of an underwriter. Espousing with zeal the cause of the Colonies, he became engaged with Jeremiah Wadsworth in the commissary department, and before the close of the war had made the acquaintance of General Philip Schuyler — similarly engaged in supplying the northern division of the army — whose daughter he married. In 1785, Mr. Church removed with his family to London, and resided there and at a country seat near Windsor Castle until 1797, when he returned to New York. The physician of King George the Third attended his family, and imparted to Mr. Church in confidence — long before it became generally known — the fact of the mental aberration of that monarch, the development of which he did not hesitate to attribute to the loss of the American Colonies.

During his residence abroad Mr. Church was returned to Parliament from Wendover, became a favorite of Pitt and Fox, and adhered to the latter gentleman when it was derisively said of him that " he and his party could drive to the House of Commons in a hackney coach."

General Alexander Hamilton, the conspicuous statesman, publicist, and financier of the Revolutionary period, married a daughter of General Schuyler and was a brother-in-law of Mr. Church. Acting as that gentleman's agent during his residence abroad, he loaned to Robert Morris $80,000, taking as security a mortgage on Morris Square, Philadelphia, but subsequently transferred the lien to 100,000 acres of land on the Morris Reserve, in what is now Allegany County. In consequence of Mr. Morris's pecuniary troubles, this tract was sold in 1800, by Roger Sprague, sheriff of Ontario County, and was bought in by Philip Church for his father. There were at the time but three white settlers in all that region. Careful training, as we have seen in the case of James Wadsworth, seems specially to fit a man for becoming the patroon of new settlements. Judge Philip Church, as he afterward became, was educated in Paris and at Eton, and studied law with his uncle, Alexander Hamilton. With advantages and connections such as fall to the lot of few men, he threw them aside for the life of a pioneer and patroon on the tract of which his father had become owner. In 1803 he erected at Belvidere on the Genesee River a frame house which for years was the only one in that section. Here he resided during more than half a century. It is said that, being an athlete in his younger days, he selected the location for his residence by climbing tall trees on the hills overlooking the river and valley. Settlement was slow in his locality, and it was not until the boatman's horn on the Genesee Canal and the screech of the locomotive on the Erie Railway resounded in that portion of the southern tier that his splendid patrimony attracted the attention of purchasers.*

Besides the hundred thousand acres foreclosed by J. B. Church, other creditors of Mr. Morris received allotments as follows: Sterritt & Harrison, of Philadelphia, 175,000 acres; Willing & Francis, 37,000 acres; the State of Connecticut and Sir William Pulteney, 100,000 acres, and LeRoy, Bayard & McEvers, 87,000 acres. It would exceed any reasonable limits to trace the subdivision and settlement of these tracts, and of the lands of the Holland Company.

Not even a sketch can be given of the pioneers on the Phelps and Gorham purchase, but portraits of some of the more prominent of them adorn the walls of the Court House in Canandaigua, and we may step in and look at their intelligent, resolute, honest faces. Here are Peter B. Porter and General Vincent Matthews, who appeared for the defense in the first jury trial held west of Herkimer County. Nathaniel W. Howell, who appeared for the prosecution; Augustus Porter, an early surveyor for Mr. Phelps and on the Holland Purchase;

* See Turner's History of the Phelps and Gorham purchase.

Moses Atwater, the first physician; and General Chapin and Jasper Parrish, the first Indian agents. (Mrs. Barlow, Mrs. Meagher, and Mrs. Crawford, of New York, are granddaughters of Captain Parrish.) There, too, are Nathaniel Rochester and Judge Fitzhugh, natives of Virginia and Maryland, and pioneers in the southern portion of Steuben and Livingston counties. These two, in connection with Charles Carroll, bought in 1802 the hundred-acre lot on which a portion of Rochester City stands, but made no move toward an improvement of that property until nearly ten years later. A member of Jefferson's cabinet is here, in the person of Gideon Granger. Here are the portraits of the gentlemen of whom some account has already been given — Oliver Phelps, Micah Brooks, William and James Wadsworth, Philip Church, and John Greig. And here is the foremost pioneer of them all, the famous sachem and orator of the Senecas — Red Jacket. He appeared for the defense in the first trial of a capital crime held in Ontario County, and saved the life of his dusky client. Mr. Greig, who as district attorney appeared for the prosecution, said of him, " I am but a reed compared to this mighty monarch of the forest." And here, too, are some of the later representatives of that aristocratic and brilliant society which made the little town famous at the bar, in the halls of legislation, and in the cabinet, during the first half of the century. They are Ambrose and John C. Spencer, Francis Granger, Mark Hopkins Sibley, Alvah Worden, Dudley Marvin, and Jared Wilson. And here, as law students, growing up amongst the giants of those days, are Stephen A. Douglas, Secretary Folger, and Senator Lapham.

The American mind is eminently practical. Our people soon tire of details and ask for results. The Californian wants to know " how the thing panned out? " and the Western man says " how did it materialize? " and the Eastern citizen inquires " whether the balance was on the right side of the ledger? " Applied to operations in lands in the Genesee Country the answer to these questions may be summed up in a general statement that the results to individual speculators in these lands were, in the main, disastrous. Very few of this class made and kept any money. Of the settlers on the Phelps and Gorham purchase the Wadsworths are almost the sole exception to this statement. They still own thousands of acres, parceled out in improved and fertile farms, and are adding to, rather than diminishing, their holdings. Col. Church still has a fine estate in Allegany County, on the Morris Reserve. Aside from these, there are very few land owners anywhere in the Genesee region whose holdings amount to so much as a thousand acres. Small farms, occupied and tilled by the owners, are the rule, and tracts of more than five hundred acres of improved land, in one body and under one control, are the exception. This is as it should be. When the head of a family becomes a proprietor of the soil, and especially when, as Pope says, he ".breathes his native air, on his own ground," he has gone far toward laying on a firm basis the foundation of good citizenship. Probably nowhere in this country is there a more intelligent, independent, and thrifty body of men than the farmers of Western New York.

Dumas says the philosophy of life is summed up in three words — "wait and hope." But very few Americans have the patience to wait or the faith that hopes on and ever. Sanguine, daring, and venturesome in the unfolding and early development of their schemes, they seldom have the courage to sit down and see them fructify. As agent and owner, James Wadsworth had as much to do with the settlement and growth of the region which he made his home as anyone connected with its history. Besides his own affairs and those of his kinsmen, he acted as agent for Phelps and Gorham, the Holland Company, Sir William Pulteney, Lady Bath, and others, and as early as 1796 had visited Europe for the purpose of interesting capitalists abroad in the lands of the Genesee Country. After a long and active acquaintance with the subject, his experience is thus expressed in a letter to a friend, he says: "It is slow realizing from new lands. I will never advise another friend to invest in them. Men generally have not the requisite patience for speculating in them."

Yet the increase in the value of the property in this section, in the last hundred years, suggests the tales of Aladdin. It was bought in 1788 for $300,000. Its assessed value in 1886 was $469,981,238 — its actual value, real and personal, to-day, is doubtless more than $600,000,000. It is often asserted that the advance in real estate is not equal to the accretion of money at compound interest. While this assertion may hold good if carried over a period of several hundred years, yet the original purchase price agreed to be paid by Phelps and Gorham to the State of Massachusetts for all the lands west of the pre-emption line would not, if compounded and doubled every ten years, be equal to one-half the value of the realty and personalty at the present time.

The London Associates realized a fair return on their American investment. With true British tenacity, they clung to their lands until the steadily-increasing tide of emigration and settlement made them valuable. A very small proportion of their sales were made for cash. Long credits were the almost universal rule, but they were quite satisfied with the legal rate of interest on bond and mortgage, and it may be set down to their credit that settlers on their tract showing any disposition to clear and improve farms were never pushed either for the interest or principal of their indebtedness.

It was the completion of the Erie Canal, however, that gave the great and lasting impetus to the Genesee region. Previous to that event, there was hardly any feasible outlet for produce. Mr. Williamson's scheme of a water route by way of Lake Ontario to Europe and New York came to naught, and Sodus Bay remains up to the present time a resort for the disciples of Isaak Walton in summer, and a bleak, boisterous, ice-locked place in winter. Navigation to Philadelphia and Baltimore by way of the creeks and rivers of the southern tier emptying into the Susquehanna was tedious, toilsome, and dangerous, and practicable only during a few weeks of high water in the spring. " Clinton's Ditch " was the " open sesame " to the treasures of Western New York. It quadrupled the value of every acre of land on the Massachusetts pre-emption. If ever any man deserved a monument to perpetuate his name and memory, Dewitt Clinton deserves one at the hands of the farmers of the Genesee region. Before the canal was finished there was, much of the time, absolutely no market for the farmer's crops and stock. Merchants often refused to take the finest quality of wheat in barter for store goods. There were many seasons when it could not be exchanged upon any terms for even tobacco and whiskey. The following items will show the expense of wagon haulage in early days and the prohibitory nature of that mode of transportation. It cost $18 to take a common wagon load from Geneva to Le Roy. The cost of hauling a load of goods from Albany to Gansons on the Holland Purchase was $120. Only when produce fetched a very high price, as it did in exceptional seasons, could it stand this mode of getting to market. A pioneer farmer says:

" In 1808 I took wheat to Canandaigua; there was no price and no sale for it there; no exchanging it for store trade. I removed it to Geneva, at a cost of 12½ cents per bushel, and paid a debt I owed there for a barrel of whiskey; the wheat netting me 12½ cents per bushel, or one gallon of whiskey for six bushels of wheat. The first cash market was at Charlotte; price 31 cents per bushel." In the same year Mr. Wadsworth writes to Colonel Troup: " It is a fact that farmers have been compelled to sell their wheat in some instances for eighteen pence per bushel, to pay taxes." In another letter he says: " The situation of the inhabitants in this part of the country has been really distressing; a farmer might have 1,000 bushels of wheat in his barn and yet not be able to buy a pound of tea." In still another letter, speaking of the scarcity of money, he says, " You would be surprised to know the rate that farmers with granaries full of wheat are paying for a little money to meet their taxes." There was, though, enough variation in the price of that product to suit the veriest Chicago or Cincinnati cornerer of to-day. Only two years previous, in 1806, wheat sold at $2.50 per bushel, and at various later periods brought high prices — selling in the cold season of 1816 as high as $3. The canal, when finished, gave a steady and reliable market for products of every sort, and " cash for wheat " met the eye thereafter on more than one signboard in every market town in the Genesee Country.

Although settlement on the lands of the Holland Company was about ten years later than on the Phelps and Gorham purchase, it did not progress very rapidly, owing to the fact that they were farther from market than the region east of the Genesee River. The company offered in 1821 to assign and turn over to anyone desiring to assume its position at that time its property of every nature and description and all its receipts to date, upon reimbursement of its original investment with interest at the rate of four per cent. per annum, and one year later offered to some well-known capitalists all its unsold lands at four shillings per acre. Neither of these offers was accepted. The company held the property until after the completion of the canal, and then realized a fair profit on its purchase.

Robert Morris died in New Jersey in 1806. Although at one time undoubtedly the richest man in the country — his estate being estimated at seven or eight millions, and his note-of-hand passing current like bank issues — he left no property. During the last years of his life, himself and wife were supported by an annuity of $1,500, granted her for life by the Holland Company, in consideration of her releasing her right of dower in the lands of the Holland Purchase.

Oliver Phelps died in Canandaigua, in 1809, a poor man. Hardly a rood was left to his family of the princely domain that he at one time might have possessed unincumbered. Like his associate, Mr. Morris, his early success in the Genesee Country led to his downfall. Elated with his good fortune there, and elected to Congress, he became smitten with the mania for speculating in wild lands, which began about 1795-96, and made rash ventures in almost every part of the country. The American Land Company and the Georgia Land Company were among the schemes with which he was connected. He became a large borrower at home and abroad. Pay day came and with it came ruin. His tombstone in Canandaigua bears this mournful inscription: "Enterprise, Industry, and Temperance cannot always secure success, but the fruits of those virtues will be felt by society."

A few words of local reminiscence will complete the sketch of the Phelps and Gorham purchase. The first sale made by them was of Township No. 11, Range 3, which then included both Farmington and Manchester. The latter town was set off in 1822. Up to that date the whole was known as Farmington. The purchasers were Nathan Comstock, Abraham Lapham, Nathan Herendeen, Doctor Daniel Brown, Nathan Aldrich, and others. Those named became settlers on the purchase. Mr. Comstock, his two sons, and Robert Hathaway arrived in 1789, made a clearing, built a cabin, and sowed wheat. John Decker Robinson and Nathaniel Sanborn were the first arrivals in the town of Phelps — coming in with Oliver Phelps in 1789. Mr. Sanborn had charge of a drove of cattle intended for beef to be distributed to the Indians, at the treaty which it was supposed would be held at Canandaigua. As soon as land sales commenced, Mr. Robinson bought lot No. 14, Township 11, Range 1, located at what was then known as East Vienna. In payment he erected for Phelps and Gorham — partly of logs and partly framed — a building in Canandaigua which was used as a land office and residence by the pioneer land agent, Mr. Walker. Mr. Robinson's son Harry was the first white male child born in the town.

Jonathan Oaks erected a large framed public house at Oaks Corners in 1794. It was the second framed tavern house west of Geneva, and was regarded as a wonder in those days, and its enterprising owner was thought to be far in advance of the times. As early as 1816, the lessees of this stand were Joel and Levi Thayer, who afterwards became residents of Buffalo. They established at Oaks — some little time before the enterprising projector of Jerome Park and Sheepshead Bay was born — the long celebrated race course which for many years attracted annual gatherings of turfmen from Long Island, New Jersey, and the South. It was for a number of years under the management of Colonel Elias Cost, a native of Maryland, who settled at Oaks in 1800, and brought with him a taste for the sports of the section from which he emigrated. After the death of his first wife, who was a daughter of Captain Shekels, Colonel Cost married the widow of Thaddeus Oaks and was for fourteen years the landlord of the old Oaks stand.

The first merchant in the town of Phelps was John R. Green, an Englishman, who opened a store at Oaks Corners. Leman Hotchkiss and David McNeil were the first merchants in the village of Phelps, then known as Vienna. Mr. McNeil was the first postmaster there, being appointed in 1804. He held the position until his death in 1841. Thirty-seven years in one office furnishes to the powers that be, and that are to be, a good lesson in civil service reform, and a good text from which to write a homily on rotation in office.

Captain Jacob Cost settled on what is now known as the Sanitarium Farm, near Clifton Springs. The fine, never-failing stream of water running through it probably attracted him to this spot. There is little doubt that this farm has been greatly improved under its present management, and it furnishes an optical illustration of what drainage, fertilizing, and tillage, backed by ample resources, can accomplish.

The following may be mentioned among the humors of local history: At the census of 1790 there were but two white inhabitants in the town of Phelps — John Decker Robinson and Pierce Granger — and they did not recognize each other. They had quarreled about some trivial matter, and did not speak as they passed by. The absurdity of the situation will be apparent the more it is reflected upon. In 1795, Mr. Charles Williamson, agent of the London Associates, learning that a body of Scotch colonists had arrived in New York, and were looking for lands upon which to settle, set out post haste to meet them and induce them to locate in the Genesee Country. He conducted a committee of them to Geneva, and from that point they visited various portions of the tract under his management. They liked the lands near the Sulphur Springs, now Clifton. Mr. Williamson, who was himself a Scotchman, commended their choice, and remarked in a joking way that the water of the springs would be handy as an antidote for the national disease. Strange to say— and in direct contradiction to Sidney Smith and his surgical operation, and to the story of the steam drill — Sandy saw the joke, and the negotiations ended then and there. The humor of this anecdote is apparent in more ways than one.

HOLLAND PURCHASE.

IF HALF the interesting and important facts were set forth concerning the transaction by which Mr. Robert Morris conveyed to a number of capitalists of the city of Amsterdam a tract of land in Western New York considerably greater in extent than the Kingdom of Holland,* they would fill a number of volumes larger than this. There is ample material for biography. More than a score of men eminent in commerce, finance, law, and statesmanship had a direct personal and pecuniary interest in this famous negotiation, from its inception in 1791 to its close in 1848. Their names will be mentioned from time to time as this story progresses, and merely mentioned, in connection with the part they took in the early history and settlement of the Genesee Country. Still more abundant materials exist for narrative that would be most interesting to local readers. But if these things were within my capacity, which I gravely doubt, they are not within the scope and plan of an undertaking the object of which is to set forth only such of the prominent facts connected with the history of the Holland Purchase as may enable the reader to form a general idea of the origin, rise, progress, and conclusion of the transaction. During his confinement for debt under the barbarous laws inherited by us from the mother country, which have been abrogated by a later and wiser generation, Mr. Morris wrote a statement of his business affairs which was published in pamphlet form, a copy of which I have been permitted to see by the courtesy of Richard Church, Esquire, of Belvidere, Allegany County. I shall therefore let Mr. Morris tell in his own words the story of his purchase from the State of Massachusetts of all the lands in the State of New York lying west of the Genesee River — except the Mill Lot, given to Messrs. Phelps and Gorham by the Seneca Indians — and a few small reservations on the lakes and Niagara River

---

* The Holland Purchase contained over 5,600 square miles. North and South Holland combined contain only 2,212, and the Kingdom of the Netherlands, including the Grand Duchy of Luxemburg, only 13,584 square miles.

upon which forts and other Government property had been erected, and his subsequent sale of the greater portion of his purchase to the Hollanders.

He says: " I shall begin with the lands purchased in the Genesee Country, acknowledging that if I had contented myself with those purchases, and employed my time and attention in disposing of the lands to the best advantage, I have every reason to believe that at this day I should have been the wealthiest citizen of the United States. That things have gone otherwise I lament, more on account of others than on my own account, for God has blessed me with a disposition of mind that enables me to submit with patient resignation to His dispensations as they regard myself.

" In the year 1790, I purchased of Messrs. Phelps and Gorham a tract of country in the Genesee district warranted to contain not less than one million of acres, and sold the whole of that purchase in the year 1791 in England to handsome profit, but which was reduced by discounts and other circumstances so as to close with less than I had at first expected.

" This purchase gave me an insight into the situation and circumstances of the remaining lands in that country, the right of pre-emptive purchase from the Indians being in the State of Massachusetts. I took measures, and in the year 1791 bought a tract of the said State, for which I paid at different periods £100,000 lawful money, equal to £125,000 Pennsylvania currency, with heavy interest, besides other sums paid for various objects in connection therewith. In this purchase, Mr. Samuel Ogden, who assisted in making it, had an interest of 300,000 acres, his brother-in-law, G. Morris, Esq. — who was expected to assist in making sales in Europe — had an interest of 250,000 acres; Richard Soderstrom, 100,000 acres; and William Constable, 50,000 acres. The whole purchase was estimated at four millions of acres, and upon actual survey yielded rather more.

" This land was by imaginary meridian lines divided into five tracts or parcels, of which No. 1 began at that point on the northern boundary line of Pennsylvania where Phelps and Gorham's western boundary intersected the same, and from thence running westerly twelve miles to a point from which the first meridian running into Lake Ontario forms the western boundary of the said Tract No. 1, Lake Ontario the northern boundary, Phelps and Gorham's west line and the Genesee River the eastern boundary, and the Pennsylvania line the southern boundary. This tract so bounded was then computed to contain 500,000 acres, but on actual survey was found to contain much more.

" No. 2 commenced at the point on the Pennsylvania line where No. 1 ended, running thence sixteen miles west, and from that point a northern meridian line to Lake Ontario formed the western boundary; Lake Ontario formed the northern boundary, the west meridian line of Tract No. 1 the eastern boundary, and the Pennsylvania line the southern boundary, and was estimated to contain 800,000 acres.

" No. 3 commenced where No. 2 ended, running sixteen miles west, then a meridian, etc., as above.

" No. 4 commenced where No. 3 ended, running sixteen miles west, then a meridian, etc., as before.

" No. 5 commenced where No. 4 ended, and runs west on the Pennsylvania line to the point on the said line where the east boundary of the land called the Pennsylvania Triangle strikes the same, and is bounded on the west by the east line of the said triangle, by Lake Erie, and by the land called the New York Reservation on the east side of Niagara River, on the north by Lake Ontario, on the east by the west line of No. 4, and on the south by the Pennsylvania line.

" I have thought this account of these divisions necessary to a true understanding of the sales and grants hereafter mentioned — especially of Tract No. 1, to an account of which I now proceed:

" In 1791 I borrowed of Colonel W. S. Smith, of New York, who was then agent to Mr. Pulteney and Governor Hornby, $100,000 and mortgaged the tract No. 1 to secure the repayment of that sum in six per cent. stock and interest.

" 100,000 acres, part of tract No. 1, was sold to Messrs. Watson, Cragie & Greenleaf in 1792.

" 86,973 acres, part of same tract, was sold to LeRoy & Bayard in January, 1793.

" 33,750 acres, part of same, was sold to Andrew Cragie in 1795.

" 50,000 acres, part of same, was sold to Samuel Ogden in 1796.

" 50,000 acres, part of same, was conveyed in trust to Captain Charles Williamson, who, as attorney for Mr. Pulteney, discharged the mortgage on tract No. 1 and accepted this 50,000 acres as security for half the debt of $100,000, the other half having been paid.

" 100,000 acres, part of said tract No. 1, was mortgaged to Alexander Hamilton for the use of John B. Church, to secure the payment of $81,679.44 with interest, which I owed him (Church). This mortgage is dated May 31, 1796.

" 175,000 acres, part of said tract No. 1, was conveyed to Samuel Sterett to secure the payment of the balance I owed to him and to Sterett & Harrison, estimated by their accounts at $400,136.92, but which upon examination of accounts I have reduced to $302,919.30, which I believe is correct, or nearly so. This conveyance is dated May 4, 1797.

" 5,120 acres, part of tract No. 1, being an undivided half of a tract called Mount Morris, given by me to my son Thomas Morris from motives of affection, and in consideration of services he had rendered, and then expected to render, and which he hath since faithfully rendered to me in that country — given by letter dated 16th February, 1793, and confirmed by deed dated 27th November, same year.

" 5,120 acres, the other undivided half of Mount Morris, conveyed to Thomas Fitzsimons by deed dated 25th January, 1798, in part security of the debt I owe him.

" 9,600 acres granted to Smith & Jones, Indian interpreters, upon terms expressed in my contract with them dated 28th April, 1792.

" 40,000 acres mortgaged to the Holland Company to secure the repayment of $40,000 they advanced to me, and after them to Messrs. Wilhelm and Jan Willink, of Amsterdam, as security for a debt due to them. This mortgage is dated December, 1796.

" 110,258 acres, part of said tract No. 1, conveyed to Thomas Fitzsimons, Joseph Higbee, and Robert Morris, Jr., in trust to secure the payment of certain debts in that deed enumerated, being debts arising from disinterested loans of money or names, or attended with circumstances that rendered them of superior claim upon my justice or integrity. This conveyance is dated 14th February, 1798, and was drawn and executed when I had not all the books and papers necessary to enable me to ascertain balances and claims accurately; which will account why many sums are mentioned in round numbers, and if any of my creditors are omitted that upon the same principles ought to have been included it is to be attributed to the absence of books and papers, and not to any desire to discriminate improperly.

" According to this disposition the tract No. 1 appears to contain 765,641 acres; but owing to one of those unfortunate mistakes which a division of large tracts of land at different periods, without actual surveys, subject the divider to make, it hath happened so that a grant to the Holland Company intersects and interferes with grants to A. Cragie, S. Ogden, G. Cottringer, and A. Hamilton; by which means a foundation is laid for disputes between the parties, which I regret very much. It is also discovered upon actual survey that the boundaries of Mount Morris and of the Jones and Smith tract intersect, so that the two together do not contain the quantity intended, and one or the other must lose the deficiency unless otherwise settled by compromise. I suppose the whole deduction from the quantity of 765,641 acres granted in tract No. 1 will not amount to 65,641 acres.

" This tract No. 1 is involved in the following circumstances: The mortgage to Colonel Smith was made by deed and defeazance. The deed was recorded in the office of the Secretary of State of New York at the time of execution or soon after. The defeazance was neglected to be put upon record until the present year. In the meantime Colonel Smith conveyed to Colonel Benj. Walker, upon the latter becoming the agent of Mr. Pulteney. Colonel Walker conveyed to Garret Cottringer in trust for me upon Captain Williamson's release. Messrs. Willings & Francis, by their attorney in New York, are pursuing in the law, as I am informed, this property as his (Cottringer's) because his name was used, but in which he had not one cent of concern or interest. Colonel Burr, as attorney for Messrs. Levi Hollingsworth & Son, obtained a judgment by process of outlawry under which it was meditated, as I have been told, to sell the whole of my purchase. I have also been informed that a judgment was obtained and some sales made by Mather and others.

" The oldest judgment against me in the State of New York was one to William Talbot and William Allum, under which (as is said) all my rights and claims in the Genesee Country have been executed and sold by the sheriff. In the mortgages to Alexander Hamilton for J. B. Church; Samuel Sterrett for Harrison & Sterrett; the Holland Company and Messrs. Willinks; and the trust deed to Messrs. Fitzsimons, Higbee, and Robert Morris, Jr., the right of redemption or surplusage, if any, was reserved to me, my heirs or assigns, which has induced me to give this long detail to enable my creditors to regulate their expectations from this source.

"Of the other four tracts, Nos. 2, 3, 4, and 5, sales were made as follows:

"1,500,000 acres were sold to Mr. Cazenove and conveyed to Herman LeRoy and John Lincklaen. This sale was made conditional by certain articles of agreement, and held at the option of the purchasers to make it a sale or a mortgage at a time fixed, and at that time they elected to make it a purchase, whereby it was supposed the deeds of conveyance became absolute, and this was my opinion, as I always after that election did consider the sale as absolute;* but after the Indian Right was purchased, Mr. Cazenove thought proper to get deeds of confirmation drawn which he presented and left for my examination, and to be executed. Instead of examining them myself I put them under the inspection of two gentlemen bred to the law, who very soon informed me that from the nature of the writings and circumstances relating to this 1,500,000 acres I had an equal right with the purchasers to elect whether it should be a sale absolute or a mortgage; in the latter case to be redeemed by repayment of the consideration money (£112,500 sterling) and interest, agreeably to the articles of agreement. And it was urged that as my affairs were then so deranged that I was obliged to keep close house, it might become my duty to reserve this right to my creditors and not to sign the deeds of confirmation. To this reasoning I submitted reluctantly because I thought the sale a fair one, intended at the time by me to be positive, and if my affairs had been in such a situation as that no creditors could have been affected I certainly would have signed the new deeds without hesitation; that I did not do it was to me a matter of regret, under which I have never felt perfectly satisfied. By this detail my creditors are informed of this claim; at the same time it must be mentioned that the Holland Company became, it is said, the purchasers of all my rights and claims in the Genesee tract under the judgment and execution of Talbot and Allum as well as that obtained by Colonel Burr.

"1,000,000 acres, sold in Holland by my son Robert as my

---

* It became an absolute sale.

attorney, was conveyed to Herman Le Roy and John Lincklaen by deed dated 27th February, 1793.

" 800,000 acres, sold by my son in Holland, were by me conveyed to John Lincklaen and Garrit Boon by deed dated 20th July, 1793.

" 200,000 acres, sold by my son in Holland, were conveyed to Le Roy & Bayard and Matthew Clarkson by deed dated 20th July, 1793.

" 100,000 acres, in two parcels of 54,000 and 46,000 each, sold by my son in Holland, were conveyed to Messrs. Le Roy, Bayard, and Clarkson by deed dated 20th July, 1793.

" The Holland Company, upon Mr. Ellicott's survey, claim reimbursement according to covenants for a deficiency of 119,562 acres within the boundaries of the conveyances made to their agents. And I am informed that according to Mr. Ellicott's survey there is a quantity of about 1,490 acres remaining to me as not being included in any of the grants, but this is included in the sale under the Talbot and Allum judgments.

" The Indians at the treaty held with them in September, 1797, reserved sundry tracts in various parts of my purchase amounting to upwards of 200,000 acres,* in which they now hold their original right and occupy the same. The purchasers within whose tracts these reservations lie look to me to purchase the Indian rights whenever the Indians shall be willing to sell."

So far Mr. Morris. Probably no better occasion will offer to correct some general impressions regarding him. It has been commonly thought that his pecuniary troubles arose from his advances to the Colonies during the Revolutionary struggle. Nothing can be farther from the truth. He was reimbursed in full, and at the time of his failure was indebted to the Government. Nor did the Genesee Country contribute toward his downfall. On the contrary, his cash profits in that section must have amounted to half a million, with 700,000 acres of land thrown in, worth at the time of his troubles at least half a million-more. It was, perhaps, this very success which led to his ultimate ruin. Take, for example, the money lost in the North American Land Company, whose capital consisted of six million acres of wild land in the States of Pennsylvania, Virginia, North Carolina, South Carolina, Georgia, and Kentucky. Mr. Morris organized a stock company with these lands as a basis, and *guar-*

---

* They amounted to over 300,000 acres.

anteed purchasers of the stock six per cent. income on their investments.   His partners in this transaction were John Nicholson and James Greenleaf, optimists of the rosiest hue, who mistakenly supposed that their associate waved the wand of Midas. But the fact is that Mr. Morris was never half as wealthy as he supposed himself to be.   He had ventures upon every sea and in every port.   His credit was high and upon that he traded. He was always a heavy borrower and the rates of interest in his day would now be thought exorbitant and crushing.   His partner Nicholson, who had been Controller General of Pennsylvania, became a public defaulter and died in prison, but not until he had ruined Mr. Morris.   I quote from the latter's statement: " Ledger C, Folio 161.   This is an unsettled account, and I suppose ever will be so.   Here began that ruin which has killed poor Nicholson and brought me to the necessity of giving an account of my affairs — but I will forbear to say more, lest I should not know when or where to stop."   The fact is that Messrs. Morris and Nicholson kited paper.   So long as the paper went without question their affairs seemed to prosper ; but the moment the least breath of distrust was blown upon it, their fabric of credit tumbled into inextricable confusion about their ears.   I quote again: " John Nicholson deceased.   Ledger C, Folios 19, 60, 84, 90, 172, 223.   A heavy balance will be found due to me on the accounts depending between this my fellow-sufferer and myself — probably upwards of $600,000 specie, when all entries are made that the transactions require.   With the purest intentions, he unfortunately laid a train that ended as it hath done.   I here say that he laid the train, because there are living witnesses that I opposed as soon as I knew it ; although, from infatuation, madness, or weakness, I gave way afterwards."   Though Mr. Morris was a patriotic citizen and a scrupulous, honorable merchant, he was at the same time a sanguine speculator upon borrowed capital, and not wholly blameless, as quotations from his own hand show, for the financial troubles that overtook him. I quote once again: " It is well known that Mr. Nicholson and myself owe a very large debt by notes drawn and endorsed by each.   The issuing of these notes is the blamable part of our conduct, which we have both felt and acknowledged."

Two or three more extracts from Mr. Morris's statement will be given for the purpose of showing his justice, integrity, and humanity.   Of his account with Garrett Cottringer he says:

" This account as it now stands on my books differs in one article from his rendered to me, wherein he charges considere   more for compensation for services than I have credited; and i   .dily declare that if I alone were to be affected by it, I would not hesitate one moment to allow all he asks, and more, for if I had not lost my fortune I should have made his, or at least have put him in a position to make one for himself. It is not personal service alone that merits compensation, but his zeal, which hath led him into embarrassments, and his fidelity entitles him to the highest consideration."

Of his wife, Mrs. Mary Morris, he says: " The sum at the credit of this account, $15,860.16, arose from the sale of two or three tracts of land or farms in Maryland left her by her father, the late Colonel Thomas White, which I sold with great reluctance when necessity pressed, and she urged me to it. I consider this a sacred debt, but have made no provision for it; therefore it depends on my creditors whether any is made or not." Of a debit against his son, Wm. W. Morris deceased, he says: " This account must be balanced by profit and loss. It is for his expenses in Europe; I gave him nothing else, and he did not live to earn anything for himself." The sacrifices Mr. Morris made to maintain his own sinking credit and that of others may be imagined from one effort in that direction. Sterrett & Harrison's account against him showed him to be indebted to them in the sum of $400,136.92. He admitted $302,919.30 of this to be correct, but adds: " I must observe that nearly $200,000 of this debt has arisen from sacrifices made to save their credit when I could not pay the balance due. And finally I gave a security on 175,000 acres of land in Genesee on which it was expected they would timeously have raised money in Holland, but the attempt to do so proved a failure, to my great affliction, as well as theirs." That identical tract is worth to-day more than six millions of dollars. The following are a few of the creditors mentioned by Mr. Morris in his statement: " Thomas Willing, William Temple Franklin (son of Benj. Franklin), Cadwalader Evans, Governeur Morris, Alex. Baring, Humphrey Marshall of Kentucky, Wade Hampton, General Walter Stewart, the French Republic, Louis Le Couteulx, Ephriam Blaine, and Benj. Harrison of Virginia, his attorney and agent in that State.

The reader will have observed that although Mr. Morris sold 3,600,000 acres of land to the Hollanders he only states the price of the first tract of 1,500,000 acres. For this he received £112,500 sterling money. The deeds recorded in the clerk's office at Canandaigua and in the office of the Secretary of State at Albany enable us, however, to arrive at the total amount received by him from the Holland Company. For the 1,000,000-acre tract he received 650,000 florins Holland money. For the 800,000-acre tract he received 600,000 florins same currency. For the 200,000 acre tract he received 175,000 florins; for the 54,000 acres he received £7,500 sterling, and for the 46,000 acres he received 60,000 Dutch guilders. Turning his purchase and sales into our currency, at the rate of five dollars to the pound sterling and forty cents each for the florin and guilder, we arrive at the following result: Cost of lands bought from Massachusetts, $500,000. Paid to extinguish native title, $100,000. Interest, commissions, and other outlays, say $100,000 additional, making a total cost to Mr. Morirs of $700,000 for 4,180,000 acres of land, or about 17 cents per acre. He sold to the Hollanders 3,600,000 acres for £120,000 sterling, and 1,485,000 florins and guilders, which are of equal value, and both amounts being reduced to our currency give a total of $1,194,000 — equal to about 33 cents per acre. Add to this the profit on the sale to the London Associates, which was £45,000 sterling gross, and could hardly have been less than $150,000 net, and it will be seen that Mr. Morris's profits on his transactions in the Genesee Country when stated at half a million were not overestimated. And besides the money profit he had remaining 700,000 acres of land, which will be known hereafter as the Morris Reserve.

So far as I have been able to obtain them, the following are the names of the gentlemen who composed the Holland Land Company: Wilhelm and Jan Willink, Nicholas Van Staphorst, Pieter and Jan Van Eeghen, Rutger Jan Schimmelpenninck, Gerrit Schimmelpenninck, son of Rutger Jan, Hendrick and Cornelius Vollenhoven, Jan Gabriel Van Staphorst, Roelif Van Staphorst the younger, Wilhelm and Jan Willink, Jr., Hendrick Seye, Egbert Jean Koch, Walrave Van Heukelom, Cornelius Isaac Vandervliet, Nicholas Van Beeftingh, and Rutger Jan's son, although I suspect this gentleman to be Mr. Gerrit Schimmelpenninck, son of Rutger Jan. Amongst these names only Mr. Rutger Jan Schimmelpenninck has a place in Dutch history. He was a statesman of distinction who in 1805 held the high position of Grand Pensionary of Holland. With genuine Dutch pride, patriotism, and courage he refused to continue in office under the upstart king, Louis Bonaparte, who had been placed on the throne of Holland by his brother Napoleon. Louis married Hortense Beauharnais, the mother of Napoleon III.

These Hollanders were grantees and grantors in a great number of real estate transactions in Western New York, and as their names are not easy, they will hereafter be known as the Holland Company. Their purchase was made in 1792 with the understanding that it was not to be paid for until the native Indian title to the lands was extinguished. As this was not effected until late in 1797, the nineteenth century had dawned before survey into townships and ranges was completed and the land ready to be offered to settlers in lots to suit. It was provided in the original contract that a deduction should be made for lakes, bays, and other bodies of water, within the boundaries, which should exceed a certain area, but all fishings, shootings, and water-power privileges were conveyed to the purchasers. It was these bodies of water, together with the fact that the Indian Reservations contained more land than was at first estimated, that made Mr. Ellicott's survey fall short nearly 120,000 acres from the amount as originally outlined by the meridian measurement. And there is little doubt that the years that elapsed between the date of his purchase and payment to Massachusetts, and the date of payment by the Holland Company, added much to the pecuniary burdens of Mr. Morris.

After the passage by the Legislature of New York of an act permitting aliens to hold real estate, the lands purchased from Mr. Morris were conveyed to the Dutch proprietors by the American trustees who originally took title, and a new subdivision was made. This subdivision consisted of three separate branches of interests, and the tract was conveyed by three deeds to the different individuals composing each branch. The different interests, however, were so closely blended that one general agent was appointed for the whole. The sub-agents also acted for the three branches, making sales for either as opportunity offered, and using the names of the different proprietors of each tract, in making conveyances to buyers. These tracts were known as the two million-acre tract, the million-acre tract, and the Willink tract. In allotting these tracts it was agreed by and between the Dutch proprietors that Messrs. Wilhelm and Jan Willink and their sons Wilhelm and Jan Willink, the younger, should have the privilege of locating their allotment (something over three hundred thousand acres) on any part of the purchase they might chose.   They accordingly selected a plat nearly square in the southeast corner of the tract, because it was nearest Philadelphia, where the general agent resided.   This selection exemplifies a strange lack of foresight and knowledge on the part of the Hollanders regarding the relative advantages of different portions of their purchase.

The number and extent of the Indian Reservations are as follows, viz. :

	Area, Square Miles.
Cannawagas Reservation	2
Little Beard and Big Tree Reservation	4
Squakie Hill Reservation	2
Gardeau — The White Woman's Reservation	28
Canadea Reservation	16
Oil Spring Reservation	1
Allegany Reservation	42
Cattaraugus Reservation	42
Buffalo Creek Reservation	130
Tonawanda Reservation	70
Tuscarora Reservation	1

The oil spring was reserved on account of the presumed medicinal qualities of the petroleum which floated on its surface.   It was called Seneca oil, and had long been known and collected by the natives of that tribe.

The first general agent of the Holland Company was Theophilus Cazenove, resident at Philadelphia.   His ancestors and brethren were merchants in Amsterdam and London, the firm in the latter city being J. H. Cazenove and Nephew.   In connection with other Hollanders resident here and abroad he owned large landed interests in Western Pennsylvania and Central New York.   His fellow countrymen and neighbors in this State were John Lincklaen and Gerrit Boon, who, having become citizens, took and held in connection with Le Roy, Bayard, McEvers, and others, title to the lands of the Holland Purchase until laws were enacted permitting foreigners to hold real estate, when they reconveyed them to the de facto owners.   The handsome town of Cazenovia was named for the early agent.

As soon as the extinguishment of the Indian right enabled Mr. Morris to give title, Mr. Cazenove engaged Mr. Joseph Ellicott as chief surveyor of the lands for which he had become agent.   The Ellicott brothers were natives of Ellicott's Mills in Maryland.   The original Mr. Ellicott emigrated from Cullupton in Wales, and was said to be " a man of high character in every respect."   His grandsons, Andrew, Joseph, Benjamin, and David possessed mechanical and mathematical genius of a high order.   Andrew was employed by Mr. Jefferson to survey the Spanish boundary line, and was afterward Surveyor General of the United States and Professor of Mathematics at West Point.   Joseph was taught mathematics and surveying by his elder brother, and was an apt scholar.   He assisted Andrew in surveying the site of the city of Washington, and in 1791 was employed by Colonel Pickering, Secretary of War, to run the boundary line between the State of Georgia and the Creek Indians.   After completing this survey he was employed by Mr. Cazenove.   Some of the men who composed his original surveying party in Western New York became distinguished in after life.   Amongst those who were not at the time foremost, Trumbull Cary was an axe and line man, and James Brisbane, not yet one-and-twenty, was commissary.

Before leaving Philadelphia for the scene of his labors, Mr. Ellicott, who knew that the variations of the magnetic needle made it difficult if not impossible to run a true meridian by the surveyor's compass, caused to be constructed by the firm of Rittenhouse & Potts, mathematical and astronomical instrument makers in Philadelphia, an instrument similar to those made use of to observe the transits of the heavenly bodies, which had no magnetic needle attached, " the prominent advantages of which were, that by means of its telescopic tube, and accurate manner of reversing, a straight line could be accurately run."   His brother Benjamin originated the idea of this instrument and assisted in its manufacture.   In order to make proper use of it, it was necessary to clear a space about four rods wide, so as to give an uninterrupted view of the heavens — no small task in a heavily timbered country; but the survey when completed was a work well done for all time.   Lawyers assert that there is much less difficulty in establishing lines and titles on the Holland than on the Phelps & Gorham purchase, because of the greater accuracy of Mr. Ellicott's survey.

Mr. Thomas Morris, acting as agent for Mr. Ellicott, furnished supplies to the surveying party, the requisition consisting of tents, bedding; towels, pork, beef, and flour; tea, coffee, and chocolate; medicines, wines, spirits, and loaf sugar; pack horses to move the tents and supplies from camp to camp, and hundreds of other things too numerous to mention. Game and fish were all around them, and we may well envy the good digestion which must have waited on appetite when this band of hardy woodsmen, sharp set by open air and exercise, assembled round the camp fires for supper.

After the meridian lines were run, the plan of Mr. Cazenove was to subdivide the tract into townships about six miles square, these again to be divided into sections about one and a half miles square, and each section subdivided into lots containing about one hundred and twenty acres ; the supposition being that a wealthy settler would buy a section (about 1,500 acres) and divide it amongst his progeny ; but when it was found that settlers wanted farms of all sizes, and of shapes to conform to the streams and topography of the country, rather than to fixed lines, the plan of Mr. Cazenove was abandoned, and thereafter the townships were simply divided into lots of about sixty chains or three-fourths of a mile square, which could be subdivided to meet the requirements of purchasers. The clashing of boundary lines between the Morris Reserve and Holland Purchase, heretofore mentioned by Mr. Morris, was settled upon the principle that the oldest conveyance was entitled to its full complement. Some of the proprietors not being satisfied with this arrangement brought suits for the purpose of getting a legal interpretation of their rights, but failed to overthrow the apparently just rule that the oldest title holds the property.

It is very easy at this distance of time and in this age of steam and electricity to write about the settlement of a new country, but a lively imagination is hardly equal to drawing a picture of the difficulties encountered by Mr. Ellicott's surveying party, backed though it was by the solid wealth of a dozen citizens of the Batavian Republic. Every article of supply was rowed, pushed, hauled, or poled in boats up the Mohawk River to Oneida Lake, through the lake into the Oswego River and through that river into Lake Ontario. From thence by sail to the mouth of the Genesee River was the only part of the journey in which hand labor was not the main motive power. Arrived at the falls

of the Genesee River, both boats and cargo had to be carried
round and relaunched, and then again man power was supplied
to move vessel and freight to Williamsburg,* where a store-
house, from which supplies were distributed, had been erected.
It cost more than half a cent to transport a ton of freight a mile
in those days.   It would be well, perhaps, for the western granger to bear these things in mind when trying to destroy the property which created his, and makes his home possible.

Let us suppose that some necessary article has been omitted in
the catalogue — left behind or lost by the way.   Mr. Ellicott
could not step to the telephone or touch a wire and order a dupli-
cate from Buffalo or Rochester, for these cities had no more existence than the telegraph and telephone.   When he first saw Buffalo, in 1798, it consisted of a double log house occupied by Mid-
daugh & Lane, a house, half log and half framed, occupied by
Captain Johnson, a two-story hewed log house kept as a tavern
by James Palmer, and three small log houses occupied by Messrs.
Ransom, Winne, and Robbins.   Rochester consisted of the mill
erected by Indian Allan, a mill much of the time without a miller,
and more of the time without grist.   This was the beginning of
a town destined within half a century to become noted as the
" Flour City."

Nor was it easy after all the materials were on the ground
to run a meridian line from the northern boundary of Pennsylvania to the shores of Lake Ontario.   It would not be easy to-day,
though most of the distance now to be traversed would be over
a cleared and cultivated country.   There are still, in the counties
of Allegany and Cattaraugus, streams which run through precipitous walls, and hills almost impossible to scale.   Mr. Ellicott's line to be of any value had to be straight, obliging him to
overcome such obstacles as these, and to measure such bodies of
unfordable water as lay in his path.   I shall venture the assertion that the men of this generation are unequal to such tasks as
were performed by their forefathers.   Without the aid of labor-
saving machinery there are not men enough engaged in agricultural employments in the Genesee Country to-day to plow,
sow, plant, and secure the products now grown.   With such
materials as the pioneer had to employ, his descendants would
stand appalled by the task he confronted and performed.   How
many farmers are there in Western New York at present who

* Near Geneseo.

know how to chop, log, and split rails, or how to sow grain broad-
cast? How many farmers' wives know how to card, spin, and
weave? Not one in a hundred under thirty-five years of age.
And I shall further venture to assert that if the prairies had
been as accessible two hundred years ago as they are now a
great part of New England would never have had an agricultural population. Her quarries of marble, granite, and slate
would have been opened, such of her forests as afforded market-
able lumber would have been felled, her streams would have been
utilized to turn the wheels of manufacturing industries, but she
would never have attempted to raise corn and wheat against
Iowa and Minnesota. No further proof of this is needed than
the fact that farming lands are constantly being abandoned
in that section. And fertile as the land is in the Genesee
Country, these remarks would apply to some extent there. The
cost of clearing an acre of our land in 1790, and fitting it for
tillage, would have paid for twenty acres of prairie ready for the
plow.

When Mr. Ellicott had completed his survey of the Company's
lands into townships and lots he was appointed local agent for
their sale. Previous to this Mr. Cazenove had retired from the
general agency and returned to Europe, fixing his residence in
London, and afterward in Paris, where he died. He was succeeded by Mr. Paul Busti, a native of Milan, in Italy, who as
a young man had entered the counting-house of his uncle in
Amsterdam, where he afterward established himself in business
— attaining a marked degree of success and a high reputation
for integrity and ability. After retiring from commercial life
he became interested with some of the gentlemen connected with
the Holland Purchase and was induced to accept the general
agency of the Company at Philadelphia, the duties of which he
continued to perform most faithfully and satisfactorily up to
the time of his decease in 1824; his term of service embracing
almost the whole active period of pioneer settlement. While he
guarded with strict integrity and rigid economy the interests
of the Company, he wisely seconded the local agencies in any
measures calculated to advance settlement. These agencies acted
under general and liberal instructions as to the opening of highways and erection of mills and public buildings, and when, as
was often the case, they advised additional or extraordinary
measures of improvement they were generously met by their chief.

Mr. Ellicott fixed upon the site of Batavia as an eligible place for opening the pioneer land office of the Company. He proposed to call it Bustiville, but the clever Italian saw the base uses to which waggery might pervert the name and promptly vetoed Mr. Ellicott's proposition. Batavia, the name of the Dutch Republic and of the capital of the Empire of the Netherlands in the East Indies, was the name selected. In regard to this site and to opening means of communication, Mr. Busti writes to Mr. Ellicott, under date Philadelphia, 15th August, 1800:

"The opening of the communication through the country is a matter deemed of such importance that it will not escape your attention that the application of money for that purpose has been appropriated on a much larger scale than you thought necessary. By extending the amount of expenditures on that head I mean to evince to you how much I am persuaded of the usefulness of having practicable roads cut out; the benefits of them being not alone confined to the lands on which the present settlement is to be undertaken, but to those of the two million-acre tract afterward to be sold. You will have to take care that the roads to be laid out at present are cut in such a direction as to become of general advantage to the whole country. The knowledge you possess of it will teach you where your attention ought to be most particularly directed. As I am speaking of roads, it will not be amiss to add a recommendation to you that in making choice of the spot on which your office and residence is to be fixed, you will select a situation of an easy and convenient approach, so as to induce the emigrants to visit you."

On Nov. 26, 1800, Mr. Ellicott was in Albany on his way to the new settlement, from which place he writes Mr. Busti that he has issued handbills offering a portion of the Company's lands for sale. These were widely circulated in England and Holland as well as in the older settled portions of this country. A part of this handbill is here given:

HOLLAND LAND COMPANY WEST GENESEO LANDS — INFORMATION.

"The Holland Land Company will open a Land Office in the ensuing month of September, for the sale of a portion of their valuable lands in the Genesee Country, State of New York, situate in the last purchase made of the Seneca Nation of Indians, on the western side of Genesee River. For the convenience of applicants, the Land Office will be established near the center of the lands intended for sale and on the main road leading from the Eastern and Middle States to Upper Canada, Presque Isle in Pennsylvania, and the Connecticut Reserve. Those lands are situate, adjoining, and contiguous to the lakes Erie, Ontario, and the streights of Niagara, possessing the advantage of the navigation and trade of all the Upper Lakes, as well as the river Saint Lawrence (from which the British settlement derive great advantage), also intersected by the Allegany River, navigable for boats of thirty or forty tons burthen, to Pittsburgh and New Orleans, and contiguous to the navigable waters of the west branch of the Susquehannah River, and almost surrounded by settlements, where provision of every kind is to be had in great abundance and on reasonable terms, renders the situation of the Holland Land Company Geneseo Lands more eligible, desirous, and advantageous for settlers than any other unsettled tract of inland country of equal magnitude in the United States. The greater part of this tract is finely watered (few exceptions) with never-failing springs and streams, affording sufficiency of water for grist-mills and other waterworks. The subscriber, during the years 1798 and 1799, surveyed and laid off the whole of these lands into townships, a portion of which, to accommodate purchasers and settlers, he is now laying off into lots and tracts from 120 acres and upwards to the quantity contained in a township.

" The lands abound with limestone, and are calculated to suit every description of purchasers and settlers. Those who prefer land timbered with black and white oak, hickory, poplar, chestnut, wild cherry, butternut, and dogwood, or the more luxuriant timbered with basswood or lynn, butternut, sugar-tree, white ash, wild cherry, cucumber tree (a species of the magnolia), and black walnut, may be suited. Those who prefer level land, or gradually ascending, affording extensive plains and valleys, will find the country adapted to their choice. In short, such are the varieties of situations in this part of the Geneseo Country, everywhere almost covered with a rich soil, that it is presumed that all purchasers who may be inclined to participate in the advantages of those lands, may select lots from 120 acres to tracts containing 100,000 acres, that would fully please and satisfy

their choice. The Holland Land Company, whose liberality is
so well known in this country, now offer to all those who may
wish to become partakers of the growing value of those lands
such portions and such parts as they may think proper to purchase. Those who may choose to pay cash will find a liberal
discount from the credit price."

Mr. Ellicott's appointment as local agent was dated Oct. 1,
1800. Mr. Asa Ransom having built a house* on the purchase
at Pine Grove a portion of it was appropriated as a pioneer land
office. Mr. James W. Stevens, who had come on from Philadelphia, acted as clerk, Mr. Brisbane occasionally assisting,
though his duties were still confined in the main to the Transit
Store House. The residence and land office at Batavia was not
finished and occupied until the autumn of 1801. Sales of land
at first were slow. Under date 16th January, 1801, Mr. Ellicott
writes to Mr. Busti: " The season of the year being such as to
prevent persons from making their establishments, prevents me at
present from making any bona fide sales." In a letter to Messrs.
Le Roy & Bayard dated May 7, 1801, he says: " In respect to
sales of land we have not as yet made rapid progress. The best
and most eligible locations only are in demand. However, we dispose of more or less every day. Settlements form more rapidly on
the east side of the purchase than on the west, owing to its con-
tiguity to the *old settlement* in the Genesee, where provisions and
necessaries for their beginning are more easily obtainable."

In a letter dated July 14th, of the same year, to Mr. Busti,
Mr. Ellicott criticises the rule laid down by the Amsterdam people requiring an advance payment in cash from all settlers
or other purchasers, and attributes the paucity of sales to this
amongst other causes. He says:

" When we reflect that there are lands for sale in every possible direction around us, that every purchaser who comes into
this quarter has to pass by almost innumerable land offices
where lands are offered on almost every kind of terms imaginable,
and that in Upper Canada adjoining this purchase, the government grants lands at sixpence, Halifax currency, per acre, we
cannot calculate to make very rapid sales until we have saw- and

---

* According to a tax roll dated October 6, 1800, and signed by Augustus
Porter and Amos Hall, of Ontario County, there were then upon the Holland
Purchase but twelve taxable inhabitants, three of whom — Johnson, Mid-
daugh, and Lane — resided in Buffalo. The Holland Company was assessed
$3,300,000.

grist-mills erected and roads opened; all of which are going forward.

"If some mode could be devised to grant lands to actual settlers who cannot pay in advance, and at the same time not destroy that part of the plan which requires some advance, I am convinced that the most salutary consequences would result, which I beg leave to suggest for Mr. Busti's consideration, as three-fourths of the applicants are of that description, and as every acre of land that is cleared, fenced, and sowed on the purchase, at the labor and expense of others, makes the contiguous district more valuable, it appears to me some mode might be devised to grant lands to such actual settlers, without restricting them to pay in advance. Married men are loth to settle before conveniences can be had, and deprive themselves of the benefits of society, which accounts for the reason why our sales have not been more extensive to that class of purchasers."

This is good reasoning, and the advice given had been adopted by the London Associates in disposing of lands on the Phelps & Gorham purchase. But the Dutchman is a phlegmatic, opinionated, slow-going person, and a dozen of them are only more so. The wealthy merchants who had bought these lands with their surplus capital could not understand how any person with proper thrift and economy could have failed to lay by a little money. Dutch farmers were all rich, why should not American farmers also have money? Land in America might be had for one-fortieth part of its cost in Holland, which seemed to them a very good reason why our people ought to be able to buy freely, and pay spot cash. Of the poverty of a great number of the inhabitants of the new world — especially of those engaged in tilling the soil — a poverty not at all discreditable — they seemed to have no notion. Nor did they at first appreciate the fact that a settler able to pay for, clear, sow, and reap, was at times absolutely unable to sell the products of his land — that their tract was farther from a market than from one end of the Kingdom of the Netherlands to the other, and that over such roads as existed a team could hardly haul a load at all.

In another letter, dated from Pine Grove as late as December 4, 1801, Mr. Ellicott writes: "I have made no actual sales this fall where the stipulated advance has been paid. I begin to be strongly of the opinion you always expressed to me (but which I must confess I rather doubted) that few purchasers will come forward and pay cash for lands in a new country." It would seem from this that Mr. Busti was an earlier convert to the credit system than the local agent.

The spot where Buffalo is built attracted attention as early as 1801. In the autumn of that year Dr. Cyrenus Chapin, of Oneida County, on his return from a visit to the purchase wrote as follows to Mr. Ellicott: " And further I would petition you for a township of land there at the Buffalo — the one that will take in the town, for since my return a number of my friends have solicited me to petition you for a township; and for that purpose forty respectable citizens that are men of good property have signed articles of agreement to take a township if it can be purchased; and we will pay the ten per cent. when we receive the article."

If this proposition had been accepted, Dr. Chapin and his friends would have secured the site of a city comprising to-day nearly half a million of inhabitants; but Mr. Busti, to whom it was submitted, did not favor the application. The following letter from the early tavern keeper at Buffalo explains itself. It is dated August 11, 1801:

" Sir: — The inhabitants of this place would take it as a particular favor if you would grant them the liberty of raising a school house on a lot in any part of the town, as the New York Missionary Society have been so good as to furnish them with a schoolmaster clear of any expense excepting boarding and finding him a school house; if you will be so good as to grant them that favor they will take it as a particular mark of esteem. By request of the inhabitants. I am yours, &c.,

" Jos. Ellicott, Esq'r.   J. R. Palmer.

" N. B.— Your answer to this would be very acceptable, as they have the timber ready to hew out."

The Buffalo of to-day will hardly be thought a proper field for missionary effort. So far as schools and churches were concerned, the Holland Company from the start laid down the rule to deed in fee half an acre to every school district on their purchase, and to give a plot of land to every organized religious society wishing to erect a house of worship. It seems hard in these days to account for the tardiness of settlement. Although Mr. Ellicott in the early months of 1801 had fixed upon Batavia as the site of the Company's office there were only three sales of

land in the village in that year.   Total sales up to 1810 were
as follows: In 1801, 40; in 1802, 56; in 1803, 230; in 1804,
300; in 1805, 415; in 1806, 524; in 1807, 607; in 1808, 612;
in 1809, 1,160.   The war of 1812 had for a time a depressing
effect upon sales, but after peace was declared settlement upon
the purchase became active.   Mr. Ellicott's agency ceased in
October, 1821.   His administration of the affairs of the Company had been active, enterprising, vigorous, and successful.
He had neither done or left undone anything that could be con-
strued as malversation, or neglect of duty.   His resignation was
his own act, and was prompted by the failure of his mental
and physical powers, which had been for some time foreshad-
owed.   It is true, that discontent had begun to prevail amongst
the settlers.   Indebtedness on land contracts had reached such
a magnitude as to press heavily on them.   Acting only as agent
for others, Mr. Ellicott had a right to insist upon the performance of contracts, but there is ample evidence that he recommended a lenient and liberal policy toward embarrassed residents and tempered justice with mercy and humanity.   But a
great number of settlers had become imbued with the idea that a
change in the local agency might bring relief, or a favorable
modification of the terms and conditions of indebtedness.   Con-
scious of this state of feeling, as well as impelled by failing
health, Mr. Ellicott resigned the agency.   The benefits anticipated from the change were not realized.   Such modifications of
the terms of contracts as were made under the incumbency of Mr.
Evans in 1827 were the work of the general agent.

   The terms of Mr. Ellicott's engagement with the Holland
Company were as follows: For the first ten years he was to
receive five per cent. cash upon all sales effected, six thousand
acres of farming lands, and five hundred acres in the village
of Batavia.   At the close of the ten years the general agent proposed, instead of a cash commission of five per cent., to assign
to him one-twentieth of all the contracts he had made.   This was
accepted by Mr. Ellicott and the amount was deeded to him in
fee by the Company.   The six thousand acres stipulated in the
contract he located along the ridge near Lockport, Niagara
County.   He afterwards added by purchase a strip of twelve
hundred acres on the south side of this plat.   In the original
survey of Buffalo he had laid out for himself a lot of one hundred
acres, which he purchased from the Company.   It was called

an *out lot*, but occupies a conspicuous position in the now widely extended city.   He bought seven hundred acres on Oak Orchard Creek embracing a fine water power, and the site of the present village of Shelby, and afterward fourteen hundred acres below this, which include the village of Medina.   And jointly with his brother Benjamin and others he was interested in other tracts on the Holland Purchase and Morris Reserve.   At the time of his death, in 1826, his property was estimated at six hundred thousand dollars, which was undoubtedly the largest estate accumulated by any individual, up to that period, west of the pre-emption line.   It would now be estimated by millions.

Mr. Ellicott was succeeded in the local agency by Mr. Jacob S. Otto, who had previously been a resident of Philadelphia engaged in commercial pursuits.   He was an amiable, courteous, methodical business man, but his previous surroundings and acquired habits and tastes were not calculated to adapt him to the place he was called to fill.   While he spared no effort to promote the interests and prosperity of the Company, he was never very popular with the backwoodsmen with whom he had to deal.   He died in May, 1827, from the effects of a cold, contracted the previous autumn, at the great canal celebration at Lockport, which he attended as a delegate.   The general agent of the Company, Mr. Busti, died during the administration of its local affairs by Mr. Otto.   He was succeeded by John J. Vander Kemp.   The new general agent was born in the city of Leyden in Holland.   He came to the United States with his parents in 1788.   The family at first settled on the Hudson near Kingston, but soon after located at Oldenbarnevelt, in the town of Trenton, Oneida County, where they enjoyed the society of their compatriots, Colonel A. G. Mappa, Gerrit Boon, Rutger B. Miller, and John Lincklaen.   Early in life Mr. Vander Kemp became clerk in the land office in charge of Colonel Mappa, succeeding H. J. Huidekoper, who was advanced to the position of chief clerk of the general agency in Philadelphia.   In 1804, Mr. Huidekoper was appointed agent for the sale of the Holland Company's lands in Pennsylvania, creating a vacancy in the chief clerkship in Philadelphia, which Mr. Vander Kemp was called to fill.   He succeeded Mr. Busti as general agent.   His whole business life was spent in the service of the Company. He continued as general agent up to the time of the final disposal of its interests in 1838, when he retired on a well-earned competency, continuing his residence in Philadelphia.

Mr. Otto was succeeded at Batavia by Mr. David E. Evans, a nephew of Mr. Ellicott. He began life as clerk for his uncle, and for many years was cashier and accountant to the agency. He had been appointed as associate with Mr. Otto, in order that that gentleman might have the benefit of his long experience in the service of the Company, and of his familiarity with all the details of its business. He, however, was able to give only a portion of his time to the affairs of the agency, his duties as a member of the State Senate calling him to Albany during the winter. He had served but one term as State Senator when he was elected to Congress. He resigned his position as Representative in the National Legislature to take upon himself the duties of the local agency. The alluring possibilities of wealth to be fairly and honestly attained in the Company's service — possibilities so splendidly realized by his uncle — were more attractive to him than the barren Congressional honors, accompanied by a then, and a still, niggardly pay.

During Mr. Otto's administration a plan of receiving cattle and grain from settlers at a price to be agreed upon — the value thereof to be endorsed on contracts — was put into operation. Depots were established on different parts of the purchase where wheat and cattle could be delivered — between certain fixed dates — once a year, and agents were appointed to receive them on behalf of the Company. The times and places were advertised yearly in advance, and a fair market price was paid. As a measure of relief to the settlers it was found beneficial, but was expensive to the Company, which was a heavy loser by these operations. In the second year of Mr. Evans's administration a general plan for the modification of land contracts was adopted. It was somewhat complicated, but to some extent was a relief from burdens that were pressing heavily upon a large class of debtors. Mr. Evans's agency continued until 1837. As early as 1835, plans for closing the entire business and interests of the Company had been formulated, and had practically been concluded before the end of his term. He was succeeded by John J. Von Hall, whose duties were confined to closing up the details of the Company's business.

As early as 1810 it was found necessary to establish other local agencies. The Company's affairs extended over an area so wide as to make it practicably impossible to transact all its business at Batavia. Offices were accordingly opened at the following places: Buffalo, Ira A. Blossom, agent; Mayville, Chautauqua County, Wm. W. Peacock, agent. Mr. Peacock was an early surveyor on the tract, assisting Mr. Ellicott, and for a time was clerk in the office at Batavia; he surveyed most of the townships in Chautauqua into farm lots. Westfield, Chautauqua County, William H. Seward, agent. His history is contemporaneous. The world knows it by heart. If it does not, then it " knows nothing of its greatest men." His connection with the Company will hereafter be alluded to more at length. Ellicottville, Cattaraugus County, David Goodwin, agent, succeeded later by Stahley N. Clark. Mr. Goodwin was also an early surveyor, and clerk in the land office. When the branch office was opened at Ellicottville he was placed in charge and remained until succeeded by Mr. Clark. These sub-agencies were established at different periods; the first being at Mayville in 1810. It was the policy of the Company to place them in charge of men familiar with the topography of the country, hence the majority of the pioneer agents had assisted to survey and plat the lands they offered for sale, and were able to describe the general features of their tracts as regards soil, water, stone, and timber. Afterward a genuine civil service reform seems to have been established by the Holland Company as well as by the Pulteney and Hornby estates. Promotion in order of merit and service was a rule with few exceptions in the management of their affairs. In addition to those heretofore mentioned the following gentlemen acted as clerks in the principal office at Batavia nearly in the order in which their names are given:

John Brandon, Andrew A. Ellicott, William Wood, David Goodwin, Walter M. Seymour, Pieter Huidekoper, Abram Van Tuyl, Stahley N. Clark, Lewis D. Stevens, Janus Milnor, William Green, John Lowber, Robert W. Lowber, Oliver G. Adams, Moses Beecher.

We will draw for a time our attention from surveyors, agents, and clerks, and turn it toward the more important factors in the settlement of the Company's domain — factors without which surveyors, agents, and clerks would have been of little account — the settlers themselves. Like the pioneers on the Phelps and Gorham Purchase, a majority of them came from the older settled portions of New York State and from New England. A glance at the names of those who took contracts up to 1820 establishes this. There is an occasional Dutchman, Irishman, or Scotchman, but more than two-thirds are undoubted Yankees. The Van Beeftinghs, Vollenhovens, Van Eeghens, Van Staphorsts, Willinks, and Schimmelpennincks seem not to any great extent to have been able to persuade their neighbor burgomasters to essay the wilderness of Western New York. The Dutchman is not of a migratory disposition. He will help to colonize Dutch settlements, but is never quite easy under any flag but his own. William of Orange, though King of England, eagerly looked forward to his escape from London and Windsor, and counted the days that must elapse ere he could set out for his favorite seat at Loo. If a session of Parliament seemed likely to delay his departure he did not hesitate to make known his desire for an adjournment, and if necessary to use his prerogative to effect it. After the colony of New Amsterdam was transferred to the English and became the colony of New York, emigration to it from Holland practically ceased. New Jersey, Pennsylvania, and Maryland contributed in a moderate way to swell the quota of settlers west of the Genesee, but the Hollander smoked his pipe with characteristic meditation upon the lands he had reclaimed from the sea, and did very little toward subduing and making productive those of the Holland Purchase.

We will let the descendant of a pioneer tell the story of his ancestor's first year in the wilderness:

"It is winter. He has the fall preceding obtained his 'Article' or had his land 'Booked' to him, and built a new log house. Cold weather came upon him before its completion and froze the ground so that he could not mix the straw mortar for his stick chimney, and that is dispensed with. He has taken possession of his new home. The oxen are browsing with the cow and three sheep, and his young wife is feeding two pigs and three fowls from her folded apron. These, together with a bed, two chairs, a pot and kettle, and a few other indispensable articles for housekeeping — few and scanty altogether, as may be supposed — for all were brought in on an ox sled, over an underbrushed woods road: these constitute the bulk of his worldly wealth. The opening in the woods is that only which has been made to get logs for his house, and browse for his cattle, for the few days he has been the occupant of his new home. He has a rousing fire; great logs blazing against his rude chim-

ney back.   His firewood is so convenient and plenty that there
is no thought of economizing that.   There is a little hay piled
on a rude hovel that gives shelter to his stock, but it is a luxury
only to be dealt out occasionally.   The roof of his house is of
peeled elm bark, and his scanty window is of oiled paper.   Glass
is a luxury that has not yet reached the ' settlements.'   The
floor of his house is made of the halves of split logs ; the door of
hewed plank — no boards to be had; a saw mill has been talked
of in the neighborhood, but has not yet been put in operation.
Miles and miles away through a dense forest is his nearest neighbor.   That forest is to be felled, logged, underbrushed, burned,
fenced, and plowed ; and the land is not only to be cleared, it is to
be paid for.   The task is a formidable one, but that rugged spot
will yet ' blossom like the rose.'   He and the helpful sharer of his
toils and privations are destined to be the founders of a settlement
and of a family ; to look out upon broad, smiling fields where once
was the dense forest, and congratulate themselves that they have
been helpers in a work of progress and improvement such as has
few parallels in an age and in a country distinguished for enterprise and accomplishment."*

It is doubtful whether the lot of the pioneer averaged as well
as the writer has outlined it.   He gives us only the bright side of
the picture.   Good health is taken for granted.   Yet it is well
known that the frontiersman was most fortunate if he escaped
the malarial and other fevers incident to all new settlements.
The loss of an ox meant the cessation of all labor which could
not be performed by hand, and in some seasons the loss of a cow
might mean starvation.   The cold year — 1816 — and the year
following were periods of great suffering.   Many of the poorer
settlers subsisted on milk, roots, boiled greens, and leeks.   Game
and fish supplemented the meager fare of those who had rod and
gun, but a majority was too poor to own such luxuries as fishing
tackle and fowling pieces.   Even the red man was reduced to the
verge of starvation, and ravenously devoured such portions of
the game he killed as are not usually thought proper for human
food.   During this period of scarcity (1816-17) wheat sold at
three dollars per bushel and corn at two dollars.   If the pioneer
had possessed the means to buy, there was not a sufficiency for
all wants.   Judge James McCall who owned a grist mill on the
purchase controlled all the surplus grain for miles around.   His

* Turner's history of the Holland Purchase.

monopoly was humanely exercised. He would sell to no one man over forty pounds of flour or meal, and to those who had teams, and the means of procuring food by going out to the older settlements, he refused to sell at all. When his supplies became reduced he declined to sell more than twenty pounds to an individual, and in this way helped to carry along the poorest and most destitute of his neighbors until the harvest of 1817. There was at all times an abundant crop of those Christian graces which adorn humanity, and of that charity and mercy " which blesseth him that gives, and him that takes." The year 1813 was also one of great distress in Niagara and Erie counties and in that part of Genesee lying west of Batavia. A circular letter dated at Canandaigua, Jan. 8, 1814, addressed to Hons. Philip Van Rensselaer, James Kent, Ambrose Spencer, Stephen Van Rensselaer, Elisha Jenkins, and to the Reverend Timothy Clowes, William Neill, and John M. Bradford, and signed by Messrs. Wm. Shepard, Thaddeus Chapin, Moses Atwater, Nathaniel Gorham, Myron Holley, Thomas Beals, and Phineas P. Bates, sets forth that " all the settlements in a section of country forty miles square have been broken up by the British invasion. Our roads are filled with people, many of whom have been reduced from competency and good prospects to the last degree of want and sorrow. So sudden was the blow by which they have been crushed that no provision could be made either to meet or elude it." After fully describing the exigencies of the situation a stirring appeal is made to their wealthy and liberal-minded fellow citizens for aid. It was promptly met by an appropriation of fifty thousand dollars by the State Legislature, three thousand by the Common Council of New York, one thousand by that of Albany, two thousand by the Holland Company, and liberal personal contributions by the citizens of New York, Albany, Canandaigua, and other localities. It is a fact worthy of mention that at this period Canandaigua was a more important town, and contained more wealth, public spirit, and liberality, than any other west of Albany, with the possible exception of Utica. The little village of Buffalo was then a heap of smoking ruins, and Rochester was still inchoate.

Following the cold season there were two years of financial crisis affecting the whole country. It was almost an impossibility to raise money for any purpose or upon any security. Men with thousands of acres of land and granaries full of wheat were unable to pay their taxes. Settlement was brought nearly to a standstill. Travel and transportation were reduced to a minimum. Many settlers abandoned the idea of trying to pay for their lands, and many others abandoned the lands and the country. Farms that had been cleared and improved at an outlay of a thousand dollars would not bring two hundred above their original cost.

Most of our timber lands have been cleared and are under cultivation. Our forests are fast disappearing. What remains of them consist principally of pine in the extreme northern and southern portions of the country, which is cut for its lumber value and not with the object of clearing the land for agricultural purposes. Associated labor, modern implements, and steam sawmills, which can be readily moved from place to place, make the task of the lumberman a comparatively easy one. Supply the hardiest and most skillful of them to-day with an axe, a log chain, and a yoke of oxen, and ask him, alone and unaided, to clear a farm of a hundred acres densely covered with oak, hickory, maple, beech, elm, and other hard and heavy timber, and he would simply say that the thing was impossible. Yet such a task confronted nearly all the pioneer settlers on the Holland Purchase. The men who accomplished that task inherited ability to perform it. They came of a race of hardy woodsmen which, having cleared New England of timber, found only the ungenerous reward of a rocky and sterile soil, from which subsistence could barely be gained by patient, unflinching toil. Inured from childhood to the work of wresting from stubborn, unfruitful nature its scanty reward, they cheerfully attacked the forests of the Genesee Country, firmly persuaded that its arable, fertile soil would, in time, abundantly recompense their labors. The men of no other country were, at that period, equal to the undertaking. Old England had long been under the plow. Holland had been rescued from the sea. It was a wonderful achievement; but when the Dutchman had said, " Hitherto shalt thou come, but no further," his eye looked out upon meadow lands, and he had no use for such accomplishments as chopping, logging, and rail splitting. The Scotch were the only people accustomed to struggle with such difficulties as were encountered by settlers upon the timber lands of North America, and they were almost the only people from abroad who, at the beginning of the century undertook the task of subduing and bringing under cultivation such lands.   And they did not attempt it to any extent.

Settlers are prone to giving home names to their new abodes, but out of one hundred and thirty towns on the Holland Purchase only one bears a Scottish title — the town of Cambria in Niagara County.   American blood and bone cleared the lands east of the prairies.   For two hundred years the settlers in the Northern States had been woodsmen, accustomed from birth to the perils and privations of frontier existence.   They had become attached to the free life of the woods, and were constantly pushing on to new settlements.   The pioneer on the Phelps and Gorham Purchase sold out his improvements and moved to the Holland Purchase.   When civilization began to press upon him, he " pulled up stakes " and started for the Western Reserve.   When the howl of the wolf and the scream of the wildcat no longer saluted his ear in Northern Ohio, he sought the familiar sounds in the heavy timber of the Wabash, and of Southern Michigan. There were living in the middle of the century hundreds of men who had helped to " clear up " half a dozen farms between New England and the Mississippi, and who in the vigor of three score and ten sighed because there were no more worlds to conquer. No foreigners did this.   If there is one who upon landing put his family and all his wordly goods on an ox sled, and, following Indian trails and blazed trees, penetrated hundreds of miles into the wilderness, settling at length upon a tract of heavy timber, and with no tools but an axe clove his way to a home and independence, he is a rare exception.   Emigrants came to us, but not in great numbers until our country had ceased to be an experiment — not until turnpike roads and the Erie Canal had made our new lands fairly accessible.   Our public works have largely been created by foreign labor, but it was gregarious.   The Irishman and Italian will work in companies, but not one in a hundred of them would to-day take a tract of heavy timber land in Wyoming or Washington as a gift, and locate on it if it was scores of miles from a town or neighbor.   Yet Wyoming and Washington are more accessible at present than the Genesee Country was at the beginning of the century, and it takes but half a dozen years out there to turn a stump field into a thriving city.   The pioneer's reward was neither certain nor adequate.   Wolves destroyed his sheep and carried off his young calves and pigs. Foxes and weasels decimated his poultry yard.   Wild pigeons by millions filled their crops with his grain. Raccoons plucked his half-ripened ears of corn, and squirrels obtained their winter supplies from his garners. Other animals besides the ass knew the master's crib. If Mr. Henry George had ever cleared up one heavily-timbered farm, the question with him of property in land would never for a moment have been in doubt. I will quote from an article on the early settlement of Northern Indiana (recently contributed to a monthly publication by Hon. Hugh McCulloh) a few well-chosen words having a direct bearing on pioneer life. He says: " I question very much whether there are any farms outside of the prairies and away from large towns which — if they were charged with the labor bestowed upon them at the rate of one dollar per day for men, and fifty cents a day for women, and with other necessary outlays (their original cost not included), and credited with the market value of their productions, and their present estimated value — would exhibit a balance on the right side of the account."

" No one who has known anything about the hardships endured by the first settlers in the timber lands of the United States, their unceasing toil, their actual want — not of the comforts but of the necessaries of life when in health, to say nothing of what they needed and could not be supplied with in sickness — during the long and wearisome years that came and went before they had cleared enough of their lands to enable them to begin to enjoy the fruits of their privations and labors; — no one who has known anything about all this will be found among those who speak of land as being God's gift, and therefore property in which there should not be absolute ownership."

Such was the lot of the pioneer on the Holland Purchase during the first quarter of the nineteenth century. In perils of wild beasts and savage men, in perils in the wilderness, in watching always, in weariness and painfulness, in hunger and thirst, in sickness, without remedies, physician, or nurse; in fastings often, in cold and heat, he clove his way — if spared — to the plain comfort and frugal competency of a farmer's life. Educated in such a school, he became a strong and rugged, though often an unpolished character — a man who knew his duties, and having performed them was prepared to assert and maintain his rights. We are told that such men constitute a state.

After the first quarter of the century the condition of pioneers on the central and northern portions of the purchase was greatly improved.   Roads that were passable intersected the settlements, and the Erie Canal opened a way to market for surplus products. But while this grand waterway doubled the value of property within twenty miles on either hand, it was at first a positive damage to settlers along the southern tier.   Overland travel to the new lands farther west, which began as early as 1805 and continued in an ever-increasing flow, went mainly through the southern counties.   Prairie schooners bound for the Western Reserve and remoter regions were a daily sight along the highways of Chemung, Steuben, Allegany, Cattaraugus, and Chautauqua, some wending their way to the navigable waters of the Allegheny, and others pushing on by land to their destination. This current of travel and transportation which had furnished a brisk trade to the towns through which it passed, was suddenly turned to the canal and the lakes.   The advantage derived from location on a great thoroughfare was lost, and another quarter of a century of isolation from markets, and from the activities of traffic, had to be endured by the settlers on the southern parts of the Holland Company's purchase.

Mr. Wadsworth was right when he said " few people have the patience necessary to make speculation in new lands successful." Even the Hollanders had not.   Famed as they are for making haste slowly, the pace in Western New York was too moderate even for Dutch phlegm.   As has already been stated in the sketch of the Phelps and Gorham Purchase, they endeavored as early as 1821 to close out their business west of the Genesee River, and for the sake of touching again their florins and guilders they offered to convey all their remaining interests and all their receipts to date upon being reimbursed their original investment and expenses, with interest at the rate of four per cent. per annum.   This offer was not accepted.

The earliest of a series of sales which resulted in 1838, in closing out the interests of the Holland Company, was made in 1828. The purchasers were James O. Morse, Levi Beardsley, and Alvin Stewart, of Otsego County.   The tract sold contained 5,397 acres — consideration one dollar per acre — location Chautauqua County.   It was known as the Cherry Valley Purchase or Cherry Valley Land Company.   The next sale was in 1835. The purchasers were Goold Hoyt, Russell H. Nevins, Rufus L. Lord, and William Kent, of New York, and Nicholas Devereux of

Utica. Eighteen thousand, nine hundred and seventy-one acres
were conveyed, the consideration being one dollar per acre. This
tract was in Allegany County. The Company's remaining lands
in Cattaraugus County were sold and conveyed to the same parties
for the same consideration — one dollar per acre. Previous to
this, sale had been made of a considerable tract in Cattaraugus
to Rutger B. Miller, of Oneida County; David E. Evans and
John Lowber, of Batavia; and The Farmers' Loan and Trust
Company, of New York.

Many sales and resales were made by the original purchasers,
and there were numerous changes in the proprietary. Wm.
Samuel Johnson, of New York, bought the interests of William
Kent, locating at Ellicottsville, where he continued to reside for
many years. Rufus L. Lord sold a part of his tract to his
brother Thomas, and they made a final sale of their holdings to
Coleman & Smith, their agents at Ellicottsville. The Lords had
previously bought a portion of Mr. Nevins' interest. Joseph
Kernochan bought from Nevins and Hoyt, and Thomas Suffern
bought from Goold Hoyt and others. Rufus King, Jacob
Ten Eyck, and Jacob H. Ten Eyck, of Albany, also had a proprietary interest by purchase. Elish Jenkins became the owner
of 1,008 acres where the city of Dunkirk now stands. It was
conveyed by him to Walter Smith, and from Smith to Russell H.
Nevins and Nicholas Devereux.

Mr. Devereux gave personal attention to his purchase, organizing the Devereux Land Company, for which Major Richard
Church, of Belvidere, acted as agent.

On the first day of October, 1836, the Holland Company con-
tracted to sell their remaining lands, land contracts, and bonds
and mortgages in the county of Chautauqua to Abraham M.
Schermerhorn, of Rochester; Trumbull Cary and George W.
Lay, of Batavia; Jared L. Rathbone, of Albany; William H.
Seward, of Auburn; and John Duer and Morris Robinson, of
New York. Each party had one-sixth interest, except Messrs.
Duer and Robinson, who owned a sixth in common. On the
fourteenth day of July, 1838, the property was conveyed by two
deeds of the Holland Company to Messrs. Duer, Robinson, and
Seward, who held it in trust for their associates. A part of
the lands, however, were divided and allotted in severalty to those
who wished to assume the personal management of their respective shares. The consideration agreed to be paid the Holland

Company was $919,175.59.   That portion of the estate belonging to Messrs. Duer, Robinson, and Seward was held by them in common and managed for their joint benefit until May 2, 1859, when they closed out their remaining interests to George W. Patterson, of Chautauqua.

The last and most important sale was consummated in October, 1838.   By a preliminary agreement executed December 31, 1835, the Holland Company agreed to sell to Heman J. Redfield, of Batavia, and Jacob Le Roy and the Farmers' Loan and Trust Company, of New York, all their unsold lands, and all their land contracts and bonds and mortgages in the counties of Genesee, Orleans, Niagara, and Erie.   The lands in Wyoming were included in these various sales, that county not having been set off until 1841.   A preliminary deed to the Trust Company and Messrs. Redfield and Le Roy was executed January 27, 1838, and a final deed specifying the location, metes, bounds, and acreage of lands was recorded on the tenth of the following October.   The consideration money was $1,462,993.27.   Mr. Redfield bought the interest of his partner, Mr. Le Roy, in 1843, and made a final disposition of all the real and personalty, and a settlement with the Trust Company in 1848.   His son-in-law, Major Glowacki, of Batavia, is authority for the statement that, in order to bring matters to a conclusion, Mr. Redfield sold land on the outskirts of the city of Buffalo for four dollars and a half an acre, which would now bring as many thousands as it then brought units.

The title of Messrs. Pulteney, Hornby, and Colquhoun, and of the Holland Company, to the lands bought of Mr. Morris has not been permitted to pass unquestioned.   Squatters have plausibly and ingeniously assailed it in the Legislature and through the courts, but decisions have been so uniformly against them that for nearly forty years no fresh attempts in that direction have been made.   Besides the treaty and deed of cession from New York to Massachusetts, the sale by the latter State to Phelps and Gorham and Robert Morris, and the deeds from these gentlemen to the foreign purchasers, their title has been confirmed by legislative acts of both States.   In April, 1798, the Legislature of New York passed an act for the special benefit of the London Associates and of the Holland Company, wherein they were empowered to hold, sell, and convey real estate.   In March, 1819, an Act declaratory of the construction and intent of the Act of 1798 was passed, empowering aliens " to give, devise, grant, sell, and convey realty, in fee or otherwise, to any other alien or aliens, and making all mortgages upon such realty good, valid, and effectual." Non-resident alien proprietors of realty in this State were also protected by the treaty of 1794, commonly known as Jay's Treaty. In 1821, an act was passed to perpetuate the testimony of Robert Troup, John Greig, and Joseph Fellowes, regarding the Pulteney and Hornby titles, the object being to make certain facts and documents pertaining to the foreign ownership matters of record, and producable as testimony in any trial between the trustees of the Pulteney and Hornby properties and squatters entering on their lands. Previous to this enactment the agents or trustees were obliged to send to England for testimony, proofs, documents, and exemplifications, in each and every petty suit of ejectment which they were obliged to bring.

In 1840, the Assembly of this State requested the Attorney-General, Hon. Willis Hall, " to investigate the title of the trustees of the Pulteney estate to the lands claimed to be owned by them in the counties of Steuben and Allegany, and report a full and perfect abstract of such title, together with his opinion of its validity, and of the right of said trustees to hold and convey such lands." An exhaustive opinion by Mr. Hall is summed up in these words: " Every link in this title is complete and perfect; the conveyances are formally and accurately drawn and executed, and the execution properly authenticated. The Attorney-General is therefore of the opinion that the title of the said trustees to the lands in Steuben and Allegany counties, and elsewhere, held by them by virtue of the will of Sir John Lowther Johnstone, is valid; and that their right to convey the same in fee simple to purchasers is unquestionable." Even this opinion did not dampen the ardor of people wishing to hold and possess land without paying for it. In 1844 a petition of 916 inhabitants of Steuben, Livingston, and Allegany counties prayed the Legislature to direct the Attorney-General to commence a suit against some person holding land by deed or contract from the heirs or trustees of the Pulteney estate, in order to test the validity of such conveyance. The petition was referred to Hon. Geo. P. Barker, Attorney-General, whose report thereon fully concurs with the opinion of his predecessor, Mr. Hall. In 1847, Hon. John VanBuren was directed by the Assembly to investigate the same title, and if he should be of the opinion that the lands had escheated to the State to bring suits for their recovery.   No report was required from him, but the fact that he brought no suit is conclusive as to his opinion of the validity of the title. The last attack through the Legislature was made in 1850, the attempt being to repeal the act of 1821, " to perpetuate certain testimony respecting the Pulteney property in this State." Messrs. L. Stetson, B. F. Tracy, and Charles L. Benedict of the Judiciary Committee reported against the repeal, and said amongst other things: " The title to the Pulteney estate has often been the subject of legislative and judicial action, and so far as your committee are advised it has in every instance been sustained as a perfect and valid title." . . . " It is manifest, therefore, that there remains to be affected by the repeal of the law only the mere squatter who has entered upon and occupied some portion of this land without the shadow of a right so to do. Such persons have no especial claim to the consideration of the Legislature.   They may be ignorant who is the true owner of the lands thus entered upon, but they assuredly know that they do not own the premises themselves, and are trespassing upon the rights of some one."

The last appearance of the Pulteney title in court was at the Livingston County General Term, July, 1849, before Justices Selden, Maynard, and Wells.   Suit of ejectment was brought against Almerin Graves, a squatter, by His Royal Highness Ernest Augustus, Duke of Cumberland, and others, trustees under the will of Sir John Lowther Johnstone, deceased.   The following are among the points made by defendant's counsel, and supported by ample quotations from the books: " The plaintiffs are bound to show who were the *cestui que trusts* of the will.   If there are none in existence then the trust is ended, and the land in question reverts.   The legal estate of these trustees in this land remains as long as necessary to execute the trusts of the will and no longer." . . . " The plaintiffs are bound to show that Henrietta Laura Pulteney did not devise the land in question." . . . " The plaintiffs are bound to produce and prove the deed of disposition referred to in the will of Sir John Lowther Johnstone, it being the power placed over the trust." . . . " None of the trustees of the will nor any of the heirs has been heard from within seven years.   The presumption therefore is that they are dead." . . . " The trustees, being aliens, could not legally take

or execute the trust." . . . " A sufficient time having elapsed
to have enabled the trustees to have fully executed the trusts of
the will of Sir John Lowther Johnstone, they are now divested of
the lands in question." But these and many other ingenious
points were brushed aside by the court, which, in an opinion
written by Judge Wells, sustained the Pulteney title and granted
the writ of ejectment.

Two other cases of litigation arising out of loans of money
on lands in the Genesee Country are deemed by me of sufficient
interest and importance to be briefly sketched. It has doubtless
been observed that the Farmers' Loan and Trust Company, of
New York, either as joint owner with others or as a loaner of
money, became interested as early as 1835 in lands in Western
New York. As its name implies, probably one of the objects of
its organization was to make loans on farm property.

Some time in 1838, Mr. Charles Carroll, of Livingston County,
borrowed from that company the sum of $52,000 for himself
individually, and, as executor and trustee of the estate of Charles
Carroll, deceased, the further sum of $43,000, making a total
of $95,000. He gave as security for the first loan 2,800 acres
of land — most of it improved — in the county of Livingston,
and for the second loan gave security on lands in the same county
and on improved property in the city of Rochester. Full
covenant warranty deeds of all the property were executed and
delivered to the Trust Company, to be held as security for the
repayment of the money loaned with interest at the then legal
rate of seven per cent. The company was empowered by Carroll
to appoint a resident agent to sell and dispose of the pledged
property, collect such sums as might become due on land contracts, and also the interest and principal of bonds and mortgages, execute deeds and contracts to purchasers, and have full
power and supervision over the property. So great was the
confidence of the company in Mr. Carroll that they appointed
him their agent.

The Loan and Trust Company did not, however, advance actual cash to Carroll, but issued to him its trust certificates for
$95,000, having twenty years to run, and bearing interest at the
rate of five per cent. per annum, every certificate of $1,000 hav-
ing forty coupons of $25 each attached. The principal, and last
coupon, became due on the first day of March, 1858.

Some time in April, 1838, Carroll obtained from Messrs.

August Belmont & Co., of New York, an advance of sixty per cent. of their face value on the Trust Company certificates, and authorized their sale in London at eighty-three or better, within forty-five days, or thereafter at the best obtainable rate. The certificates were sold during the summer by Messrs. N. M. Rothschild & Sons, and the proceeds, amounting to $82,575.23, were paid over to the Trust Company to the credit of Carroll, by Messrs. Belmont & Co.   Carroll withdrew the money and paid interest on the $95,000 up to September first, 1839 (eighteen months), and thereafter made no further payments either of interest or principal.   On the 16th day of August, 1842, the Trust Company wrote him urging payment of the interest past due, but he paid no attention to the demand nor did he reply to the letter.   The amount then due the company was $19,950. Soon thereafter the company sent another letter by the hands of Robert W. Lowber, Esquire, instructing him to make a personal demand on Carroll, and hear his reasons, if any, for non-payment.   In reply to this demand, Carroll denied any indebtedness to the Loan and Trust Company and requested it either to desist setting up any claim against him or at once proceed to adjudicate the same.   From this it was evident that he meant to set up a plea of usury in bar of his indebtedness.   The Trust Company accepted the alternative and brought suit.   The case reached a final trial at a General Term of the Supreme Court, held at Bath, Steuben County, in September, 1849, before Justices Maynard, Wells, and Marvin.   William Curtis Noyes and Hiram Denio appeared for the plaintiff and John C. Spencer and Alvah Worden for the defendant.   Verdict for defendant. Opinion written by Jus'ice Wells.   He held the transaction to be a loan, and to be usurious *per se*.   He said: " Suppose A. agrees to lend B. one thousand dollars and it is a part of the agreement that B. shall receive the loan in negotiable promissory notes of a third person, due at a future day and bearing legal interest from the time of making the loan, and that B. shall repay the amount by the time the notes become due, with interest from the date of the loan at the rate of nine per cent.   Will any one deny that such a transaction would be usurious? "

If a layman may be permitted to reply to the question of the learned judge, he would say that of course such a transaction would be usurious because nine per cent. is above the legal rate. The judge further says: " And if nine per cent. would be illegal seven per cent. would be equally so, if the notes borrowed bore an interest of only five per cent." This is not clear to the lay mind. An agreement at that date to pay seven per cent. was surely not usurious. The Judge compares the trust certificates to promissory notes, but later in his decision he says they " possess none of the qualities of commercial paper." He further held that " though the conveyances by Carroll to the Trust Company were absolute in terms and assumed to convey the entire fee, yet as the agreement between the parties showed that they were intended only as securities in the nature of mortgages for the repayment of the certificates issued to Carroll, that they were to be considered as mortgages; and further, that the agreement could not be enforced as a loan — first, because the company did not possess the power of making loans; and, second, because the loan and all securities relating to it were illegal and void, as being in violation of the usury laws."

The lay mind easily assents to the latter of these propositions because it bows to the legal mind, but how a warranty deed, after it has been executed and recorded, can be transformed into a mortgage is puzzling. And if the Farmers' Loan and Trust Company had not, and has not, the power to make loans it should change its name.

He further decided that " holders or assignees of the certificates could not enforce payment of them, as they took them *cum onere*, and as they did not possess the qualities of commercial paper, the fact was sufficient to put all persons dealing in them upon inquiry, and thereby deprived them of protection as innocent or bona fide holders."

The Loan and Trust Company of course paid the certificates at maturity. It seems to have rested satisfied under the decision of the General Term, though Mr. Geo. F. Talman, so long identified with the company, was always of opinion that if an appeal could have been taken to the United States Supreme Court a reversal of Judge Wells' decision would have resulted.

A case almost exactly parallel arose out of the sale by the Holland Company to Messrs. Duer, Seward, Schermerhorn, and others. The lands bought having been divided and allotted to the several purchasers, a part of the money to pay for them was borrowed from the American Loan & Trust Co., a financial institution of Baltimore having branches or agencies in New York and elsewhere. This company issued to the borrowers its sterling certificates payable in London, having twenty years to run and bearing five per cent. interest, to the amount of £147,700. Abraham M. Schermerhorn's proportion of this borrowed money was (in our currency) $151,933.44, for which he gave his personal bond, and a mortgage on his allotment of the Chautauqua lands. Not long thereafter Mr. Schermerhorn failed, and the Baltimore company foreclosed and took possession of the mortgaged premises. Meantime the assignee in bankruptcy of the Schermerhorn estate closed up its affairs, and in 1843 his client obtained a discharge. As a part of his duties the assignee advertised and sold at auction all the right, title, and interest of the bankrupt in and to the foreclosed Chautauqua lands; Schermerhorn himself becoming the purchaser for the sum of two dollars. Previous to this the Baltimore company became embarrassed, and assigned its effects, including the bond of Schermerhorn, to Geo. F. Talman and others of New York in trust to pay its creditors.

Mr. Schermerhorn having by his discharge in bankruptcy obtained a new lease of business life, brought an action against Messrs. Duer, Robinson, and Seward, and against Talman and others, assignees of the American Loan and Trust Company, to repossess himself of his Chautauqua lands, alleging amongst other things usury on the part of the Baltimore company. A preliminary trial was had before Chancellor Whittlesey, who decided that the transaction was usurious. The case was carried to the Court of Appeals, which by a majority of one reversed the Chancellor's decision. The gist of the opinion of the majority was summed up in the allegation that a litigant must come into court with clean hands, and that Schermerhorn "must do equity before he could ask for relief." Although it would have benefited him as well as Schermerhorn had the plea of usury been sustained, Mr. Seward strongly opposed it, and after the decision of Chancellor Whittlesey promptly made over to Mr. Talman and his co-assignees his entire interest in the purchase from the Holland Company for the benefit of the creditors of the Baltimore institution. Honorable business men will heartily endorse the statement that no act of Mr. Seward's long, useful, and distinguished career reflects greater credit upon him than this, and will rejoice that the decision of the Court of Appeals rendered the sacrifice he was willing to make unnecessary.

The names of William L. Marcy and Heman J. Redfield having been mentioned in these sketches, the way Mr. Marcy, representing the Albany Regency, paid a political debt in 1853 which was contracted in 1824, is interesting, as showing the Regency's good faith towards those who obeyed its behests. Mr. Redfield, residing in Batavia, represented his home district in the State Senate in 1824. The Albany Regency had views regarding the presidential election of that year which they thought would be promoted by the defeat of a bill pending in the Legislature, taking from that body the choice of presidential electors and giving it to the people. The measure was popular in Mr. Redfield's section, and very few members west of Cayuga Bridge dared to brave their constituents by opposing it. On a close count it was found that the vote of Mr. Redfield was needed to defeat the bill in the State Senate. He was asked by Mr. Marcy, speaking for the Regency, for that vote. He frankly said to Marcy, who was his intimate friend, that if he opposed the measure it would be political death to him, so far as any elective office in his section was concerned. " Do as we wish you to and we will take care of you," was Marcy's reply; and Mr. Redfield voted as the Regency desired. The political results were such as he predicted.

For reasons best known to themselves, the Regency, which had previously opposed De Witt Clinton, supported him for Governor in 1826, and he was, of course, elected. It was natural to suppose that the support of such a powerful junta carried with it obligations on Mr. Clinton's part, but to a great extent he ignored them and turned a deaf ear to the Regency's requests. Amongst other things they asked him to appoint Mr. Redfield a Circuit Judge of the district in which he lived, but the Governor had other views and declined to make the appointment.

Parties at the time were in a chaotic state. Clintonians and Bucktails were merging into Jacksonians and National Republicans, and these, especially in Western New York, disintegrated to a great extent and formed the parties known as Mason and Anti-Mason, all to be finally marshaled under two banners, Whig and Democratic. The Whig party carried but two presidential contests — those of 1840 and 1848 — and then gave way to the present Republican party. The Democratic party still exists, but the men composing the Albany Regency who dominated it in State politics up to 1860 are, to this generation, only names. They were William L. Marcy, Martin Van Buren, Benjamin Knower, pious Ben Butler, Silas Wright, Edwin Croswell, Peter

Cagger, and Dean Richmond, a bold, shrewd, brainy, and powerful combination.

In this self-constituted cabinet of all the talents, Marcy, in mental caliber, if not in clever political chicanery, stood at the head. To very few of the human family have equal powers of mind been vouchsafed. His famous saying that " To the victors belong the spoils of the enemy " has passed into a proverb. He was easily the brains of two Democratic administrations — those of Polk and Pierce.

Among many other well-known characters in the Genesee Country, developed during the pioneer period, but in their maturity more properly belonging to the second generation of settlers, was a farmer of Livingston County, by the name of Abel. Although perhaps not more entitled to special mention than hundreds of others, I shall give some space to a sketch of him because of his selection by Leonard W. Jerome to undertake a delicate and most important diplomatic mission. It is hardly necessary to say that I have Mr. Jerome's permission to make public this episode of the Civil War.

The farmer was a man of great natural shrewdness and tomb-like reticence. He could not, like Von Moltke, hold his tongue in seven languages, but in his own he was not excelled by anyone. These qualities had attracted the attention of some of the leading politicians of the farmer's party, and with two of them — Mr. Seward and Thurlow Weed — he formed a life-long intimacy. Bold but impenetrable, aggressive but not rash, he was for many years the right-hand man of those gentlemen in the stronghold of their power west of Cayuga Bridge.

It may as well be confessed at once that as a politician his aims were not elevated nor his methods scrupulous. The higher law of his creed was to get the better of his adversaries. The men who fought the Albany Regency were obliged to adopt the weapons of their opponents and the motto that " all's fair in war and politics " became so thoroughly established as a leading tenet of the farmer's faith that he came in time, if it served his purpose, to apply it to friend and foe alike.

The farmer was a wit and humorist as well as a politician. One or two instances will establish his reputation in this respect. As he was driving along one day he met an old friend, a gentleman of wealth and position at the bar, who said to him, " Farmer, I am going to Europe for a three months' vacation. Come along with me." " I should like to, of all things," replied Abel, " but I can't possibly get away just now." " Why not? " said the other. " Your farm won't run away while you are gone." " Maybe not," was the rejoinder, " but something else might." " How's that? said the Judge. " Well, to tell the truth," replied Abel, " I have just been appointed executor of a large estate, and if I go off to Europe I'm afraid the heirs will get away with all the money." Although an active politician, the farmer was not an office-seeker, preferring, like his coadjutor, Mr. Weed, to be the king-maker rather than the occupant of the throne. On one occasion, however, his constituents having placed him in nomination for the State Senate, he was persuaded to stand. Shortly afterward as he was driving along the road he met Judge Martin Grover coming from the opposite direction. The judge, as well as the farmer, was noted for a rather sarcastic humor. After the usual salutations, the judge said: " I see, farmer, you have been put in nomination for the State Senate; now if you will promise to be half-way honest I'll vote for you." Quick as a flash Abel replied: " Judge Grover, if I am sent to Albany this winter, I must go there untrammeled by any pledges whatever."

Leonard W. Jerome was a prominent figure in finance during the War of the Rebellion. It would not be too much to say that from 1861 to 1865 he was easily at the head of money-making and money-spending Americans. He had early imbibed the correct notion that the enormous issues of paper money by the Government must inflate values, and being a man of bold and broad views, he had in the autumn of 1861 already become a large holder of stocks, and a leader of the bull forces in Wall Street. Among the properties in which he had thus early become a heavy owner was the stock of the Pacific Mail Steamship Company, which he had carried from about seventy to a point considerably above par. Things were going on to Mr. Jerome's entire satisfaction, when one morning in November, 1861, a piece of intelligence was printed in the daily journals which startled everyone, and delighted all but a few reflecting, sober-minded, thoughtful persons. The " Trent," a British West-India mail steamer which left Havana on the seventh of November was boarded on the eighth by the United States man-of-war " San Jacinto," commanded by Captain Wilkes, and four passengers — Messrs. Mason and Slidell, Confederate Commissioners to London and Paris, and their secretaries, were forcibly taken from the British vessel, against the energetic protest of its commander, and the admiralty agent in charge of the mail.   No event since the firing upon Sumpter had inflamed the public mind equal to this act of Captain Wilkes. He was lauded to the skies, and, until the popular judgment had time to cool, was the hero of the hour.   International law, comity, and courtesy were thrown to the winds by hot-headed enthusiasts, who boastingly proclaimed our ability " to whip all creation." If within eight-and-forty hours after the seizure of the Confederate Commissioners became known a popular vote upon the question of their surrender could have been taken it would have resulted five to one in favor of holding them and taking the consequences.   A panic seized the stock market.   Shares tumbled pellmell; whilst the premium on gold correspondingly arose.

This was death financially to Mr. Jerome, or soon would be. Although a firm believer in the inflation of values certain to result from large issues of paper money, his patriotism and unwavering confidence in the great future of his country inspired him with the belief that the paper would ultimately be " as good as gold." Time showed both opinions to be correct, but meanwhile he was ground between the upper and nether millstones — he was long of stocks and short of gold.   The shares of the Pacific Mail Company were specially vulnerable, and dropped to the neighborhood of fifty.   War with Great Britain would have swept the company's vessels from the seas.   After a few days of such mental suffering as must inevitably come to a proud-spirited man who sees ruin staring him in the face, Mr. Jerome bethought him of a plan by which he not only extricated himself from peril but added largely to his fortune.   It was a stroke of real genius. There was probably but one man in the United States who could have procured for him the information it was vital for him to secure, and he hit upon that man.

In the early part of his career Mr. Jerome had been something of a politician, and was for some time editor and proprietor of a daily journal in the city of Rochester which supported the measures of the Whig party, of which Mr. Seward was the acknowledged head in the State of New York.   In this way he had become acquainted with farmer Abel, and with the fact that Mr. Seward and the farmer had long been upon terms of friendly intercourse and intimacy.   He at once sent a telegraphic dispatch to Abel to take the first train to New York, as he wished

to see him upon business of great importance to both.   The fame
of Mr. Jerome's exploits in the financial world had already been
spread abroad, and the shrewd old farmer promptly responded
to the dispatch, presenting himself next morning at Jerome's
office.   After the usual civilities, Jerome took Abel into a private
room and closing the door said to him in an off-hand sort of way:
"Farmer, would you like to make some money?"   "Indeed I
would, Leonard," was the reply.   "How much would you like
to make?"   "Well, I have been building and fixing up —"
"Never mind the details," broke in Jerome — "how much?"
"Well, if you are in such a devil of a hurry, Leonard, I think it
will take between thirty-seven and thirty-eight hundred dollars
to put me straight with the world."   "I can show you how to
make the money," said Jerome.   The farmer's eyes glistened.
Though he had long been a forehanded man he was unaccus-
tomed to making in a day or in a single transaction such a sum
as he needed to "square him up."   "Well, Leonard, what's your
scheme?" said he.   "You know Secretary Seward, don't you?"
"Know him! I should think I did!   Didn't Thurlow Weed and I
take him out of the Holland Land Company's office up there at
Westfield and make him Governor?   Why, bless you, he has visited at my house times and again, and when he was Governor I
always put up at his house when I went to Albany.   Did I ever
tell you about —"   "No time for stories, farmer — are you
still on visiting terms with him?"   "Bless you, yes; been to his
house in Washington a number of times when he was Senator.
But what's all this leading up to, Leonard?"   "I want you to
go to Washington and find out whether he is going to surrender
Mason and Slidell or hold them," replied Jerome.

The farmer "caught on" in a moment.   He gave a long, low
whistle, apparently for the purpose of gaining time for reflection, and then said: "My God, Leonard, you play for pretty
high stakes, don't you?   It's a mighty ticklish job you want me
to undertake, do you know it?"   "I do know it," replied Jerome,
"and you are the only man in the world who has the slightest
chance of succeeding in it.   Are you willing to try it?"   "I
believe you are right," said the farmer.   "If I can't get that
information out of the governor no one can.   I'll try it, anyhow.
When do you want me to start?"   "At once," said Jerome.
"Hours are years just now."   Hastily penning two dispatches
he handed them to Abel, saying: "There, takes these with you,

and guard them more carefully than you do your money. I have kept copies. There is a government censorship over all dispatches, but these are harmless on their face, and mean nothing except to you and me. One of them tells me that Mason & Co. are to be given up, the other that they are to be held. Have marked both plainly so that there may be no danger of your getting them mixed. Now post haste and catch the next train to Washington."

Away went the farmer. Next morning early he registered at Willard's Hotel. Bath, barber, breakfast, and fresh linen, put him in good shape by 11 o'clock to call on the Secretary of State. There were very few men in the world who could have had an audience of Mr. Seward on that day, but he was delighted to see the farmer and gave orders that he be at once admitted to the private room where work at that moment was going forward upon the letter to the British Government surrendering the rebel commissioners. He was pleased to see his old friend and said to him frankly: " Farmer, it is a comfort and a relief to me to see your honest, sunbrowned face. I shall be very busy all day, but I want you to send your luggage to my house and be there at eight o'clock to dinner. Afterward we will talk over old times." The farmer was much too shrewd a man to turn a visit into a visitation, and left Mr. Seward to his labors, promising to be on hand promptly for dinner. They dined and wined. After the cloth was removed, Mr. Seward, under the genial influence of a glass of old Madeira and a fragrant cigar, became delightfully chatty and reminiscent. He spoke of the great accession to the Whigs by the disruption of the Anti-Masonic party, and of the wonderful revolution in public sentiment caused by General Jackson's veto of the bill to recharter the United States Bank, of the withdrawal of deposits from the banks and Mr. Van Buren's scheme of the Independent Treasury, remarking that, whether rightfully or not, the people attributed the hard times of 1836-37 to these measures, and had in a single year demolished the apparently impregnable majority of the Democracy, and returned him as Governor. These and many other topics the great Secretary discussed as he only could, until the wee sma' hours were approaching. Abel had been no dummy during the evening. His shrewd, humorous comments upon men and affairs, and his racy anecdotes had greatly amused the Secretary.

" The farmer told his queerest stories,
   The statesman's laugh was ready chorus."

But no opportunity had as yet presented for introducing the subject that was uppermost in the guest's mind. He was far too shrewd to explode it like a bomb upon the conversation, knowing that it must flow naturally and easily into the evening talk or there would be no possible chance of bringing out the information he was so anxious to gain.

After a momentary pause, Mr. Seward said: "Why, farmer, I think I must be losing my memory or my manners. I have been Mrs. Abel's guest so often that I should have inquired after her long ago. I hope she is very well." Although not just the opportunity that the farmer desired, it seemed to be the only one likely to offer, so he replied: "Thank you, governor, Roxy (the familiar name by which he always spoke to or of Mrs. Abel) is pretty well for a woman of her years, or has been 'til lately, but jess now she's real miserable." "I am very sorry to hear it," replied Mr. Seward. "Of what does she complain?" "Well, to tell you the truth, governor, she seems to carry the whole burden of this war on her mind. It was bad enough before we took them cussed rebels out of that English ship, but since that she has hardly slept a wink. She says if we have a war with England the Union will be broken up, and the slave holders will lord it over us here at the North same as they do over their niggers, and she never wants to live to see the day. The poor woman takes on so that she has nearly broken me up too."

Mr. Seward was touched, and in a moment of sympathy gave utterance to a few words which five minutes later he would probably have given anything in the world to have recalled. He said: "Farmer, you go home and tell Mrs. Abel to sleep on both ears — we are not going to have a war with England." Then suddenly seeming to arouse he straightened up in his chair, leaned forward, and added in an impressive tone: "Abel, I have known you more than thirty years and never heard of your betraying a friend or a political secret. The information I have imparted to you will be public property within thirty-six hours. In the meantime it is known to but one man outside of this room, and he is President of the United States. The Cabinet know nothing about it. The "Trent" affair was referred to Mr. Lincoln and myself for settlement. They know that we have considered the matter, but do not know that we have arrived at a conclusion, or what that conclusion is. Having gone thus far, I may as well tell you that I have to-day — or yesterday, rather, for it is now past midnight — completed the draft of a memorandum to the British Government surrendering the Confederate Commissioners. I know that this will for a time be unpopular, but I tell you, farmer, we haven't got a leg to stand on. The act of Captain Wilkes cannot be justified, and no nation having the slightest respect for the honor of its flag would submit to it. I am to meet the President at the department in the morning to look over our memorandum and give it a final revision if necessary. The following morning it will be given to the press and the world. If you will look in about eleven o'clock I will introduce you to Mr. Lincoln. Meantime it is time honest people were abed. We breakfast at nine." After expressing to Mr. Seward, his delight with the action about to be taken, they bade one another good-night and retired.

The farmer's habit of early rising stood him in good stead. He was out next morning by daybreak wending his way to the telegraph office at Willard's Hotel.

The fact that Mr. Seward had not expressly enjoined him from imparting the information of the previous night, was sufficient, under the farmer's code of morals, to justify the use he was about to make of it. " All's fair in war and politics," was still his motto.

He had to wait nearly an hour for the censor and operator. When they arrived he handed them the following dispatch addressed to Mr. Jerome:

" My daughter has been seriously ill, but is out of danger."

This dispatch being entirely harmless on its face was at once forwarded, and when Jerome arrived at his office he was the fourth man in the world who knew that our Government had decided to surrender the Confederate Commissioners. As sporting men say, he had a day all to himself. Confining himself pretty closely to a private room in his office, he gave out orders right and left to buy stocks and sell gold. The street was puzzled, and when they traced these operations to Jerome they were in a greater quandry than ever, for he was believed to be already loaded to the danger line. " Night came, but no Blucher." Not a word or sign from Washington. Could the farmer have been mistaken? It was beyond a doubt a *mauvais nuit* for the great speculator. The morning brought welcome and splendid relief. It was known in every part of the globe reached by telegraphic wires that our Government was to surrender Messrs. Mason and

Slidell with their secretaries.   Long before the usual hour for
business an excited crowd gathered in the vicinity of the Stock
Exchange and began to buy and sell — a custom continued during all the speculative period of the war.   Prices went up with a
bound, and before night had in many instances reached figures
higher than those current before the " Trent affair " was made
public.

Very soon after being introduced to Mr. Lincoln the farmer
took leave of Mr. Seward, saying he would like to be the bearer
of the good news to his wife and neighbors.   He arrived in New
York next morning, and after breakfast at the Astor House
walked down to Jerome's office.   Being a stout man the exercise
had put him in a glow.   As Mr. Jerome tells the story, " He
came puffing and blowing into my office, took off his hat and set
it down on my desk, pulled a big bandana handkerchief from his
pocket, wiped his forehead, and said, ' Leonard, I'll take a check
for that money.'   ' All right, farmer — how much did you say it
was? '   ' Better make it thirty-eight hundred.'   ' Very good.' "
Mr. Jerome went into his business office and returned with a check
for five thousand dollars which he handed to Abel, saying: " You
have been to some trouble and expense in this matter, and it has
turned out pretty well, so I've made the check for an even
amount."   The farmer looked at it and said: " Thank you,
Leonard.   I reckon you can pretty well afford it."   That night,
with money enough to " square up with the world " and give him
a balance in the bank, the farmer set out to carry the news to
Roxy.

Mr. Jerome was too shrewd a diplomat to breathe a word about
his achievement, and it was not until some time after Mr. Seward and farmer Abel had joined the silent majority that he disclosed to a few friends the means by which he found out —
twenty-four hours in advance — what was to be the outcome
of the " Trent affair."   The crowning evidence of great gen-
eralship is the ability to seize the right moment and the right
means for turning defeat into triumph.

CLIFTON SPRINGS, N. Y., Jan'y 18, 1890.

To the Clerk of Niagara County,

Lockport, N. Y.

Dear Sir:

The Holland Land Co. closed out its remaining properties in Western New York in 1838 to Heman J. Redfield of Batavia and Jacob Le Roy and the Farmers' Loan and Trust Co. of New York. Conveyances in Genesee and Erie counties were dated Octo. 10th of that year, in the former by one deed of 55,848.20 acres, and in the latter by three deeds granting a total of 160,435.77 acres. Consideration in each case one dollar.

Will you be good enough to give me the number of acres conveyed in Niagara County with the consideration, and oblige,

Yours resp'l'y,

E. W. VANDERHOOF.

NIAGARA COUNTY CLERK'S OFFICE, Jan. 22, 1890.

Reply:

I find three conveyances from Willink, et al., to The Farmers' Loan & Trust Co., each dated Jan'y 27, 1838. 1st. cons'd $749,733.05 — conveys all of the 983,000-acre tract they were seized of on Dec. 31, 1835. 2d. cons'd $1,462,993.27 and conveys all of the 2,000,000-acre tract of which they were seized Dec. 31, 1835, and 3d, all of the "Willink Tract" in Niagara and Erie Co's or either, of which they were seized, Dec. 31, '35, cons'd $69,656.31.

Very truly yours,

DAN'L CARROLL,

Clerk.

CLIFTON SPRINGS, Jan'y 25, 1890.

Dear Sir:

I have your reply of 22d current. I think the deeds you mention from Willink, et al., to the Loan & T. Co., dated Jan'y 27, 1838, were preliminary, and that a subsequent conveyance or conveyances giving metes and bounds and acreage was executed later. That was the case in Genesee and Erie Co's, the later deeds bearing date Octo. 10, '38. Was it not so in Niagara?

Yours resp'l'y,

E. W. VANDERHOOF.

DANIEL CARROLL, Esq., Clerk, etc., Lockport, N. Y.

NIAGARA COUNTY CLERK'S OFFICE, Jan'y 28, 1890.
Reply:

I find it as you state. Three deeds bearing date Oct. 10, 1838, and recorded in Book of Deeds 25, at pages 1, 18, and 30.

Yours truly,
DAN'L CARROLL.

MARY JEMISON.

THE story of Mary Jemison was a familiar one around the pioneer fireside. Without regarding the polite phrase of the French, *place aux dames*, the " white woman of the Genesee," by reason of her interesting and remarkable career as an Indian captive, and by her priority as a white settler on the Genesee River, easily takes her place as a prominent and dramatic figure in the early history of Western New York. She was born on the ship " William and Mary " during its voyage from a port in Ireland to Philadelphia in the winter of 1742-43; her father, Thomas Jemison, and mother, Jane Erwin Jemison, with three older children — two sons and a daughter — having embarked on that vessel to try their fortunes in the then new and far-off world. The father, having been bred a farmer, removed his family soon after landing to the western frontier of Pennsylvania, where he cleared a large tract of land, and for a number of years enjoyed undisturbed the fruits of his industry. Here two sons were born to him, so that his family at the outbreak of the French War consisted of himself, his wife, four sons, and two daughters, the subject of this sketch being the fourth child. Recounting in her eighty-second year her early recollections, she says: " The morning of my childish, happy days will ever stand fresh in my memory. Even at this remote period the recollection of my pleasant home, of my parents, brothers, and sister, and of the manner in which I was so suddenly and terribly deprived of them affects me so powerfully that I am sometimes overwhelmed with a grief that seems insupportable."

In the spring of 1752 and succeeding seasons, reports of Indian atrocities were circulated in Mr. Jemison's neighborhood. In 1754, an army for the protection of the frontier, and to drive back the French and Indians, was raised — Colonel George Washington being second in command. In that army John Jemison, an uncle of Mary, served as a private, and was killed at the battle of Great Meadows or Fort Necessity. After the surrender of this fort by Washington, the French and Indians became a greater terror than ever to the English settlements, but the beginning of the year 1755 found Mr. Jemison and his family still unmolested. Their repose, however, was destined to be short. On a pleasant spring morning of that year, while her brothers were at the barn making ready to go afield, her father at the side of the house shaving an axe helve, and her mother busy with preparations for breakfast, they were startled by an explosion of fire-arms, and the whoop of a band of Shawnee Indians. They surrounded Mr. Jemison's dwelling and took his family prisoners with the exception of the two older boys, who, being at the barn, made good their escape. Included among their captives were the wife and three children of a neighbor, the husband and father having been killed by the first discharge of the attacking party's guns. After plundering the dwelling of its portable valuables, and taking as much in way of provisions as they could conveniently carry, the scouting party, which consisted of six Indians and four Frenchmen, set out with their prisoners for Fort Du Quesne — now Pittsburg. During the march an Indian followed the party with a whip to scourge the children and quicken their pace. It is probable that the original intention of the captors was to take the entire party as prisoners to Fort Du Quesne, but this design was relinquished, and on the morning of the second day they butchered, scalped, and mutilated their helpless captives with the exception of little Mary and the son of the neighbor killed at the outset by the attacking band. Mary at this time — 1755 — was about thirteen years of age. Her fellow-captive, whom she always referred to as "the little boy," was probably a year or two her junior. Putting moccasins upon the feet of their youthful prisoners and arraying them as far as possible in Indian dress the party set forward, and after a toilsome march, which was interrupted for three days by a heavy storm, arrived on the ninth day after the capture at the fort. During the journey the Indians had succeeded in making little Mary understand that the lives of the party would have been spared if they had not feared pursuit and capture by the whites. A number of times during their trip her young cavalier, with a courage beyond his years, had endeavored to induce her to join him in an attempt to escape; but Mary, knowing the danger and apparent impossibility of making their way without a guide through the pathless woods to a white settlement, declined to join her enterprising fellow-captive in his precocious effort for freedom.   Arrived at Pittsburg, her boyish companion in captivity was turned over to the French, and was never again heard of or seen by her.   What happened to her will be stated in her own words.   She says: " I was left alone in the fort, deprived of my former companions and of everything dear to me but life.   But it was not long before I was partially relieved by the appearance of two pleasant-looking squaws of the Seneca tribe, who examined me attentively for a short time and then went out.   After a few minutes' absence they returned in company with my captors, who gave me to the squaws to dispose of as they pleased."   She was accordingly embarked in a small canoe with the two Indian women and conveyed down the Ohio.   Her female custodians resided at a small Seneca village about eighty miles below the fort.   On reaching home, the squaws divested her of the tattered remains of her civilized wardrobe, and dressed her in a new and complete Indian costume.   They had recently lost a brother in battle, and, according to the custom of the Indians, little Mary was given to them to supply their loss.   It was their privilege either to torture and take her life to satisfy their vengeance, or to adopt her into their family in place of the lost.   They chose the latter course, and from that time until her death, at the advanced age of ninety-one, she was as thoroughly an Indian woman as the squaws who cared for and reared her.

The ceremony of her adoption very much resembled a wake. All the squaws in the village gathered in the wigwam of the Seneca women, surrounded little Mary, and set up a most dismal howling, weeping bitterly, and bemoaning the death of the brother who had been slain.   Tears flowed freely, and all the signs of genuine grief were manifested.   One of the sisters in a broken voice bewailed their loss, and extolled the virtues and prowess of the deceased.   Her eulogium ended with these words : " Oh, friends, he is happy ! then dry up your tears.   His spirit has seen our distress and sent a solace whom with pleasure we greet.   Deh-he-wa-mis has come, then let us receive her with joy. She is handsome and pleasant.   Oh, she is our sister, and gladly we welcome her.   In the place of our brother she stands in our tribe."   As the sister ceased speaking the grief of the party turned to joy, and they rejoiced over the little white girl as over a long-lost child. Her Indian name, Deh-he-wa-mis, signifies a low, musical voice, or, perhaps more literally, two falling voices, and was probably given her because of the great difference between her sweet, childish tones and the harsh, grunting gutteral to which the sisters were accustomed. Her life as a Seneca woman now began. She lived in the summer in a town her people had built on the Ohio River, called by them Wi-ish-to, and assisted at first in the care of the papooses and in carrying the small game killed in the vicinity, and as her strength increased began to work in the cornfields with other squaws. After the crops were gathered the tribe moved each season down the Ohio to its junction with the Sciota. The forests in this region abounded with elk and deer which, in addition to their skins, furnished an abundant supply of meat, while the marshes and streams afforded liberal supplies of peltry in way of muskrat, mink, and beaver. These the women assisted to dry, tan, and fit for market at Sandusky and other trading stations on Lake Erie.

Two years passed in this way, when peace was declared between the French and English, and the Indians went up to Fort Pitt to make a treaty with the latter, taking Miss Jemison with them. She here met for the first time since leaving Fort Du Quesne — the name of which had been changed to Pitt — with people of her own race and tongue, who were much surprised to see so young and apparently delicate a girl enduring the hardships of a savage life. They asked her name, inquired into the circumstances of her capture, and appeared much interested in her behalf. Her Indian sisters becoming alarmed, and fearing she would be taken from them, hurried her into their canoe and never once stopped paddling until they reached home. Their fears were not groundless, as the English had determined to offer her a home and freedom. While living at Wi-ish-to the Senecas were joined by a party of Delawares who took up their abode there, and lived in common with them. The Delawares were one of the subjugated tribes ruled by the Iroquois. They had not been settled very long with the Senecas before Miss Jemison's sisters told her she must go and live with one of them, whose name was Shen-in-jee, and she was accordingly married, before she had reached her seventeenth year, to the Delaware brave. She says of her husband: "He was a noble man, large in stature, elegant in appearance, generous in his conduct, corteous in war, a friend to peace, and a lover of justice. The idea of spending my days with him was at first repugnant to my feelings, but his good nature, generosity, and tenderness toward me soon gained my affection, and, strange as it may seem, I loved him. We lived happily together until our final separation, which happened two or three years after our marriage." Her first Indian child — a girl — lived only two days, and nearly cost its young mother her life; her second, a son, was born in the fifth winter of her captivity, and proved to be a strong and healthy child, living until 1811, when he was killed in a quarrel by his younger brother John. Her eldest boy she called Thomas, after her murdered father. When this child was about nine months old she set out on foot for Little Beards town on the Genesee River. Her two sisters had preceded her by more than a year. She was accompanied on the journey by her husband and her three brothers, the latter belonging to the Seneca tribe. Arrived in the neighborhood of Sandusky, her husband, Sen-in-jee, concluded to return to Wi-ish-to and spend the winter hunting with his friends. He accordingly sent her forward with her brothers, promising to join them in the spring on the Genesee.

Now began a march which for unflinching fortitude and plucky endurance has scarcely a parallel. Let us hear her own account of it. She says: " Those only who have traveled on foot a distance of five or six hundred miles through an almost pathless wilderness can form an idea of the fatigue and suffering I endured on that journey. My clothing was thin and illy calculated to defend me from the drenching rains with which I was almost daily wet, and at night, with nothing but my wet blanket to cover me, I had to sleep on the bare ground, without shelter, save such as nature provided. In addition to all this, I had to carry my boy, then about nine months old, every step of the journey, on my back, and provide for his comfort and prevent his suffering, as far as the poverty of my means would admit."

Be it remembered that the woods were pathless and continuous, that the streams were swollen and bridgeless, and that but one of the party was acquainted with the trail, over which he had passed in going to and returning from the Cherokee wars. Sherman's march to the sea was a holiday parade compared with the heroism of this tramp by the plucky little Irish woman. Her brothers had caught two horses near a deserted Indian

village, but with that noble disdain of toil characteristic of the
red man they bestrode the steeds, and left the delicate under-
sized white woman with her burden to struggle after them on
foot, never apparently having heard of Dogberry's remark upon
" two riding of a horse." But all things have an end, and the
party at last arrived at Little Beards town on the Genesee, where
they were received with every demonstration of welcome by the
sisters who had preceded them, and by other members of the Indian family. Mrs. Jemison says: " I spent the winter com-
fortably and as agreeably as could have been expected in the
absence of my kind husband." It will be seen from this that,
although just past her eighteenth year, she had already become
thoroughly identified and satisfied with her mode of life and
surroundings. But she was never again to see her kind husband.
He died at Wi-ish-to the winter after leaving her. This, she
says, " was a heavy blow, but after a few months my grief wore
off and I became contented." Another, and to her an apparently heavier, blow was impending. Peace had been declared
between the French and English and a bounty had been offered
to any one who would bring in the prisoners that had been taken
during the war to the military post at Niagara, where they were
to be redeemed and set at liberty. She preferred death to liberty,
and an agreement was made with one of her Indian brothers that
sooner than see her delivered up to the whites and freedom she
was to die by his hand. It will hardly be necessary after this
statement to again assert how strongly she had become attached
to her Indian mode of life. She remained in hiding until all
danger of her being set at liberty had passed, and then joyfully
resumed her place in the tribe. She soon after married a Seneca
warrior whose name was Hiokatoo, though commonly called
Gardeau, by whom she had four daughters and two sons. Her
affection for her relatives from whom she was so terribly parted
seems still to have been strong, as she named her children for
them, calling the girls Jane, Nancy, Betsy, and Polly, and the
boys John and Jesse. Thoroughly satisfied with her surroundings, she thus describes them: " No people can live more happily
than the Indians did in times of peace before the introduction of spirituous liquors among them. Their lives were a con-
tinual round of pleasure. Their cares were few, their wants
were only for to-day, their thoughts not extending to the uncer-
tainties of to-morrow." She pays high tribute to the honesty

and morality of the Indians, tells us they despised deception and falsehood, and held chastity in such veneration that a violation of it was considered sacrilege. They were living this peaceful, virtuous, arcadian life, according to Mrs. Jemison, when the trouble that had long been brewing between King and Colonies was about to break forth in rebellious war.

Anxious to secure the neutrality of the Six Nations, the Colonies called their sachems, chiefs, and warriors together in a general council, which was held at German Flats, in order to ascertain in good time whom they should consider and treat as friends and whom as enemies in the war then about to break out. The result was a treaty of peace in which the Iroquois solemnly agreed that in event of the outbreak of hostilities they would not take up arms on either side, but would observe a strict neutrality. About a year after this, agents were sent to the Six Nations requesting them to convene in general council at Oswego for the purpose of conferring with British Commissioners, who were desirous to secure their assistance in subduing the rebels who had risen against the good King, their master, and were about to rob him of a great part of his possessions and wealth. The council having convened, and its object having been stated by the British envoys, the sachems arose and informed them of the nature of the treaty they had made the year previous with the people of the States, and declared they would not violate it by taking up the hatchet for either side. The Commissioners, however, were not to be denied. They represented to the Indians that the people of the Colonies were few, poor, and easily to be subdued; while the good King was rich and powerful, both in money and subjects; that his rum was as plentiful as the waters of Lake Ontario and his soldiers as numerous as the sands on its shores, and if they would assist their great father, the good King, they should never want for money, arms, rum, or blankets.

Here Mrs. Jemison's dusky idols step down from their pedestals. Their fidelity is no longer perfect. They no longer despise deception and falsehood. They are no longer candid and honorable in their sentiments. In a moment they become dishonorable, false, and treacherous. Stimulated by bloodthirstiness and greed they concluded a treaty with the British Commissioners in which they agreed to take up arms against the Colonies and continue in his Majesty's service until his rebellious

subjects were subdued.   As soon as the treaty was ratified, the
Commissioners made a present to each Indian of a suit of clothes,
a brass kettle, a gun, a tomahawk and scalping knife, a quantity
of powder and lead, a piece of gold, and promised a bounty on
every scalp that should be brought in.   Thus equipped, these
merciless devils went forth to torture, slaughter, and scalp men,
women, and children, who had given them no offense, and with
whom they had but a short time before made a treaty of strict
neutrality.   It would be idle to write words denouncing the red
man.   He acted up to his lights and instincts.   His white em-
ployers acted according to their instincts, but not according to
their lights.   Their conduct may be safely left to the just judgment of mankind.

For a time all went well with the red men, and they burned,
scalped, and tortured the frontier settlers almost without opposition, but the cry for relief at length was heeded, and in the
autumn of 1779, General Sullivan was sent with an army to
devastate the Indian country and destroy their means of subsistence.   He performed the work effectually, and the allies of
the good King learned by sad experience that in war there are
blows to receive as well as blows to give.   It is plainly to be
seen from Mrs. Jemison's narrative that her sympathies were
wholly with the Indians and against the whites in the war then
going on.   She says of Sullivan and his army : " They destroyed
every article of food they could lay their hands on.   They burnt
our houses, killed what few cattle and horses they could find,
destroyed our fruit trees, and left nothing but the bare soil and
timber."   She congratulates herself that " The Indians had
eloped and were nowhere to be found."   The noble red man left
his squaw and pappooses to shift for themselves, and took to the
woods.   The result, so far as Mrs. Jemison and her offspring
were concerned, was that she was obliged to husk corn for two
negroes whose crops were not destroyed, and through this labor
accumulated twenty-five bushels of shelled grain which kept her
family in samp and cakes for the winter.

Soon after the close of the Revolutionary War the Indians, by
treaty, agreed to surrender all prisoners held by them, and Mary
was again offered her liberty, which she again refused to accept.
The Indians were pleased with her loyalty, and told her if it was
her choice to live among them she should have a piece of land
which she could call her own, and bequeath at her decease to her

children.   For a long time no attempt was made to fulfill this
promise, but when the great council was held at Big Tree,
Farmers Brother sent for her to attend.   He presented and
urged her claim to the land that had been promised her.   Red
Jacket opposed the gift with all his influence and eloquence, but
the little white woman had able champions in the United States
Commissioners, two of whom, Jasper Parrish and Horatio Jones,
having been many years in captivity among the Indians, were
able to argue her case with Red Jacket in his own tongue, and
at length convinced him that it was the white people and not the
Indians who were giving the land, and gained his assent to the
transfer.   In this way she became possessed of what has been
known ever since as the Gardeau Reservation, which is situated
on both sides of the Genesee River, near Mount Morris, and contains about 18,000 acres of land.   Mr. James Wadsworth, of
Geneseo, who now owns a part of the tract, estimates the value
of the whole reservation at $45 per acre, or a total of $800,000,
as the present worth of the gift to the white woman.   Referring
to her property she says: " My flats were extremely fertile but
needed more labor than my daughters and myself were able to perform.   In order that we might live with greater ease, Captain
Parrish, with the consent of the chiefs, gave me liberty to let or
lease my land to white people to till on shares.   This made my
task less burdensome, while at the same time I was better supplied
with the means of support."

Although now a rich landed proprietress and able to live at
her ease, Mrs. Jemison was by no means free from trouble and
sorrow.   She was destined again to encounter severe domestic
afflictions.   Her second husband, Hiokatoo, was about fifty-five
years of age when she married him — she about twenty-two.
A more merciless wretch and red-handed fiend never breathed.
To burn the cabin of a white settler and throw his helpless children into the flames before their parents' eyes, to take an infant
child from its mother's arms and dash its brains out against a
stump or stone, to practice every torture upon prisoners that
ingenious deviltry could invent, was pastime to this gentle
savage.   Yet Madam Hiokatoo says he " was a kind and attentive husband, and uniformly treated me with all the tenderness
due a wife."   Her estimate of the Indian character must be received with many grains of allowance.   General Sheridan's is
preferable: " The only good Indian is a dead one."   Even Mrs.

Jemison is forced to admit that her loving partner's " cruelties to his enemies were unparalleled, and not to be palliated."

Her punishment for association with him came in bearing children to him who inherited his disposition. Two of her sons were murdered by a third. The fratricide seems to have possessed all his sire's bad traits and none of his good ones — if he had any. In a quarrel with his elder half-brother, Thomas (son of Shen-in-jee), he seized him by the scalp and dragged him out of their cabin and dispatched him with a tomahawk. The sachems assembled in council, tried John, the offender, according to their laws, and acquitted him. A statement of the grounds of this decision will give us some insight into Indian notions of justice. Thomas, for some cause not known, had always called his brother John a witch, and as they grew to manhood this was the cause of frequent quarrels between them. Another source of contention arose from the fact that John had two wives, which Thomas held to be wrong, although polygamy was at the time tolerated by the tribe. When sober, Thomas was peaceful, but when under the influence of liquor, he was quarrelsome and seemed to lose all reason and act like a maniac. In one of these fits of delirium he had threatened his mother for having given birth to a witch (John), and had gone so far as to raise a tomahawk to brain her. In July, 1811, he came to her house in her absence, and, being intoxicated, at once began a quarrel with his brother, who dispatched him as stated. In view of all the facts, the sachems adjudged Thomas to be the aggressor, and acquitted John. It would be a mistake to conclude from this relation that John Jemison was dangerous only when assailed. On the contrary, he was fiendish and aggressive in the extreme. His mother says of him that " from childhood he carried something in his features indicative of an evil disposition, and it was the opinion of those who knew him that he would be guilty of some crime deserving death." Such a crime he committed within a twelvemonth after having killed Thomas, by murdering his younger brother Jesse in a drunken quarrel. No notice seems to have been taken of this butchery either by whites or natives, and its perpetrator lived unmolested until some time in 1817, when he met his death at the hands of two Squakie Hill Indians named Doctor and Jack. The sins of the father were visited upon the children of Mrs. Jemison, all of her sons having met violent deaths. To her youngest son, Jesse, she was af-

fectionately devoted.   She describes him as being mild-tempered,
good-mannered, intimate with the white people, whose habits
of industry he copied, and willing in every way to assist her in
her labors, and make her burdens lighter.   He shunned the
company of his brothers, and this, she says, " together with my
partiality for him, excited in his brother John a degree of envy
that nothing short of death would satisfy."

Border warfare develops many remarkable characters, both
good and evil.   One of these who obtained a bad eminence during the Revolutionary struggle, and was a prominent figure in
the early history of the Genesee Country, was Ebenezer, or Indian,
Allen.   He was sheltered and protected by the White Woman,
with whom he established a cordial and proper intimacy.   She
was to him a most faithful friend and ally.   Menace and en-
treaty were alike powerless to shake her loyalty to the backwoods
renegade.   Her recital of some of the incidents of his career
will be given in her own words: " Some time near the close of
the Revolutionary War, a white man, by the name of Ebenezer
Allen, left his people, in the State of Pennsylvania, on account
of some disaffection toward his countrymen, and came to the
Genesee River to reside with the Indians.   He tarried at Geni-
shau a few days, and came up to Gardeau, where I then resided.
He was, apparently, without any business that would support him; but he soon became acquainted with my son Thomas,
with whom he hunted for a long time, and made his home with
him at my house.   Winter came on, and he continued his
stay.*

" When Allen came to my house I had a white man living on
my land, who had a Nanticoke squaw for his wife, wi⁺h whom he
had lived very peaceably ; for he was a moderate man, commonly,
and she was a kind, gentle, cunning creature.   It so happened
that he had no hay for his cattle; so that in the winter he was
obliged to drive them every day perhaps a mile from his house to
let them feed on the rushes, which in those days were so numerous
as to nearly cover the ground.

" Allen, having frequently seen the squaw in the fall, took the
opportunity when her husband was absent with his cows daily to
make her a visit; and in return for his kindnesses she made and

---

* Ebenezer Allen was no hero, but rather, a desperado.   He warred
against his own race, country, and color; and vied with his savage allies in
deeds of cruelty and bloodshed.   He was a native of New Jersey."
— TURNER'S HISTORY OF THE HOLLAND PURCHASE, p. 297.

gave him a red cap, finished and decorated in the highest Indian style.

" The husband had for some considerable length of time felt a degree of jealousy that Allen was trespassing upon his rights, with the consent of his squaw; but when he saw Allen dressed in so fine an Indian cap, and found that his dear Nanticoke had presented it to him, his doubts all left him, and he became so violently enraged that he caught her by the hair of her head, dragged her on the ground to my house, a distance of forty rods, and threw her in at the door. Hiokatoo, my husband, exasperated at the sight of so much inhumanity, hastily took down his old tomahawk, which for a while had lain idle, shook it over the cuckold's head, and bade him jogo (i. e., go off). The enraged husband, well knowing that he should feel a blow if he waited to hear the order repeated, instantly retreated, and went down the river to his cattle. We protected the poor Nanticoke woman, and gave her victuals; and Allen sympathized with her in her misfortunes till spring, when her husband came to her, acknowledged his former errors, and that he had abused her without a cause, promised a reformation, and she received him with every mark of a renewal of her affection. They went home lovingly, and soon after removed to Niagara.

" The same spring, Allen commenced working my flats, and continued to labor there till after the peace of 1783. He then went to Philadelphia on some business that detained him but a few days, and returned with a horse and some dry goods, which he carried to a place that is now called Mount Morris, where he built or bought a small house.

" The British and Indians on the Niagara frontier, dissatisfied with the treaty of peace, were determined, at all hazards, to continue their depredations upon the white settlements which lay between them and Albany. They actually made ready, and were about setting out on an expedition to that effect, when Allen (who by this time understood their system of war) took a belt of wampum, which he had fraudulently procured, and carried it as a token of peace from the Indians to the commander of the nearest American military post. The Indians were soon answered by the American officer, that the wampum was cordially accepted, and that a continuance of peace was ardently wished for. The Indians, at this, were chagrined and disappointed beyond measure; but, as they held the wampum to be a sacred thing, they dared not go against the import of its meaning, and immediately buried the hatchet, as it respected the people of the United States, and smoked the pipe of peace. They, however, resolved to punish Allen for his officiousness in meddling with their national affairs, by presenting the sacred wampum without their knowledge; and went about devising means for his detection. A party was accordingly dispatched from Fort Niagara to apprehend him, with orders to conduct him to that post for trial, or for safe keeping, till such time as his fate should be determined upon in a legal manner.

" The party came on; but before it arrived at Gardeau, Allen got news of its approach, and fled for safety, leaving the horse and goods that he had brought from Philadelphia an easy prey to his enemies. He had not been long absent when they arrived at Gardeau, where they made diligent search for him till they were satisfied that they could not find him, and then seized the effects which he had left and returned to Niagara. My son Thomas went with them, with Allen's horse, and carried the goods.

" Allen, on finding that his enemies had gone, came back to my house, where he lived as before; but of his return they were soon notified at Niagara, and Nettles (who married Priscilla Ramsay), with a small party of Indians, came on to take him. He, however, by some means found that they were near, and gave me his box of money and trinkets to keep safely till he called for it, and again took to the woods. Nettles came on, determined, at all events, to take him before he went back; and, in order to accomplish his design, he, with his Indians, hunted in the day time, and lay by at night at my house; and in that way they practiced for a number of days. Allen watched the motions of his pursuers, and every night after they had gone to rest, came home and got some food, and then returned to his retreat. It was in the fall, and the weather was cold and rainy, so that he suffered extremely. Some nights he sat in my chamber till nearly daybreak, while his enemies were below; and when the time arrived, I assisted him to escape unnoticed.

" Nettles at length abandoned the chase, went home, and Allen, all in tatters, came in. By running in the woods his clothing had become torn into rags, so that he was in a suffering condition, almost naked. Hiokatoo gave him a blanket, and a piece of broadcloth for a pair of trousers. Allen made his trousers himself, and then built a raft, on which he went down the river to his own place at Mount Morris.

"About that time he married a squaw, whose name was Sally.

"The Niagara people, finding that he was at his own house, came and took him by surprise, and carried him to Niagara. Fortunately for him, it so happened that just as they arrived at the fort, a house took fire, and his keepers all left him, to save the building if possible. Allen had supposed his doom to be nearly sealed; but, finding himself at liberty, he took to his heels, left his escort to put out the fire, and ran to Tonawanda. There an Indian gave him some refreshments, and a good gun, with which he hastened on to Little Beard's Town, where he found his squaw. Not daring to risk himself at that place, for fear of being given up, he made her but a short visit, and came immediately to Gardeau.

"Just as he got to the top of the hill above the Gardeau Flats, he discovered a party of British soldiers and Indians in pursuit of him; and, in fact, they were so near that he was satisfied that they saw him, and concluded that it would be impossible for him to escape. The love of liberty, however, added to his natural swiftness, gave him sufficient strength to make his escape to his former castle of safety. His pursuers came immediately to my house, where they expected to have found him secreted, and under my protection. They told me where they had seen him but a few moments before, and that they were confident that it was within my power to put him into their hands. As I was perfectly clear of having had any hand in his escape, I told them plainly that I had not seen him since he was taken to Niagara, and that I could give them no information at all respecting him. Still unsatisfied, and doubting my veracity, they advised my Indian brother to use his influence to draw from me the secret of his concealment, which they had an idea that I considered of great importance, not only to him but to myself. I persisted in my ignorance of his situation, and finally they left me.

"Although I had not seen Allen, I knew his place of security, and was well aware that, if I told them the place where he had formerly hid himself, they would have no difficulty in making him a prisoner.

"He came to my house in the night, and awoke me with the greatest caution, fearing that some of his enemies might be watching to take him at a time when, and in a place where, it would be impossible for him to make his escape.   I got up, and assured him that he was then safe; but that his enemies would return early in the morning, and search him out if it should be possible. Having given him some victuals, which he received thankfully, I told him to go, but to return the next night to a certain corner of the fence near my house, where he would find a quantity of meal that I would have prepared and deposited there for his use.

"Early the next morning, Nettles and his company came in while I was pounding the meal for Allen, and insisted upon my giving him up.   I again told them that I did not know where he was, and that I could not, neither would I, tell them anything about him.   I well knew that Allen considered his life in my hands; and although it was my intention not to lie, I was fully determined to keep his situation a profound secret.   They continued their labor, and examined, as they supposed, every crevice, gully, tree, and hollow log in the neighboring woods, and at last concluded that he had left the country, gave him up for lost, and returned home.

"At that time Allen lay in a secret place in the gulf, a short distance above my flats, in a hole that he accidentally found in a rock near the river.   At night he came and got the meal at the corner of the fence as I had directed him, and afterward lived in the gulf two weeks.   Each night he came to the pasture and milked one of my cows, without any other vessel in which to receive the milk than his hat, out of which he drank it.   I supplied him with meal, but, fearing to build a fire, he was obliged to eat it raw, and wash it down with the milk.   Nettles having left our neighborhood, and Allen considering himself safe, left his little cave, and came home.   I gave him his box of money and trinkets, and he went to his own house at Mount Morris.   It was generally considered, by the Indians of our tribe, that Allen was an innocent man, and that the Niagara people were persecuting him without a just cause.   Little Beard, then about to go to the eastward on public business, charged his Indians not to meddle with Allen, but to let him live among them peaceably, and enjoy himself with his family and property if he could.   Having the protection of the chief, he felt himself safe, and let his situation be known to the whites, from whom he suspected no harm. They, however, were more inimical than our Indians, and were easily bribed by Nettles to assist in bringing him to justice.

Nettles came on, and the whites, as they had agreed, gave poor Allen up to him. He was bound, and carried to Niagara, where he was confined in prison through the winter. In the spring he was taken to Montreal or Quebec for trial, and was honorably acquitted. The crime for which he was tried was for having carried the wampum to the Americans, and thereby putting too sudden a stop to their war.

" From the place of his trial he went directly to Philadelphia, and purchased on credit a boat load of goods, which he brought by water to Conhocton, where he left them, and came to Mount Morris for assistance to get them brought on. The Indians readily went with horses, and brought them to his house, where he disposed of his drygoods; but not daring to let the Indians begin to drink strong liquor, for fear of the quarrels which would naturally follow, he sent his spirits to my place, where we sold them. For his goods he received ginseng roots, principally, and a few skins. Ginseng at that time was plenty, and commanded a high price. We prepared the whole that he received for the market, expecting that he would carry them to Philadelphia. In that I was disappointed; for, when he had disposed of, and got pay for, all his goods, he took the ginseng and skins to Niagara, and there sold them, and came home.

" Tired of dealing in goods, he planted a large field of corn on or near his own land, attended to it faithfully, and succeeded in raising a large crop, which he harvested, loaded into canoes, and carried down the river to the mouth of Allen's Creek, then called by the Indians Gin-is-a-ga, where he unloaded it, built him a house, and lived with his family.

" The next season he planted corn at that place, and built a grist-mill and sawmill on Genesee Falls, now called Rochester.

" At the time Allen built the mills, he had an old German living with him by the name of Andrews, whom he sent in a canoe down the river with his mill irons. Allen went down at the same time; but, before they got to the mills, Allen threw the old man overboard, as it was then generally believed, for he was never seen or heard of afterward.

" In the course of the season in which Allen built his mills, he became acquainted with the daughter of a white man who was moving to Niagara. She was handsome, and Allen soon got into her good graces, so that he married and took her home, to be a joint partner with Sally, the squaw, whom she had never heard of till she got home and found her in full possession; but it was too late to retrace the hasty steps she had taken, for her father had left her in the care of a tender husband, and gone on. She, however, found that she enjoyed at least an equal half of her husband's affections, and made herself contented. Her father's name I have forgotten, but hers was Lucy.

" Allen was not contented with two wives, for in a short time after he had married Lucy he came up to my house, where he found a young woman who had an old husband with her. They had been on a long journey, and called at my place to recruit and rest themselves. She filled Allen's eye, and he accordingly fixed upon a plan to get her into his possession. He praised his situation, enumerated his advantages, and finally persuaded them to go home and tarry with him a few days at least, and partake of a part of his comforts. They accepted his generous invitation, and went home with him. But they had been there but two or three days, when Allen took the old gentleman out to view his flats; and as they were deliberately walking on the bank of the river pushed him into the water. The old man, almost strangled, succeeded in getting out; but his fall and exertions had so powerful an effect upon his system that he died in two or three days, and left his young widow to the protection of his murderer. She lived with him about one year in a state of concubinage, and then left him.

" How long Allen lived at Allen's Creek I am unable to state; but soon after the young widow left him, he removed to his old place at Mount Morris, and built a house, where he made Sally — his squaw, by whom he had two daughters — a slave to Lucy, by whom he had one son; still, however, he considered Sally to be his wife. After Allen came to Mount Morris at that time, he married a girl by the name of Morilla Gregory, whose father, at the time, lived on Genesee Flats. The ceremony being over, he took her home to live in common with his other wives; but his house was too small for his family — for Sally and Lucy, conceiving that their lawful privileges would be abridged if they received a partner, united their strength, and whipped poor Morilla so cruelly that Allen was obliged to keep her in a small Indian house, a short distance from his own, or lose her entirely. Morilla, before she left Mount Morris, had four children.

" One of Morilla's sisters lived with Allen about a year after Morilla was married, and then quit him.

" A short time after they had been living at Mount Morris, Allen prevailed upon the chiefs to give to his Indian children a tract of land two miles square, where he then resided. The chiefs gave them the land, but he so artfully contrived the conveyance that he could apply it to his own use, and by alienating his right destroy the claim of his children.

" Having secured the land in that way to himself, he sent his two Indian girls to Trenton, N. J., and his white son to Philadelphia, for the purpose of giving each of them a respectable English education.

" While his children were at school, he went to Philadelphia and sold his right to the land, which he had begged of the Indians for his children, to Robert Morris. After that, he sent for his daughters to come home, which they did.

" Having disposed of the whole of his property on the Genesee River, he took his two white wives and their children, together with his effects, and removed to Delaware Town, on the River De Trench, in Upper Canada.* When he left Mount Morris, Sally, his squaw, insisted upon going with him, and actually followed him, crying bitterly, and praying for his protection, some two or three miles, till he absolutely bade her leave him, or he would punish her with severity. At length, finding her case hopeless, she returned to the Indians.

" At the great treaty in 1797, one of Allen's daughters claimed the Mount Morris tract which her father had sold to Robert Morris. The claim was examined, and decided against her, in favor of Morris's creditors.

" He died at the Delaware Town, on the River De Trench, in the year 1814 or 1815, and left two white widows and one squaw, with a number of children to lament his loss.

" By his last will, he gave all his property to his last wife, Morilla, and her children, without providing in the least for the support of Lucy or any of the other members of his family. Lucy, soon after his death, went with her children down the Ohio River to receive assistance from her friends.

" In the Revolutionary War, Allen was a Tory, and by that

* Governor Simcoe granted him three thousand acres of land, upon condition that he would build a sawmill, a grist-mill, and a church. All but the church to be his property. He performed his part of the contract, and the title to his land was confirmed. In a few years, he had his mills, a comfortable dwelling, large improvements, was a good liver, and those who knew him at that period represent him as hospitable and obliging.

means became acquainted with our Indians, when they were in the neighborhood of his native place desolating the settlements on the Susquehanna. In those predatory battles he joined them, and for cruelty was not exceeded by his Indian comrades.

" At one time, when he was scouting with the Indians, he entered a house very early in the morning, where he found a man, his wife, and one child, in bed. The man instantly sprang on the floor, for the purpose of defending himself and little family; but Allen dispatched him at one blow. He then cut off his head, and threw it, bleeding, into the bed with the terrified woman; took the little infant from its mother's breast, dashed its head against the jamb, and left the unhappy widow and mother to mourn alone over her murdered family. It has been said by some, that after he had killed the child he opened the fire and buried it under the coals and embers; but of that I am not certain. I have often heard him speak of that transaction with a great degree of sorrow, and as the foulest crime he had ever committed — one for which I have no doubt he repented.

" About the year 1806, or 1807, reverses began to overtake him. At one period he was arrested and tried for forgery; at another, for passing counterfeit money; at another, for larceny. He was acquitted of each offense upon trial. He was obnoxious to many of his white neighbors, and it is likely that at least two of the charges against him arose out of a combination that was promoted by personal enmity. All this brought on embarrassments, which terminated in an almost entire loss of his large property. He died in 1814."— TURNER'S HISTORY OF THE HOLLAND PURCHASE, pp. 302-3.

In the year 1816, Micah Brooks, of Bloomfield, Ontario County, and his neighbor, Jellis Clute, began negotiations for the purchase of Mrs. Jemison's land; and on the 23d of April, 1817, they bought the entire Gardeau Reservation from her for the sum of three thousand dollars, or about seventeen cents per acre. As the London Associates had paid Mr. Morris twenty-seven cents per acre for the unsold balance of the Phelps and Gorham lands more than a quarter of a century previous, and as Alexander Hamilton had loaned eighty cents per acre on one hundred thousand acres of the Morris Reserve nearly twenty years before the sale to Messrs. Brooks and Clute, it will be seen that the price agreed to be paid by them for Mrs. Jemison's land was not excessive. Perhaps further investigations into

CORN PLANTER

pioneer history may reveal to me some instance in which the
Red Man got the better of the bargain.   If so it shall not fail to
be recorded.   Although deed of the property was given to the
purchasers, and placed upon the records of Genesee County, the
sale was annulled, because of the fact that Mrs. Jemison's title
was defective, she not being a natural born or naturalized citizen,
and the consent of the chiefs of the Seneca Nation being necessary to a legal transfer.   To surmount the first part of this
difficulty, Messrs. Brooks and Clute procured the passage, on
April 11, 1817, of a special act of the Legislature for the relief
of Mary Jemison, which authorized her to take, hold, and convey
real estate, by purchase, devise, or descent, in like manner as
any naturalized citizen, and confirmed to her the grant of the
Gardeau Reservation.   The sale was not concluded until the
lapse of about five years.   She says: " After much delay and
vexation in ascertaining what was necessary to be done to effect
a legal transfer, and having consulted my children and friends,
I agreed in the winter of 1822-23 with Messrs. Brooks and
Clute that if they would get the chiefs of our nation and a United
States Commissioner of Indian lands to meet in Moscow, Livingston County, N. Y., I would sell to them all my right and
title to the Gardeau Reservation, containing 17,927 acres, with
the exception of a tract for my own benefit two miles long by one
mile wide, where I should choose it, and also reserving a lot I had
promised to give to Thomas Clute as a recompense for his faithful
guardianship over me and my property for a long time.   The arrangement was agreed to and the council assembled on the third
day of September, 1823, at the place appointed.   It consisted of
Major Carroll, Judge Howell, and Nathaniel Gorham, acting
for and in behalf of the United States; Jasper Parrish, Indian
agent; Horatio Jones, interpreter; and a large number of Seneca chiefs.   The bargain was assented to unanimously, and a
deed was executed and delivered by me and upward of twenty
chiefs, conveying all my right and title to the Gardeau Reservation except the reservations before mentioned, to Henry B. Gibson, Micah Brooks, and Jellis Clute, their heirs and assigns forever.   The tract I reserved for myself begins at the center of
the Great Slide, thence west one mile, thence north two miles,
thence east about a mile to the Genesee River, and thence south-
erly, along the west bank of the river, to the place of beginning.
In consideration, Messrs. Gibson, Brooks, and Clute — among

other things — bound themselves, their heirs and assigns, to pay me, my heirs and successors, three hundred dollars a year forever."

What the " other things " were that the purchasers bound themselves to do I have not been able to ascertain; but in the year 1830 she sold her remaining two square miles of land to Messrs. Gibson and Clute, and, commuting her annuity for a lump sum in ready money, removed to the Buffalo Creek reservation, where she purchased the Indian right of possession to a small piece of land on which she resided until her decease.   In this, the last prominent incident in her career, she showed, as she had done a number of times in her earlier history, her thorough attachment to her adopted friends and their mode of life. The Senecas, in 1825, sold all their reservations on the Genesee River and removed with their families to the Tonawanda, Buffalo Creek, and Cattaraugus reservations, leaving Mrs. Jemison alone among the white people.   This was more than she could endure, and she accordingly disposed of her remaining lands and joined her red brethren at Buffalo Creek.   Misfortune attended her here.   After paying for the land and cabin which she had purchased, the remaining proceeds of the sale of her Genesee lands — a sum barely sufficient to make her last days comfortable — were entrusted to a white man who lost them in unfortunate speculations.   She died in her own house on the 19th day of September, 1833, aged about ninety-one years.   She was small in stature, had a very white skin, golden yellow hair, blue eyes, delicate hands and feet, and pleasing, regular features. She was, in fact, a handsome type of Irish blonde beauty.   Her endurance was little short of marvelous.   For seventy-five years she performed daily such tasks as fall to the lot of men employed in agricultural labor.   She planted, hoed, and husked her own corn, fed and milked her own cows, and chopped her own firewood.   She slept upon skins without any bedstead, sat upon the floor or on a bench without a back, and when she ate held her food on her lap or in her hands in Indian fashion.   Her way of life was thoroughly that of the people with whom she lived for more than three-quarters of a century.

The attempts that have been made to treat her as a heroine and model worthy of imitation are not well advised.   She was in fact, a generous, plucky, little Irish peasant woman who loved a fight as dearly as any one of her countrymen who ever trailed his coat and flourished his shillelah at Donnybrook fair. When past her eightieth year, and telling for publication the story of her life, she extolled the good qualities of the red-handed fiend, her husband — Hiokatoo — and though admitting that his atrocities were unparalleled, there is no evidence that she ever tried to stay his hand. She aided, abetted, sheltered, and encouraged the Bluebeard desperado, outlaw, and cutthroat of the Genesee — Indian Allen. Her fortitude and self-control were Indian traits, and good ones. She was a pagan until her ninety-first year. Her profession of Christianity after that date, when her faculties were dimmed by years, may be taken at any valuation the reader chooses to put upon it. The good missionary lady who visited her in her first and last illness, and tried to administer to her the consolations of religion, says in her narrative: "My visit evidently excited and wearied her, and she seemed quite exhausted, and toward the last quite sleepy; which warned me that I ought to bring it to a close."

Mrs. Jemison's remains were buried in the graveyard of the Seneca Mission Church near Buffalo. Red Jacket was interred but a few feet from her tomb. It was not their last resting place. The famous sachem sleeps on the Cattaraugus Reservation;* and the White Woman sleeps on the banks of the Genesee.

The following account of her removal and reinterment is taken from the *Buffalo Courier* of March 10, 1874:

MARY JEMISON.

THE REMAINS OF THE " WHITE WOMAN OF THE GENESEE "
REMOVED TO HER OLD HOME.

The remains of Mary Jemison, or Deh-he-wa-mis, commonly known as the " White Woman of the Genesee," were taken up last week from the old Mission burying ground at Red Jacket, near Buffalo, where they had been buried about forty years ago, and conveyed to the neighborhood of her home and life-long associations on the Genesee River. The stone that had marked her grave had been nearly destroyed by remorseless relic hunters, by whom it had been broken and carried away piece by piece until but a small portion of it remained above the ground. It was feared by those interested in preserving whatever pertained to the history of this remarkable character that in a few years all trace of her resting place would be obliterated.

---

* At a later date, the remains of Red Jacket were removed to Buffalo and interred in Forest Lawn Cemetery, where a stately shaft marks the spot.

The removal of the remains took place under the direction of "Dr. James Shongo," a favorite grandson of the deceased, son of her daughter Polly by marriage with John Shongo. James was born under the "White Woman's" roof, and was a member of her family during his boyhood, and was present at her death and funeral. He also assisted in the removal of his grandmother to Buffalo, at the time she left the Gardeau Reservation, a few years prior to her death.

The spot selected for the final resting place of her remains is a high eminence on the left bank of the Genesee River, overlooking the Upper and Middle Falls. The point is one commanding the finest views of the picturesque scenery of Portage — including both the Upper and Middle Falls and railroad bridge. Upon this eminence and quite near to her present grave is the ancient Seneca Council-house, removed a year or two since from Caneadea, within which it is believed Mary Jemison rested for the first time after her long and fatiguing journey of six hundred miles from Ohio, during which she carried her infant upon her back. The reinterment took place on Saturday afternoon in the presence of a large concourse of people, some of whom were old citizens from the Reservation which she once owned, who had known her during her life and held her memory in esteem. The remains were borne from Castile village to the old Council-house, within which appropriate exercises were conducted by Rev. W. D. McKinley of Castile. They consisted of the reading of selections from Scripture, a brief but very interesting reminiscence of the eventful life of the subject, and prayer. From the Council-house the remains were taken to the grave, a few feet northerly of the building. The following gentlemen officiated as pall-bearers:

George Wheeler, D. W. Bishop, Giles Davis, Benjamin Burlingham, John Peter Kelly, Isaac McNair.

Mary Jemison's former residence on the Gardeau Flats is but a few miles from the spot where her ashes now repose, and, standing by her grave, the murmur of the Genesee may be heard as she heard it during nearly seventy years that she lived upon its banks. We are informed that the grounds about her grave are to be enclosed with an iron fence, and that it has already or soon will be conveyed by its present owner in perpetuity to the State of New York. It is also in contemplation to erect a suitable memorial within the enclosure.

JEMIMA WILKINSON.

Imposture most securely lurks under the cloak of religion. Men are most apt to believe what they least understand.—MONTAIGNE.

JEMIMA WILKINSON, a preacher and prophet of the latter part of the eighteenth century, was born in the State of Rhode Island in the year 1751. Her parents, Jeremiah and Amy Whipple Wilkinson, were of the customary poor but reputable class. Their family was large, consisting of six sons and an equal number of daughters, Jemima being the eighth child of the marriage. The father, though not a member of the Society of Friends, usually attended the meetings of that sect, of which his wife was a strict adherent. She was an amiable and intelligent person, a devoted wife and affectionate mother, whose life, while spared, was given up to the care and training of her large family. She died in giving birth to her twelfth child — the subject of this sketch being then eight years of age. The father never remarried, and his numerous offspring received but the simplest rudiments of education, and were taught such branches of labor and domestic economy as were common in New England farm houses in colonial times. By the time Miss Jemima had reached an age when she was expected to assist in household labor and duties she began to develop some of the peculiar traits of character which later in life made her so marked a personality. An unconquerable aversion to labor, an unusual cunning in shifting upon others the tasks assigned to her, an imperious will, and a strong propensity to dictate and rule, together with a love for idleness, finery, pomposity, and superiority were marked features of her character before she had reached her seventeenth year. Finding her unmanageable at home, and yielding to her solicitations, her father permitted her to go to a neighboring town for the purpose of learning the trade of a tailor, and it would have been well in later years for many of her ruined dupes if she had made herself mistress of that useful occupation, and remained a tailor instead of becoming a prophet. Steady employment was her pet aversion, and after an apprenticeship of a few months she was dismissed and sent back to her father's house.

Her life for the next few years was uneventful — her contempt for industry and fondness for dress, excitement, and pleasure being its chief features. About the year 1774 she attended a series of meetings held by a sect styling themselves New-Lights. They were fanatical zealots, who professed to live continually under the power and spirit of religion, and to be guided and illuminated directly from on high. Under their ministrations Jemima became serious, her airy gayety was exchanged for sedateness and reflection, and she appeared to have received a strong impression as to the nature and necessity of religion. She discarded all other reading for the Bible, discontinued her visits abroad, and after a time secluded herself altogether from company, confining herself to her own room and, after a time, to her bed. A physician called by her family was unable to locate or trace any symptoms of disease, she complained of no pain or distress, and told him plainly that she had no occasion for his services. He therefore gave it as his opinion to her friends that she was under some strong mental delusion, the removal of which could not be effected by medical treatment. She soon after confined herself altogether to her bed, became pale and wan, and began to speak of having visions from heaven and of seeing celestial forms hovering about her. Her family, believing her about to die, watched by her bedside both day and night for many weary weeks. At length this consummate actress played the last scene in the ghastly farce she had so long been enacting. She lay pale, motionless, and apparently lifeless during an entire afternoon and evening, but those who watched her closely saw that respiration was going on, though so softly as almost to defy detection. When the clock struck the hour of midnight she arose from the bed, declared that she had passed the gates of death, and was a new and immortal being, risen from the dead, and in a tone of voice consonant with her old imperious manner demanded her clothing, in which she arrayed herself and went forth apparently as well as ever, though pale and somewhat enfeebled by her long fasting and confinement. To her friends who congratulated her on her recovery she promptly and vehemently denied that she was Jemima Wilkinson, and boldly asserted that she was a new being, reanimated by the power and spirit of God, and commissioned from on high to save a lost and dying world. She alluded to her body as the tabernacle that had formerly been inhabited by Jemima, but proclaimed that it was now immortal — that she would live and reign on earth a thousand years, at the end of which time she would be taken up to heaven in a cloud of glory. Her first public address was delivered the Sabbath after she had risen from the dead, or bed, as the case may be. She attended public worship at the Meeting House in the neighborhood, and, as she no doubt expected and wished, was an object of much curiosity to the assembly, many of whom had heard the tale of her death and resurrection. During the intermission between the morning and afternoon services she retired to the shade of a tree at some little distance from the church and was soon surrounded by the entire congregation. Here she delivered her first public address. Having for more than a year devoted her time to a study of the Bible and other religious books, she displayed a knowledge of the subject she was discussing which quite astonished her hearers, and led some of the more credulous among them to believe that her utterances were inspired, and from this class the nucleus of a sect was formed which for nearly half a century followed her footsteps, and were ruled and governed by her with an imperious and unquestioned sway. She formulated no creed, but announced herself as " The Universal Friend of Mankind, whom the mouth of the Lord hath named." She did not at first gather her followers about her and establish a church and society, but became for a time a sort of itinerant; her inordinate vanity being fed by the attention she attracted wherever her meetings were held. During the first year of her ministry she visited and preached in Newport, Providence, New Bedford, and other towns in Rhode Island, Massachusetts, and Connecticut. During her stay in Newport she attracted the attention of a number of British officers stationed there, to one of whom she became engaged to be married.

It was a genuine affair of the heart on the part of both, and preparations were made for a honeymoon voyage to England, but military operations intervened to postpone the happy event, and a bullet encountered by her lover put an end to it. Jemima was greatly distressed, but with the almost supernatural command over her feelings which she possessed, she resumed her ministry, and thenceforward denounced matrimony as a sin and an abomination in the sight of the Lord, and prohibited it amongst her followers. About the year 1781 she proposed to

a number of her confidential advisers the desirability of a tour
into the State of Pennsylvania, the object being to draw proselytes from the Quakers, who were numerous and wealthy in
Philadelphia and its vicinity.   She represented to her people that
she had received a special mandate from heaven to visit these
Friends, who were anxiously awaiting the coming of the Lord's
messenger.   A generous subscription was made by the faithful
to defray the expenses of the journey, which she undertook in
company with four or five of her most devoted followers.   They
traveled leisurely, and with as much comfort as the conditions
of that period afforded.   The story of her death, resurrection,
divine mission, power to heal the sick and raise the dead had
preceded her, and had lost nothing in the telling, and it is not
surprising that her appearance in Philadelphia produced a considerable degree of sensation and curiosity, and that crowds
followed her in the streets and flocked to hear her in
such numbers that it was with difficulty that any place
could be obtained of sufficient capacity to contain them.
After a time, curiosity regarding her began to wane.   No
politician, however astute, could excel Jemima in detecting the
advancing and receding waves of popular excitement, and when
her audiences began to diminish she promptly had a vision from
on high commanding her to return to her flock in Rhode Island.
She remained with her New England followers until the summer
of 1784, when she again took her departure for the State of
Pennsylvania, locating this time in the town of Worcester, Montgomery County, where one of the wealthiest and most devoted
of her adherents resided.   This gentleman was an extensive
landed proprietor, owning a number of large and fertile farms in
the vicinity of his residence.   Upon one of these Jemima and the
retinue of personal disciples and attendants who composed her
household took up their abode.   Upon the premises were a commodious stone dwelling, barns, carriage house, and stables, with
all the stock and utensils usually belonging to a prosperous
farmer.   Of all this the Universal Friend took possession, as
though she had been its owner in fee.   Nor did her exactions
stop here.   Whatever else she coveted her infatuated adherent
was weak enough to yield, until his estates became encumbered
and ruin began to stare him in the face.   " The Lord hath need
of it," was her impious phrase in levying exactions upon this
deluded man, and this command seemed to him a mandate from

on high that could not be disregarded. A year or two of ease
and comfort were passed by her on the farm of her disciple before
symptoms of revolt and returning reason on his part began to
exhibit themselves. She was quick to detect the change and
prompt in discovering what she believed to be the grounds for it.
She rightly attributed the decline of her influence to the following causes: the increase of education, the circulation of news-
papers, the general spread of useful knowledge, and the fact
that in a thickly settled and intelligent community her dupes
were likely to be influenced by their environments, and begin to
question, while she wished them only to believe. To counteract
these baleful influences she resolved to emigrate with her
remaining followers to a new and unpopulated region, where
intelligence and doubt could never come to arouse the minds and
unsettle the faith of her disciples. She had heard glowing
accounts of the Genesee Country, or, as she called it, the " Lake
Country," then a continuous wilderness; and thither she proposed to emigrate with her followers, believing in her narrow-
mindedness that there she could live and reign a thousand years
undisturbed by the meddlesome and caviling influences of civilization. The generation now inhabiting the Lake Country may
be pardoned for irreverently regarding the gift of prophecy
which consigned their fertile and beautiful region to a thousand
years of ignorance and solitude. To raise funds for her emigration scheme, Jemima made a third and — as it proved — a last
visit to Rhode Island. During her absence in Pennsylvania
many of her New England followers had become lukewarm, and
collections for the scheme came in slowly. Those who had money
to give were not at all enthusiastic about surrendering good
homes and society, with all the pleasures afforded by a highly
cultivated country, for a frontier life, with its privations, dan-
gers, and vicissitudes, even though lands were cheap, and the
country was described as a veritable New Jerusalem, where the
wicked would cease from troubling and the weary be at rest.
But where there is a will there is a way, though in this case it
proved to be dishonest and dangerous. One of Jemima's female
abettors was a resident in the family of the treasurer of the State
of Rhode Island. " The Lord hath need of money," so these
worthy teachers of religion and morality abstracted about two
thousand dollars from the strong box of the State.

The discovery of the robbery created great consternation

among Jemima's followers, and she, fearing criminal prosecution as a participant in the theft, absconded in the night in company with three or four of her adherents and made the best of her way again to Worcester, Pa. Here she was followed by an officer, who arrived almost at the same time with herself. He boldly accused her of having the purloined money in her possession, and demanded its restoration. With the utmost hardihood and composure Jemima denied all knowledge of the missing funds, and appealed to the great Searcher of Hearts to show her pursuer the error of his accusation and the great wrong he was doing to an upright and holy person. The officer, feeling sure she had the money, was not to be thwarted by impious and hypocritical appeals of any sort. He instituted an immediate and thorough search of the house, under such surveillance as would preclude any possibility of removing or concealing the money, and in one of Jemima's traveling trunks found eight hundred dollars of the missing funds. She denied all knowledge of the money thus found, said it had been put in her trunk by some person unknown to her, and without her privity or consent; that it was not hers, and she knew not to whom it belonged, and if he claimed it he was welcome to take it, which he did, and returned to Rhode Island without finding trace of the residue. The balance was made good by two or three wealthy persons whose relatives were implicated, and in order to shield them the affair was allowed to drop. Jemima, however, " fearing every bush an officer," hastened her departure for the land of promise, where she arrived with a number of her followers in the month of April, 1789. Their route was overland to Wilkesbarre, and thence by the Susquehannah River to Elmira, then called Newtown. Here this worthy saint and her vicegerent, one Sarah Richards, undertook to cheat the boatman who had brought them up the river out of a part of the stipulated sum agreed to be paid him; and upon being threatened with prosecution endeavored to suborn two young men of their party to swear that they were to be allowed twenty dollars for assisting the boatman over rapids and places where the current was swift. In order to defraud the laborer of his hire, these young men were asked to commit perjury, and were threatened with the dire displeasure of their saintly mistress if they refused to do so. In spite of threats and entreaties the young men declined to make oath to a falsehood, and the canting would-be swindlers were obliged to pay the boatman's honest demand. In a few days, Jemima found means to convey her followers and their goods and chattels to a tract of land near Crooked Lake, in the present county of Yates. To the new settlement she gave the name of Jerusalem, which is still the name of the town in that county in which it is located. Although expecting to live and reign in undisturbed solitude with her adherents, they had hardly provided themselves with shelter when they found that two enterprising New Englanders, Messrs. Phelps and Gorham, claimed to be owners of the land upon which they had settled. This was wholly unexpected by Jemima, who had relied upon wheedling the Indians out of the tract, and, by persuading them that she was an ambassadress from the Great Spirit, to secure such further portions of their domain as her grasping nature might covet. As she had collected nearly one hundred followers about her, and as Messrs. Phelps and Gorham were anxious to forward the settlement of the country, they made her a generous donation of land, and gave to her people such easy terms and prices as to satisfy all parties.

Jemima, in her character of having put off the earthly and assumed the heavenly, could not be expected to deal in real estate, hence a deed of the tract which she had selected as her resting place during her mundane sojourn was taken in the name of her right-hand maiden and coadjutor, Sarah Richards. It was well selected as to location, having in general a southern and eastern exposure, was finely timbered, and was then, and is still, a most excellent quality of land for agricultural purposes. Her disciples purchased their lands in severalty — the common-stock project was abandoned, and contributions for the support of the Friend and the retinue of personal adherents and servants who composed her household were freely made by the faithful. They plowed, planted, and reaped her fields, supplied her with horses, cattle, sheep, and other domestic animals; made contributions of money, labor, and goods, and seemed only too happy to neglect their own affairs to attend to those of the beloved Friend. As her domain contained about fourteen hundred acres, Jemima lived in greater ease and comfort than was common to the pioneers a hundred years ago. Her household consisted of from fifteen to twenty persons. Of these only four were admitted to her personal intimacy: Sarah Richards and her daughter Eliza, and Rachel and Margaret Malin. The rest were only too happy to do her drudgery indoors and out for a mere subsistence, in order to be near the sacred person of the adored Friend. So far as her sway over her followers was concerned, Jemima's anticipations in removing to the Lake Country were for a time realized.   She ruled and governed them with a rod of iron, punishing with the utmost severity any infractions of the discipline laid down for their guidance.   Being thus secure in her power over her own people, she conceived the idea of converting the Indians — thinking that success would add greatly to her fame as a prophet, and that once established as their spiritual guide she would be able to inveigle them into making her grants of some of their valuable lands.   To further this design she visited Canandaigua at a time when the sachems, chiefs, and warriors of the Seneca Nation were assembled there in council, and while they were engaged in deep consultation burst in upon them without previous notice or introduction, and began a long and vehement address, which, though intended to be a prayer, turned out to be a sort of religious harangue or exhortation. Indian councils are always conducted with the utmost gravity, and the sachems were deeply offended at this interruption.* They showed their impatience by frowns, groans, and grimaces. When she ceased speaking she surveyed her audience attentively to discover what effect she had produced, and was much chagrined to see them at once resume their deliberations without paying the least attention to her or her presence.   She was not discouraged by this rebuff.   Not long after this failure, an Indian treaty was held at Elmira which was attended by a deputation of Oneida chiefs.   In passing through Seneca Lake they encamped for the Sabbath at Norris Landing, in the vicinity of Jemima's settlement.   She embraced the opportunity of preaching to them, and in the course of her sermon endeavored to persuade them that she was Christ, their Saviour.   They listened to her with their usual gravity and attention.   When she had finished one of the chiefs arose and delivered a short and animated address in his own tongue.   When he had concluded Jemima sought the interpreter who was with the Oneidas, and asked him to explain what the speaker had said.   Her wish being made known to the chief who had spoken, he at once promptly replied that she was an impostor, for if she were Jesus Christ she would know what a poor Indian said without being told.   He

---

* The Indians are good listeners.   They consider it the height of rudeness to interrupt anyone who is speaking.

and his party contemptuously turned away and took no further notice of her. To be treated with contempt by savages before her own people was so galling to Jemima's pride that she thenceforward abandoned all attempts upon their morals and lands.

Although pretending to devote her life wholly to spiritual concerns, she was inordinately avaricious and grasping, and was constantly inventing plans to secure by gift, devise, or grant the property of her deluded disciples. In the accomplishment of her purposes she knew no law but her own imperious will, and did not hesitate to alter and amend wills, and other legal instruments which came into her possession, in order to obtain property to which she had no right. Her ignorance, stubbornness, and dishonesty kept her involved a greater part of the time during the last twenty years of her life in a variety of law suits which, though not prosecuted or defended in her name, were in reality litigated in her sole interest. Forgetting the adage about having a fool for a client, she procured and studied legal works from which she probably derived more litigation than law. She did not hesitate for a moment to tell her disciples what she expected them to swear to, asserting that they *must know* that the facts were as the Friend stated them, that they had the word of the Lord for their truth, and that they need not fear man who, at the worst, could only kill the body, while the Lord could kill the soul. These facts became so notorious that her opponents would submit to nonsuit rather than try a case upon which one of her people sat as a juror, and in a number of instances decisions were given against her in the teeth of the most positive evidence on the part of her deluded dupes. The arrest and conviction of one of them for perjury put a stop for a time to her mill for grinding out testimony to order. Being reluctant to employ professional men to attend to her legal matters, and relying upon the little learning which is so dangerous, she in a number of instances was obliged to surrender property which the devisor fully intended to convey to the society. In one instance a large and valuable tract of land devised to the " Universal Friend's Society " reverted to the giver's heirs, because the " Society," not being a body politic or corporate, was incapable of accepting the gift.

Having examined a few of the worldly points of Jemima's character, let us glance briefly at her spiritual traits, with a view to ascertaining whether she was altogether lovely in her assumed role of priest and prophet. As has been stated, she claimed to have arisen from the dead, to have put off the mortal and put on immortality, and to be endued directly with wisdom and power from on high. This, she asserted, rendered her capable of reading the hearts and secret thoughts of mankind, and of performing all miracles mentioned in the Bible. If a scrutiny of her spiritual methods shall reveal her as an impious fraud and sham, not unwilling to commit crime in order to establish her character as a foreteller of events and miracle worker, the fault is hers alone. Firstly, she had accomplices. Some of these resided in her household and formed what may be termed her cabinet council. Others remained in Rhode Island and Pennsylvania to look after and watch over her flock in those States. With these she kept up a close and voluminous correspondence, requring them to report to her fully whatever was said, done, or contemplated by the faithful. In this way not only their acts but their thoughts and desires were communicated to Jemima, and when they joined her in the Lake Country it was as easy as lying for her to tell them what they had been saying and doing, and what they had been wishing and thinking as well. Ignorant, unsuspecting, and credulous, they attributed miraculous power and divination to the person who simply repeated to them what had been reported by her accomplices. Similar means were resorted to with the followers by whom she was surrounded, her cabinet council being very clever in searching out and reporting the wishes, desires, and thoughts of these deluded people, who were awestruck to hear the Beloved Friend announce to them simply what they had told her accomplices.

As to her ability to heal the sick, this was on a par with her mind-reading. When necessary, cases of extreme and apparently mortal illness were made to order, some one of the cabinet council or a devoted follower residing in her household enacting the role of invalid. Tales of healing that were past mortal aid were vouched for by her accomplices, and readily believed by the rest of her community. In visiting any of her flock who were really ill, she was careful to note their condition and apply her miraculous power of healing only to such young and vigorous persons as were already well advanced toward convalescence. With such she prayed fervently, and laying her hands upon them promised them a restoration to health. In nine cases out of ten the promise was fulfilled, and the Divinely empowered Friend was given credit for performing a miraculous cure.

Her attempts to raise the dead were, of course, fraudulent. The first was made before she left Rhode Island. The ghastly farce began with the illness and sudden demise of one of her most devoted and best-beloved adherents. The coffin containing the remains of the deceased was placed in a room where a number of the faithful were congregated. There were also present two or three outsiders, among them a military officer who was disposed to question Jemima's ability to restore the dead to life. After a long prayer in which she earnestly besought power from on high to reanimate the departed, she approached the coffin and was about to command the dead to come forth, when the officer called a halt. He said, " In order that there may be no mistake as to the restoration, I wish to be sure that the person lying enshrouded here is dead, and will run my sword through the body previous to its being reanimated." The presumed cadaver gave a shriek, and in anything but sepulchral language protested against the soldier and his weapon. A second attempt of this kind was arranged to be performed in the Lake Country, but the young woman who was to sicken, die, and be raised, after being coached by Jemima for a number of weeks, became frightened at the shocking and ghastly part she was required to enact, and positively declined all further participation in the impious fraud. She had been shown by an associate to whom she entrusted the secret the infamous nature of the imposture to which she was a party, and was persuaded that it would not be improbable that her Maker, offended at such horrible profanation, should strike her dead the moment her pretended decease was announced.

Jemima was now in a quandry. She had long been meditating this project, and in preparing for carrying it out had permitted no one to attend upon the patient but herself, and was beside herself with vexation at the prospect of the miscarriage of a scheme that was to establish on a firm basis her God-given power to raise the dead. But threats, entreaties, and persuasion were powerless to induce her patient to continue the fraud. Jemima, notwithstanding, managed to turn the affair to considerable purpose. She extorted from the young woman a promise of absolute secrecy, and induced her to consent to be raised from a bed of mortal illness to perfect health. The faithful were accordingly assembled to witness the farce. Jemima exhorted and prayed with more than usual fervor, ending with a petition that the dearly beloved and dying sister might be made whole. The door of the sick room was then thrown open, disclosing a small table on which were three lighted candles. Between this table and the bed the miracle-worker stood, surrounded by her cabinet council of confederates, who pretty effectually shut out from the audience all view of the proceedings. Taking her patient by the hands she commanded her to arise, and of course was easily obeyed. To a question asked by her healer she replied in a distinct and strong voice, convincing the assembly that she was as well as ever. Jemima then gave thanks for the restoration of this dearly beloved lamb of the flock, gave those assembled her blessing, and dismissed them, thoroughly convinced, and ready to positively affirm, that they had witnessed a most wonderful miracle. The young woman upon whom it was performed became so shocked, terrified, and disgusted with the blasphemous frauds and shams by whom she was surrounded that she took an early opportunity to abandon the society and denounce the deception in which she had participated. This availed nothing so far as the Friend's fanatical dupes were concerned, apostacy being powerless to shake their faith in their divinely empowered idol. Before leaving Rhode Island she had attempted the feat of walking on the water. The brethren and sisterhood of the fraternity and a large assembly of " the world," as she designated everyone outside of her flock, had gathered to witness the performance. As usual, she entertained her hearers with a long exhortation; this time upon the importance of faith; and endeavored to persuade them that if she failed to do what they had assembled to witness, it would be owing to their unbelief; and cited the case of Peter, who had walked on the water until his own and his brethren's faith departed from them, when he began to sink, but was saved by the outstretched arm of the Master, who cried, " O thou of little faith: wherefore didst thou doubt? "

At the conclusion of her harangue she approached the margin of the river, but the unstable water refused to sustain her hallowed person. Turning upon the spectators she upbraided and reproved them for their lack of faith, denounced them as an evil generation who were seeking a sign, but unto whom no sign should be given, and dismissed them, very much humiliated and ashamed (her adherents at least) of having been the cause of the failure of her aquatic miracle. Her historian

JEMIMA WILKINSON

asks to be excused for dropping into slang and asserting that Miss Wilkinson had a gall.

A similar experiment undertaken in " The Lake Country " had a better issue. Only her flock were apprised of the attempt, and as they were posted on a hill more than a quarter of a mile from the water, they were unable to detect a staging two or three inches beneath the surface upon which their Messiah trod. By such frauds as have been recounted the Universal Friend of Mankind sought to convince an unbelieving world of the sanctity of her person and the divinity of her mission. It is doubtful whether these pretended miracles added half a dozen to the number of her followers. Those who withheld their belief were denounced as the children of wrath, who were on the broad road to perdition.

Jemima's prohibition and denunciation of matrimony was an afterthought. In the early part of her ministry she was a skillful matchmaker, and succeeded in providing husbands for a number of her community who had anticipated wedlock by becoming mothers before they were wives. After the unfortunate termination of her own early love affair she pretended to have received new light upon the subject of marriage, and believing it to be inconsistent with the character she had assumed, she denounced it as a sin and an abomination in the sight of the Lord, which would consign anyone committing it to eternal perdition. She was too shortsighted to discover that even if she succeeded in setting at naught the laws of nature and restraining the strongest of human passions she would inevitably have decreed the dissolution of her society. She denied that marriage was an institution sanctified by the divine authority, and cited as many texts in support of her theory as her successor, Joseph Smith, Jr., could quote in behalf of his. It is certain that no end of misery resulted from the teachings of these two persons, who would have us believe they were inspired from on high, the one to preach celibacy and the other polygamy.

In cases where husband and wife became members of Jemima's community she laid down the law of non-intercourse, but it was not always strictly observed. Some time after the promulgation of her family interdict a Mrs. W——, who with her husband were influential and prominent members of her community, gave birth to a fine, healthy boy. Jemima was highly incensed, as the compliance of this couple with all the requirements of her religious system was of the utmost importance in its bearing upon the obedience of her other followers.   As soon as the mother's health was re-established Jemima paid the husband and wife a visit, and denounced in vigorous terms their criminal departure from duty, told them they had committed a heinous sin, and that only by sincere repentance and future obedience could they atone in the sight of the Lord for the crime of which they had been guilty, and in order that a remembrance of their offense might be constantly before them she named the child Lamentation.   The poor mother protested, but the father acquiesced, and the child was so christened. This, however, did not prevent the birth about three years later of a fine girl.   Armed with all the terrors of her wrath and indignation Jemima again visited these perse-vering offenders, and delivered a stormy denunciation of their continued disobedience.   She became violent and abusive, and ended by declaring that the child should be called Abomination. The good mother's heart rebelled at this second attempt to stig-matize her innocent babe, and she gave vent to her feelings by ordering Jemima to leave the house.   The latter, finding she had gone too far, endeavored to recall the most galling of her words, and bring matters to an amicable understanding, but the indignant mother was more than willing to come to an open rup-ture and plainly told the Friend she was actuated by spleen, envy, and malevolence in her endeavors to destroy the happiness of married people, and that her hostility to matrimony arose from her own misconduct in early life, when she bore an illegitimate child to her lover, the British officer, and that notwithstanding all her present pretensions to purity she was no better than she should be regarding her acquaintance with men, and peremp-torily ordered her to go about her business and never show her detested face in their house again.   The husband on this occasion sustained his resolute helpmeet, and as he had been generous in contributing when " the Lord had need," and had often been held up by Jemima as an example of piety and liberality, she smothered her resentment, not daring to denounce vengeance against him, or persevere in her attempts to regulate his do-mestic affairs.   But this was an almost solitary instance on her part of a relaxation of the laws laid down for the government of her flock.   As a rule, her will was theirs, she never conde-scended to explain the reasons for actions nor would she permit others to do so.   It was her prerogative to give orders and

directions and theirs to obey — which they usually did without
a murmur, as they believed the Friend to be more than mortal,
and invested with Divine authority, power, and wisdom.

To sustain the character of a prophet, which she had assumed,
she was — if a contemporary writer in the *Pittsburg Mercury*
is to be believed — not incapable of committing heinous crimes.
Dating from Philadelphia, 1819, he says: " Our next door
neighbor, Mrs. Sarah M—, became one of her proselytes, and
when Jemima took her departure from our city this infatuated
lady forsook her husband and children and accompanied the
Friend to her new settlement. She had not been very long absent from her family before she returned, heartily disgusted
with the impostor whom she had followed. Some trouble having
arisen between them, Jemima, when her adherents were gathered
in chapel, rose from her seat after a long silence, and addressing
Mrs. M —, proclaimed in a loud voice, ' Sarah! Sarah!!
Sarah!!! I have a message from God unto thee! This night
will thy soul be required of thee !' She then sat down. Not
another word was uttered, but an indescribable terror seized
upon the minds of all present, they having implicit faith in
Jemima as a prophetess. The assembly dispersed and the victim of the denunciation went with a palpitating heart to her bed-
chamber. A remarkable providence intervened to save her.
The house was crowded, and unknown to Jemima a domestic
female servant was obliged to occupy a part of Mrs. M—'s bed.
The girl, in consequence of having a heavy ironing to do in the
evening, did not retire until near midnight. Twice previous to
that hour Jemima dressed in white, with a veil over her head, and
holding a lighted candle in each hand had entered the room,
passed close to the bed, looked at Mrs. M—, and retired without uttering a word. Before the hour of 12 the girl came in and
Mrs. M—, moving to the back of the bed, gave the tired servant
her place. The girl was soon asleep. Not so her companion.
Soon the door opened again. This time all was darkness, and
Mrs. M— could not see the object which entered, but heard it
approaching the bed. On a sudden the girl began a desperate
struggle with an unseen foe. Mrs. M— screamed and gave the
alarm, shouting robbers! murderers!! and a person fled precipi-
tately from the room. On being interrogated as to the cause of
her struggle the girl replied that some one had her by the throat
and was trying to strangle her. It need hardly be said that

Mrs. M— left the house early next morning, giving the prophetess no further opportunity to fulfill her own prediction."

During the first twenty years of her residence in the Genesee Country Jemima led a tolerably active life, taking carriage exercise in fine weather, and visiting, from time to time, the members of her community; but as age crept on she grew stout and lethargic, and during the last ten years of her life she confined herself to her house, and mainly to her own room, seldom crossing its threshold even when preaching to her people. This sedentary existence impaired her health, but as she claimed to have put off the mortal, and as her adherents thoroughly believed she would never again taste death, but little attention was paid to her ailments and evidently declining strength. It would have been inconsistent with the character she had assumed to have called a physician, and she endured during the last year or two of her life all the suffering incident to a dreadful complaint — the dropsy — with a fortitude and uncomplaining composure which half redeem the many other faults of her character. She seemed more anxious to perpetuate a belief in her divinity than to prolong or render comfortable her existence. And this she succeeded in doing. It would have been easier to persuade her infatuated flock that the great globe itself was about to dissolve than that the life of their divine Idol was drawing to a close. When asked, as they often were, " How does the Friend? " they admitted that " the tabernacle which she inhabited " was frail and disordered, but denied that her life was endangered, and became angry and impatient whenever the possibility of her decease was mentioned.

But Jemima knew well that the supreme hour was approaching. The day preceding her death she said to those about her that she " must soon leave them." Towards evening she began to sink rapidly, and again said, " My friends, I must soon depart. I am going — this night I leave ye." She passed away on the morning of Thursday, July 1, 1819, in the sixty-eighth year of her age. A few of the more intelligent of her adherents admitted the " departure of the Friend," but the majority of them could not, and did not, believe that she was dead, but zealously declared that she would live to see all the wicked cut off from the earth. Those living at a distance, upon hearing the report of her decease, started at once to visit the " Beloved " and inform her of the false rumor that the unregenerate had

spread abroad concerning her. Confronted with the dread reality, they seemed lost in a maze of astonishment, doubt, and
fear. Her cabinet council — knowing that it was necessary in
order to perpetuate the system established by their mistress —
to allay the doubts of their fellow worshipers, informed them
that the departure of the beloved Friend was but temporary,
that she would reappear and secure their eternal happiness
provided they continued firm in the faith unto the end. Believing she would rise again, her remains were kept until the
evening of the fourth day after her " departure," and were then
taken away by her household council, and no man knoweth the
place of her sepulchre unto this day. There was no funeral and
no burial, and those of her neighbors not members of her flock,
who came to pay the last tribute of their respect, were received
with gloomy silence except when questions were asked, and these
were answered in a manner which showed they were considered
inquisitive and offensive.

I shall attempt no summary of the character of the remarkable
woman whose career has been so summarily recounted, but will
quote a contemporary sketch by the Duke de la Rochefoucauld
Liancourt, who traveled extensively in this country a hundred
years ago. He says:

" We saw Jemima and attended her meeting, which is held in
her own house. We found there about thirty persons, men,
women, and children. Jemima stood at the door of her bed-
chamber, on a carpet, with an arm chair behind her. She had
on a white morning gown and waistcoat, such as men wear, and a
petticoat of the same color. Her black hair was cut short, carefully combed, and divided behind into three ringlets; she wore a
stock and white silk cravat, which was tied about her neck with
affected negligence. In point of delivery she preached with more
ease than any other Quaker I have yet heard; but the subject matter of her discourse was an eternal repetition of the same
topics — death, sin, and repentance. She is said to be about
forty years of age, but she did not appear to be more than thirty.
She is of a middle stature, well made, of florid countenance, and
has fine teeth, and beautiful eyes. Her action is studied; she
aims at simplicity, but is somewhat pedantic in her manner.
In her chamber we found her friend, Rachel Malin, a young
woman about twenty-eight or thirty years of age, her follower
and admirer, who is entirely devoted to her. All the land which

Jemima possesses is purchased in the name of Rachel Malin, an advantage she owes to her influence over her adherents, and to her dexterity in captivating their affections. Jemima, or the Friend, as she is called by way of eminence, inculcates, as her leading tenet, poverty and resignation of all earthly possessions. If you talk to her of her house, she always calls it ' the house which I inhabit.' This house, however, though built only of the trunks of trees, is extremely pretty and commodious. Her room is exquisitely neat, and resembles more the *boudoir* of a fine lady than the cell of a nun. It contains a looking glass, a clock, and an armchair, a good bed, a warming pan, and a silver saucer. Her garden is kept in good order; her spring house is full of milk, cheese, butter, butcher's meat, and game. Her hypocrisy may be traced in all her discourses, actions, and conduct, and even in the very manner in which she manages her countenance. She seldom speaks without quoting the Bible, or introducing a serious sentence about death, and the necessity of making our peace with God. Whatever does not belong to her own sect is with her an object of distaste and steadfast aversion. She sows dissensions in families, to deprive the lawful heir of his right of inheritance, in order to appropriate it to herself; and all this she does under the name and agency of her companion, who receives all presents brought by the faithful, and preserves them for her reverend friend, who, being wholly absorbed in her communion with Christ, whose prophetess she is, would absolutely forget the supply of her bodily wants if she were not well taken care of. The number of her votaries has, of late, much decreased. Many of the families who followed her to Jerusalem are no longer the dupes of her self-interested policy. Some still keep up the outward appearance of attachment to her; while others have openly disclaimed their connection with Jemima. Such, however, as still continue her adherents appear to be entirely devoted to her. With these she passes for a prophetess, an indescribable being; she is not Jemima Wilkinson, but a spirit of a peculiar name, which remains a profound secret to all who are not true believers; she is the Friend, the All-Friend. Six or seven girls of different ages, but all young and handsome, wait upon her with surprising emulation, to enjoy the peculiar satisfaction of being permitted to approach this celestial being. Her fields and her garden are plowed and dug by the Friends, who neglect their own business

to take care of hers; and the All-Friend is so condescending as
not to refuse their services; she comforts them with a kind word
now and then, makes inquiries after, and provides for, their
health and welfare, and has the art of effectually captivating
their affections, the more, perhaps, because she knows how to keep
her votaries at a respectful distance. When the service was
over, Jemima invited us to dinner. The hope of watching her
more narrowly induced us to accept the invitation; but we did not
then know that it forms a part of the character she acts never
to eat with anyone. She soon left us; and locking herself up
with her female friend, sat down without other company to an
excellent dinner; we did not get ours till after she had dined.
When our dinner was over, and also another, which was served
up after ours, the sanctuary was opened again. And now Jemima
appeared once more at the door of her room, and conversed with
us seated in an arm chair. When strangers are with her, she
never comes over the threshold of her bedroom; and when by herself, she is constantly engaged in deliberation how to improve the
demesne of her friend. The house was, this day, very full.
Our company consisted of exactly ten persons; after us, dined
another company of the same number; and as many more dined
in the kitchen. Our plates, as well as the table linen, were perfectly clean and neat; our repast, although frugal, was yet better in quality than any of which we had partaken since we had left
Philadelphia; it consisted of good fresh meat, with pudding, an
excellent salad, and a beverage of peculiar, yet charming, flavor,
with which we were plentifully supplied out of Jemima's apart-
ment, where it was prepared. The devout guests observed, all
this while, a profound silence; they either cast down their eyes
or lifted them up to heaven with a rapturous sigh; to me they
appeared not unlike a party of the faithful, in the primitive
ages, dining in a church. The All-Friend had by this time exchanged her former dress for that of a fine Indian lady, which
however, was cut out in the same fashion as the former. Her
hair and eyebrows had again been combed. She did not utter
a syllable respecting our dinner; nor did she offer to make any
apology for her absence. Constantly engaged in personating
the part she had assumed, she descanted in a sanctimonious,
mystic tone, on death, and on the happiness of having been an
useful instrument to others in the way of their salvation. She
afterwards gave us a rhapsody of prophecies to read, ascribed

to one Dr. Love, who was beheaded in Cromwell's time; wherein she clearly discerned, according to her accounts, the French Revolution, the decline and downfall of popery, and the impending end of the world.   Finding, however, that this conversation was but ill adapted to engage our attention she cut short her harangue at once.

"We had, indeed, already seen more than enough to estimate the character of this bad actress, whose pretended sanctity only inspired us with contempt and disgust, and who is altogether incapable of imposing upon any person of common understanding, unless those of the most simple minds, or downright enthusiasts.   Her speeches are so strongly contradicted by the tenor of her actions; her whole conduct; her expense compared to that of other families within a circumference of fifty miles; her way of living, and her dress, form such a striking contrast with her harangues on the subject of condemning earthly enjoyments; and the extreme assiduity with which she is continually endeavoring to induce children, over whom she has any influence, to leave their parents and form a part of her community; all those particulars so strongly militate against the doctrine of peace and universal love, which she is incessantly preaching, that we were all actually struck with abhorrence at her duplicity and hypocrisy, as soon as the first emotions of our curiosity subsided.   Her fraudulent conduct, indeed, has been discovered by so many persons, and so much has been said against it, that it is difficult to account for her having any adherents at all, even for a short time.   And yet she will probably retain a sufficient number to increase still further a fortune which is already considerable for the country in which she resides, and fully adequate to the only end which she now seems anxious to attain — namely, to live independent, in a decent, plentiful, and even elegant manner.   There are so many weak-minded religionists, and Jemima is so particularly careful to select her disciples among persons who are either very old or very young, that her imposture, however gross and palpable to the discerning, may yet be carried on for some time with success sufficient to answer her ultimate purpose.   If her credit should sink too low, she would find herself constrained to transplant her holiness to some other region; and, in fact, she had last year harbored the design of removing her family and establishment, and of settling on Carlton Island, in the Lake of Ontario, where she would enjoy the satisfaction of living under the English Government, which, by her account, has offered her a grant of land."

If comment were in order it might be said that deference to the sex and the universal law which forbids criticism of accepted hospitality should have softened the duke's account of his visit to the Friend, though it must be admitted that if he was to publish his impressions at all they should have been his real ones, unvarnished by sentiment of any kind.

Another contemporary account, taken from manuscript left by the late Thomas Morris, is submitted as corroborative of what has preceded. He certainly was not a man whose inclinations would lead him to " set down aught in malice " against any one. He says:

" Prior to my having settled at Canandaigua, Jemima Wilkinson and her followers had established themselves on a tract of land, purchased by them, and called the Friend's settlement. Her disciples were a very orderly, sober, industrious, and, some of them, a well-educated and intelligent set of people; and many of them possessed of handsome properties. She called herself the Universal Friend, and would not permit herself to be designated by any other appellation. She pretended to have had revelations from heaven, in which she had been directed to devote her labors to the conversion of sinners. Her disciples placed the most unbounded confidence in her and yielded in all things the most implicit obedience to her mandates. She would punish those among them who were guilty of the slightest deviation from her orders; in some instances, she would order the offending culprit to wear a cow bell round his neck for weeks, or months, according to the nature of the offense, and in no instance was she known to have been disobeyed. For some offense, committed by one of her people, she banished him to Nova Scotia, for three years, where he went, and from whence he returned only after the expiration of his sentence. When any of her people killed a calf or sheep, or purchased an article of dress, the Friend was asked what portion of it she would have, and the answer would sometimes be, that the Lord hath need of the one-half, and sometimes, that the Lord hath need of the whole. Her house, her grounds, and her farms, were kept in the neatest order by her followers, who, of course, labored for her without compensation. She was attended by two young women, always neatly dressed. Those who acted in that capacity, and enjoyed the most of her favored confidence, at the time I was there, were named Sarah Richards and Rachel Malin. Jemima prohibited her followers from marrying; and even those who had joined her after having been united in wedlock were made to separate and live apart from each other. This was attributed to her desire to inherit the property of those who died.

" Having discovered that bequests to the Universal Friend would be invalid, and not recognizing the name of Jemima Wilkinson, she caused devises to be made by the dying to Sarah Richards, in the first instance. Sarah Richards, however, died, and her heir-at-law claimed the property thus bequeathed; litigation ensued, and after the controversy had gone from court to court, it was finally decided in Jemima's favor, it appearing that Sarah Richards had held the property in trust for her. After the death of Sarah Richards, devises were made in favor of Rachel Malin; but Rachel took it into her head to marry, and her husband claimed, in behalf of his wife, the property thus devised to her. Among Jemima's followers was an artful, cunning, and intelligent man, by the name of Elijah Parker; she dubbed him a prophet, and called him the Prophet Elijah. He would, before prophesying, wear around the lower part of his waist, a bandage or girdle, tied very tight, and when it had caused the upper part of his stomach to swell, he would pretend to be filled with the prophetic visions which he would impart to the community. But after some time, Jemima and her Prophet quarreled, and he then denounced her as an impostor, declared that she had imposed on his credulity, and that he had never been a prophet. After having divested himself of his prophetic character he became a justice of the peace, and in that capacity issued a warrant against Jemima, charging her with blasphemy. She was accordingly brought to Canandaigua, by virtue of this warrant, and at a circuit court held there in 1796, by the late Governor Lewis, judge of the Supreme Court of the State, a bill of indictment, prepared by Judge Howell, of Canandaigua, then district attorney, was laid before the grand jury. Judge Lewis having told the grand jury, that by the laws and constitution of this State blasphemy was not an indictable offense, no bill was found. Judge Howell has informed me that a similar question having been brought before a full bench of the Supreme Court, that Judge Lewis' opinion was overruled by all the other

judges, and that blasphemy was decided to be an indictable offense. These litigations, however, had considerably lessened the
number of her followers, but she, as I am informed, retained until
her death her influence over a considerable portion of them.

"Prior to these occurrences, Jemima had been attacked with
a violent disease, and she expected to die. Under this conviction,
she caused her disciples to be assembled in her sick chamber,
when she told them that her Heavenly Father, finding that the
wickedness of the world was so great that there was no prospect of her succeeding in reclaiming it, had determined that she
should soon quit it, and rejoin Him in heaven. Having unex-
pectedly recovered, she again assembled them, when she announced to them that her Heavenly Father had again commanded
her to remain on earth and make one more trial.

"When I first saw Jemima, she was a fine looking woman,
of good height; and, though not corpulent, inclined to embon-
point. Her hair was jet black, short, curled on her shoulders;
she had fine eyes and good teeth and complexion. Her dress consisted of a silk purple robe, open in front; her underdress was of
the finest white cambric or muslin. Round her throat she wore
a large cravat, brodered with fine lace. She was very ignorant,
but possessed an uncommon memory; though she could neither
read nor write, it was said that she knew the Bible by heart,
from its having been read to her. The sermon I heard her
preach was bad in point of language, and almost unintelligible;
aware of her deficiencies in this respect, she caused one of her
followers to tell me, that in her discourses she did not aim at
expressing herself in fine language, preferring to adapt her
style to the capacity of the most illiterate of her hearers."

I am inclined to think Mr. Morris mistaken as to Jemima's
inability to read. The evidence is almost conclusive that she
had not only read the Bible and other religious works but law
books as well. That she did not wield the pen of a ready writer
is evidenced by the fact that her X mark was affixed to her last
will and testament.

In the year 1750, a contemporary of Jemima — Joanna
Southcott — was born in Devonshire, England. Like her
American prototype, she was of humble birth, illiterate, and in
early life had joined the Methodists — a sect then regarded by
Church of England people as religious zealots and fanatics.
Becoming acquainted with a man by the name of Sanderson,

who claimed to be endued with the spirit of prophecy, Joanna made like pretensions herself. She gave forth that she was the woman driven into the wilderness mentioned in the Book of Revelations, and though very illiterate, wrote many letters, pamphlets, and predictions in prose and verse. She also issued papers which she called her seals, which, she assured her followers, would protect them from the judgments of God here and hereafter, and be the means of their eternal salvation. Thousands of both sexes — amongst whom were many persons of good education and respectable position — received these seals with implicit confidence. When she had passed the age of sixty she imagined she was to give birth to a new Prince of Peace, and her followers, having the utmost faith in the announcement, prepared a handsome cradle, and made other expensive arrangements befitting so great an event. Joanna, however, simply had the dropsy, a disease which carried her off in 1814, as it did the American prophet a few years later. The similarity of their methods for raising the wind is amusing. Joanna writes to one of her adherents as follows: " I am the Lord thy God! Tell M— to pay thee five pounds for thy expenses in coming up to London; and he must give thee twenty pounds to relieve the perplexity of thy handmaid and thee, that thy thoughts may be free to serve me, the Lord, in the care of my Shiloh."

There is nothing so marvelous about these two women as the influence they exercised over the minds of their followers, many of whom — especially as regards Joanna — were people of intelligence and cultivated minds. What Macaulay says of her may well apply to both: " We have seen an old woman with no ability beyond the cunning of a fortune-teller, and with the education of a scullion, surrounded by devoted followers, many of whom were in station and knowledge immeasurably her superiors; and all this in the nineteenth century and in London. Yet why not? For the dealings of God with man have no more been revealed to the nineteenth century than to the first, or to London than to the wildest parish in the Hebrides."

" The last Will and Testament of the person called the Universal Friend, of Jerusalem, in the county of Ontario, and State of New York — who in the year one thousand seven hundred and seventy-six, was called Jemima Wilkinson, and ever since that time the Universal Friend, a new name which the mouth of the Lord hath named.

" Considering the uncertainty of this mortal life, and being of sound mind and memory, blessed be the Lord of Sabaoth and Father of Mercies therefor — I do make and publish this my last Will and Testament —

" I.   My Will is, that all my just debts be paid by my Executors, hereafter named.

" II.   I give, bequeath and devise unto Rachel Malin and Margaret Malin, now of said Jerusalem, all my earthly property, both real and personal: that is to say, all my land lying in said Jerusalem and in Benton, or elsewhere in the county of Ontario, together with all the buildings thereon, to them, the said Rachel and Margaret, and their heirs and assigns forever, to be equally and amicably shared between them, the said Rachel and Margaret.   And I do also give and bequeath to the said Rachel and Margaret Malin, all my wearing apparel, all my household furniture, and all my horses, cattle, sheep, and swine, of every kind and description, and also all my carriages, wagons, and carts, of every kind, together with all my farming tools and utensils, and all my movable property, of every nature and description whatever.

" III.   My Will is, that all the present members of my family, and each of them, be employed, if they please, and if employed, supported during natural life, by the said Rachel and Margaret, and when any of them become unable to help themselves, they are according to such inability, kindly to be taken care of by the said Rachel and Margaret.   And my will also is, that all poor persons belonging to the Society of Universal Friends shall receive from the said Rachel and Margaret such assistance, comfort, and support during natural life as they need — and in case any, either of my family, or elsewhere in the Society, shall turn away, such shall forfeit the provisions herein made for them.

" IV.   I hereby ordain and appoint the above named Rachel and Margaret Malin Executors of this my last Will and Testament.— In witness whereof, I, the person once called Jemima Wilkinson, but in, and ever since the year 1777, known as and called the Public Universal Friend, hereunto set my name and seal, the twenty-fifth day of the second month, in the year of the Lord eighteen hundred and eighteen.

THE PUBLIC UNIVERSAL FRIEND.   [L. s.]

IN THE PRESENCE OF, &C., &C.

" *Be it remembered,* That in order to remove all doubts of the due execution of the foregoing Will and Testament, being the person who before the year one thousand seven hundred and seventy-seven was known and called by the name of Jemima Wilkinson, but since that time as the Universal Friend, do make, publish, and declare the within instrument as my last Will and Testament — as witness my Hand and Seal, this seventeenth day of the seventh month (July), in the year one thousand eight hundred and eighteen.

HER

JEMIMA × WILKINSON.   [L. s.]

CROSS *or* MARK.

OR UNIVERSAL FRIEND."

WITNESSES, &C.

JOSEPH SMITH, JR., AND MORMONISM.

NO QUESTIONS that engage the human understanding are more interesting in their analysis or more vital in their import than those which deal with man's origin and destiny. Why are we here, and whither are we tending? What are our relations to the Creator, and His intentions toward us, now and hereafter? Wise men in all ages have given their best thought to the solution of these questions. Buddhist priests and Jewish rabbis, skilled in all the mystical lore of the East, pondered them, ages before the Wise Men saw Bethlehem's star. From them the Nazarene learned his lesson, and the best evidence that he was more than man is that he bettered their instruction. A majority of the Christian world holds Christ's doctrines to be emanations from Deity itself. In this they perhaps do wisely. Better accept the immaculate birth, incarnation, miracles, atonement on the cross, resurrection and ascension, as taught in the New Testament, and guide the bark of faith by them, than to drift without compass or rudder on a boundless sea of speculation, doubt, and uncertainty. There is at least safety in the beaten path. And yet we cannot keep man's feet in that path. Reason, protest, denounce, and anathematize as we may, he will go astray. The check-rein of church authority no longer curbs or guides the human mind. The faith of this generation may be the fable of the next. The Episcopalian is not content with his prayer-book, and the Presbyterian is dissatisfied with his creed. Even " The Word of the Lord " which " endureth forever " has recently been revised. If we accept it, either in its original or revised form, we are little wiser so far as our relations to the Deity and His intentions toward us are concerned than were those who lived before the Scriptures were given to mankind. All faiths and all lack of faiths, all beliefs and all doubts, have been drawn from Holy Writ. No one has been able to lift the veil and disclose the ultimate truth, though the greatest minds in all ages have been earnestly busy with the attempt.   And not great minds alone but little ones. Enriched by credulity and superstition, imposture has found in religious speculation a fertile field of effort.   Such a field was opened nearly sixty years ago in Western New York by the promulgation of the Book of Mormon.   As a part of pioneer history I shall try to give some account of the origin of a faith that has spread over half the globe, and has for years defied one of the strongest of existing governments.

Joseph Smith, Jr., the bearer of the new evangel, and founder of the Church of Jesus Christ on earth of Latter Day Saints, was born in Sharon, Vermont, in 1805.   His parents, Joseph, Sr., and Lucy Smith, can be truthfully described as poor, but it is doubtful whether the rest of the customary phrase can be applied.   The father was a shiftless, ignorant, underwitted, and credulous person, given to idle and speculative religious vagaries, and had embraced, from time to time, all the creeds and isms that had come in his way.   He changed his beliefs more easily than his costumes, for he had more of them.   He was a smatterer in Biblical knowledge and theology, but the seed was sown on barren soil and produced nothing but idle and shallow discussion.   A believer in the marvelous and a money digger, prone to difficulties with his neighbors and to petty lawsuits, he was the last person in the world who would have been suspected by those who knew him of being the father of a prophet.

The wife was much superior to her husband.   She was a woman of strong though uncultivated mind; was bold, artful, and ambitious; believed that the world owed her a better living than had ever been provided by her husband, and saw her way to get it by interesting those who had money and credulity in some new and wonderful scheme of revelation in which they were to be co-workers.   Her religious enthusiasm was not well regulated, and at the start had probably no higher aim than to provide for the temporal wants of herself and family without labor.   The first hints that a prophet was to spring from her humble household came from her, but her husband was her faithful ally in all that promised to enable the family to prosper without work.

Nothing definite was formulated until after their removal to the Genesee Country, which took place in 1816.   The family, consisting of six sons and three daughters — Joseph being the fourth child in order of birth — settled at Palmyra, Wayne County, New York, and opened there a small shop for the sale of cakes, candies, spruce beer, and tobacco, adding, on the fourth of July and general muster days, pies, boiled eggs, gingerbread, and chestnuts, which they peddled from a rude cart constructed by the proprietor.   The profits of this limited trade were insufficient for the maintenance of Mr. Smith's large family, and were supplemented by occasional jobs of gardening and wood-sawing for the villagers, and by well-digging and harvest work for the surrounding farmers.   A constitutional aversion to labor rendered the income from these sources small, and after a residence in Palmyra of about two and a half years the Smiths abandoned their shop and removed to a piece of wild or timbered land in the northeast corner of the town of Manchester, Ontario County, about two miles south of Palmyra.   On this land they had built, previous to removing, a small one-story log house, having two apartments on the ground floor, and a low garret above similarly divided.   The property belonged to non-resident minor heirs, and the rights of squatter sovereignty were exercised by the Smiths for a number of years; but at length they purchased it on contract, paying a small sum down, and in this way continued their occupancy until the exploiting of the Mormon scheme in 1829.

Removal from the village failed to improve the pecuniary status of the Smiths.   There was no quarter day, but there were also no cakes and ale.   They underbrushed half an acre or so about their cabin, and when Mrs. Smith's tea or sugar gave out, driven by her and necessity, they would cut a jag of firewood and haul it to Palmyra, and from its sale replenish in a scanty way their stock of groceries.   Turner, the author of a " History of the Holland Purchase," at that time a journeyman printer in Palmyra, thus describes Joseph, Jr.: " My recollections of him are distinct ones. He used to come into the village from his backwoods home with little jags of wood, sometimes patronizing the saloon too freely, and sometimes finding an odd job to do about the store of Seymour Scovell.   Once a week he would stroll into the office of the old *Palmyra Register* for his father's paper.   How impious in us to occasionally blacken the face of the future prophet with the old-fashioned ink-balls when his inquisitiveness put him in the way of the working of the old Ramage press."

The father and his elder sons, Alvin and Hyrum, still did odd jobs of well-digging and harvesting, but the greater portion of their time was spent in hunting, fishing, trapping mink and muskrat, digging wood chucks out of their holes to supply vacancies in the family larder, and lounging around the shops and stores in Palmyra.   Joseph was too lazy to hunt or dig — just lazy enough to fish, at which meditative sport he would pass whole days without moving from the spot where he made his first cast, possibly revolving the scheme which was to make him a marked if not an estimable character, but more likely lost in visions of an earthly nature, such as locating buried treasures or devising other means for circumventing the original penalty — " In the sweat of thy face shalt thou eat bread."   At lounging about he was the equal of his brethren and their progenitor.   A large and thriftless family, without habits of industry or visible means of support, occupies an unfortunate place amongst industrious and honest neighbors.

Suspicion was often turned toward them in connection with nocturnal depredations on hen roosts, smokehouses, and sheep-folds, which they in turn charged upon four-footed marauders. The pioneer, however, was too familiar with the tracks of wolves, foxes, and weasels to mistake them for human footprints. But it must in all fairness be said that, whatever may have been the suspicions of their neighbors, no judicial proceedings ever traced missing property to Smith's door.

The general repute of the family may be learned from the following statements.   Any old resident of Palmyra or Manchester will recognize among the signatures the names of the best people living at that time in those towns.

" MANCHESTER, ONTARIO CO., N. Y., Nov. 3, 1833.
" We, the undersigned, being personally acquainted with the family of Joseph Smith, Sen., with whom the Gold Bible, so called, originated, state that they were not only a lazy, indolent set of men, but also intemperate, and their word was not to be depended upon, and that we are truly glad to dispense with their society.

PARDON BUTTS,	WARREN A. REED,
HIRAM SMITH,	ALFRED STAFFORD,
JAMES GEE,	ABEL CHASE,
A. H. WENTWORTH,	MOSES C. SMITH,
JOSEPH FISH,	HORACE N. BARNES,

SYLVESTER WORDEN."

"PALMYRA, Dec. 4, 1833.

"We, the undersigned, have been acquainted with the Smith family for a number of years, while they resided near this place, and we have no hesitation in saying that we consider them destitute of that moral character which ought to entitle them to the confidence of any community. They were particularly famous for visionary projects, spent much of their time in digging for money which they pretended was hid in the earth; and, to this day, large excavations may be seen in the earth, not far from their residence, where they used to spend their time in digging for hidden treasures. Joseph Smith, Senior, and his son Joseph, were, in particular, considered entirely destitute of moral character, and addicted to vicious habits.

"Martin Harris was a man who had acquired a handsome property, and in matters of business his word was considered good; but on moral and religious subjects he was perfectly visionary — sometimes advocating one sentiment and sometimes another. And in reference to all with whom we were acquainted that have embraced Mormonism from this neighborhood, we are compelled to say were very visionary, and most of them destitute of moral character and without influence in this community: and this may account why they were permitted to go on with their impositions undisturbed. It was not supposed that any of them were possessed of sufficient character or influence to make anyone believe their book or their sentiments, and we know not of a single individual in this vicinity that puts the least confidence in their pretended revelations.

GEORGE N. WILLIAMS,	CLARK ROBINSON,
LEMUEL DURFEE,	E. S. TOWNSEND,
HENRY P. ALGER,	C. E. THAYER,
G. W. ANDERSON,	H. P. THAYER,
L. WILLIAMS,	GEORGE W. CROSBY,
LEVI THAYER,	R. S. WILLIAMS,
P. SEXTON,	M. BUTTERFIELD,
S. P. SEYMOUR,	D. S. JACKWAYS,
JOHN HURLBUT,	H. LINNELL,
JAMES JENNER,	S. ACKLEY,
JOSIAH RICE,	JESSE TOWNSEND,
RICHARD D. CLARK,	TH. P. BALDWIN,
JOHN SOTHINGTON,	DURFEY CHASE,
WELLS ANDERSON,	N. H. BECKWITH,

PHILO DURFEE,	GILES S. ELY,
R. W. SMITH,	PELATIAH WEST,
HENRY JESSUP,	LINUS NORTH,
THOMAS ROGERS, 2D,	WM. PARKE,
JOSIAH FRANCIS,	AMOS HOLLISTER,
G. A. HATHAWAY,	DAVID G. ELY,
H. K. JEROME,	G. BECKWITH,
LEWIS FOSTER,	HIRAM PAYNE,
P. GRANDIN,	L. HURD,
JOEL THAYER,	E. D. ROBINSON,
ASAHEL MILLARD,	A. ENSWORTH,

ISRAEL F. CHILSON."

In September, 1819, a trifling and apparently unimportant event occurred which, however, had much to do in establishing the Mormon Church. This was the discovery of the celebrated Peek Stone. It was unearthed by the Prophet's father and elder sons while engaged in digging a well near Palmyra for Mr. Clark Chase. It first attracted the attention of Mr. Chase's children by the peculiarity of its shape, which nearly resembled the foot of a young child. When washed it was whitish, glossy, and opaque in appearance. Joseph, Jr., who was an idle looker-on at the labors of his father and brethren, at once possessed himself of this geological oddity, but not without strenuous protest on the part of the children, who claimed it by right of discovery, and because it was found upon their father's premises. Joseph, however, kept it, and though frequent demands were made, after it became famous, for its restoration, it was never returned to the claimants. Very soon it became noised abroad that by means of this stone the inchoate Prophet could locate buried treasure and discover the whereabouts of stolen property. In the latter case he might not have had to look a great way. People from far and near who had lost valuables consulted Joseph. With his eyes bandaged and his Peek Stone at the bottom of a tall white hat, he satisfied all inquirers for a fee of seventy-five cents. My grandfather paid that sum to learn what had become of a valuable mare stolen from his stable, and he was a tolerably shrewd and prosperous Dutchman for those days. He recovered his beast, which Joe said was somewhere on the lake shore, and about to be run over to Canada. Anybody could have told him that, as it was invariably the way a horsethief would take to dispose of a stolen animal in those days.

It was not long before Joe discovered that with his stone he could locate hidden treasures of great value. Glittering heaps of gold and silver, contained in earthen pots and iron chests, buried in the earth, were revealed to his vision and their exact locality indicated by its aid. When we consider the attractiveness of suddenly-acquired wealth to the generality of mankind, and the fascination which gold hunting has possessed from the days when Jason and Captain Kidd sailed the main down to the time when the Argonauts of '49 went 'round the Horn, we cannot wonder that some of the poorer and more credulous of Joe's neighbors believed his stories and helped him to unearth his fabulous treasures. The shining hoards he pretended to see had this advantage: they were in stamped and minted coin, unmixed with baser matter. There was no occasion for a washer, smelter, or assayer. His money-digging operations were organized much in the usual way. The working capital was labor and whiskey. The former was contributed by toiling men who were to share in the profits of the enterprise. The whiskey was supplied by Joe from funds raised in the vicinity from credulous and good-natured people who were taken in on the ground plan, and promised a thousand-fold for every dollar invested. From those who were not prepared to pay in cash, contributions of grain, flour, fat sheep, calves, and pigs were received. It seems hardly credible, but it is true, that for nearly five years the Smiths found dupes who supported them in considerable comfort by contributions to their fortune-telling and money-digging schemes.

Joe's delving parties were organized with much secrecy and mystery. He usually named some unfrequented spot and the dead hour of night as the place and time of rendezvous. Thither the party repaired with lanterns, spades, shovels, and pickaxes. After some preparatory mystic ceremonies, such as the waving of a magic wand, and the utterance of some foolish incantation gibberish, Joe would look at the Peek Stone in his hat, and then indicate the spot where the digging was to begin. Absolute silence was the condition of success. Work would go on for hours and hours without a word being spoken. At length some tired and perhaps disgusted digger, " tempted by the Spirit of Evil," would speak, and the treasure would vanish. The company were always assured by Joe that if the spell had not been broken a few more blows would have revealed the glittering heaps. But the spell always was broken, and the wonder remains that Smith should have been able to continue these operations until the surface of the earth in his neighborhood was full of holes, digged by his dupes.   I copy an account of one of these delving operations from Pomeroy Tucker's " History of the Rise and Progress of Mormonism." He says: " A single instance of Smith's style of conducting these money-diggings will suffice for the whole series, and illustrate his low cunning and the strange infatuation of the people who yielded to his unprincipled designs. Assuming his accustomed air of mystery on one of these occasions, and pretending to see by his miraculous stone just where the sought-for chest of money had lodged in its underground transits, he gave out the revelation that a black sheep would be required as a sacrificial offering upon the enchanted ground before entering upon the work of exhumation.   He knew that his kind-hearted neighbor, Wm. Stafford — a farmer in comfortable worldly circumstances — possessed a fine, fat, black wether, intended for division between his household and the village market.   Joe also knew that Mr. Stafford had been for many years a sailor, and was prone toward the vagaries and superstitions of his class.   He therefore proposed that his friend should invest the wether as his share in the speculation, a proposition to which the credulous sailor readily acceded.   At the appointed hour of night the diggers with lanterns and the fatted sheep for the sacrifice were conducted by Joseph to the spot where the treasure was to be obtained.   There he described a circle on the ground around the buried chest.   As usual, not a word was to be spoken until after the prize was brought forth.   Everything being in readiness, the throat of the sheep was cut, and the poor animal made to pour out its blood around the circle.   Then the digging began in a vigorous and solemn way.   In this case it was continued for three hours, when some one, instigated by the devil, ' spoke,' and the plan was again frustrated, exactly as on repeated former trials !   In the meantime the elder Smith, aided by one of his sons, had withdrawn the sacrificial carcass and dressed it for family use."   Perhaps there was more than one black sheep in that party.

Although human credulity seems to be unbounded, yet the same unsuccessful schemes being worked upon a few persons over a

series of years become at length a trifle stale and monotonous, and
it is no wonder that Joe's neighbors began after a while to tire of
making contributions of labor, money, and barter to his money-
digging operations.   The fame of these nocturnal adventures,
however, had been sounded near and far, and the miraculous Peek
Stone, though it had never been the means of bringing
forth a dime except from the pocket of some credulous neighbor, had become nearly as celebrated as the
lamp of Aladdin.   Among those who had heard of it was
the Rev. Sidney Rigdon, who appeared at the log hut of the
Smiths in the summer of 1827 and had an interview with the
money digger.   I give it as my deliberate opinion that the
credit or discredit of being the founder of the Mormon faith be-
longs to Mr. Rigdon.   The Smiths never had brains enough to
exploit it.   It is true that Mrs. Smith had given out that she was
to be the mother of a prophet, but she had fixed upon her eldest
son Alvin to be the wearer of Elijah's mantle, and with his death
all her hopes in that direction were blasted.   I am furthermore
of opinion that if Alvin Smith had lived the Gold Bible and
Mormonism would never have been heard of.   He seems to have
been the only level-headed, honest member of the family.   He
had some habits of industry, and his neighbors were willing to
exchange work with him, or trust him for a bag of wheat or
corn, for a ham or a jag of fodder, upon his promise to pay for
the same in labor.   He had no faith in the Peek Stone or the
money-digging schemes, was not given to religious vagaries, and
it is very doubtful whether he could have been induced by Rigdon
to become a party to the fraud upon which the Mormon faith
is based.   An examination of the facts will go far toward establishing Mr. Rigdon's claim to be the founder of the Mormon
Church.

If contemporary evidence is of any value, it settles beyond dispute the fact that Joseph Smith, Jr., was not a person of sufficient education to have written the Book of Mormon.   In fact,
he could hardly write at all, his efforts in the way of caligraphy
being confined in the main to inscribing in an awkward and
laborious manner his own name.   His reading was confined to
works of fiction of the dime-novel class, and to stories of piracy
and criminality.   The lives of Stephen Burroughs and Captain
Kidd captivated his fancy and satisfied his mental cravings.   Up
to the time when Mr. Rigdon appeared on the scene Joe's principal

characteristics were taciturnity, secretiveness, and mysterious pretensions; when disposed to be communicative, which was not often, he was so mendacious and extravagant in statement as to bring upon himself the aversion and contempt of his auditors. His religious views were unique and original at first, but degenerated into unbelief and blasphemy, and finally led him to the conclusion that " all sects were wrong, all churches on a false foundation, and the Bible a fable." Yet we are asked to believe that a new revelation from God to man was made through such a medium as this. The only other person in any way connected with the production of the Mormon Bible was Oliver Cowdery. He was a country schoolmaster whose education was limited to a superficial acquaintance with the three R's. Perhaps a claim to celestial inspiration might be urged in his behalf from the fact that he taught school two winters in the district that was afterward the home of the Fox Sisters, who originated modern Spiritualism. But the main reason of his association with Smith and Rigdon was that they wanted a scribe who wrote a legible hand, which Smith certainly did not. Rigdon was the only one of the triumvirate who could pretend to any literary ability, and he — as the sequel will show — was a compiler, and not an originator. Previous to his acquaintance with Smith he had been preacher, printer, and lecturer, in short, a sort of versatile tramp who was willing to turn his hand to anything except honest labor. Just how he became acquainted with the Smiths is not known, but it is probable he had heard of their miraculous stone, and believing he could turn it to good use, or rather to personal advantage, sought them out and introduced himself. For nearly two years his visits to them were secret and incognito, a style of thing that suited Joe exactly. He was known to the neighbors as the mysterious stranger. Though not susceptible of absolute proof, it is reasonably certain that he furnished Joe with two things which formed the basis of the Mormon Bible. The first was a set of plates " having the appearance of gold," upon which were engraved curious hieroglyphics; the second, a manuscript tale concerning certain lost tribes which had formerly inhabited North America, one of which had been exterminated by the other — the remnant of the remaining tribe being the native Indians found here when the country was discovered. From this tale, mixed up with copious quotations and paraphrases from the Old and New Testament, the Book of Mormon was compiled.

How did Rigdon become possessed of the plates?   In answer, I quote from Mr. Tucker's history: " Among American antiquities found in the Western country and preserved by the curious in such matters, are what are called glyphs, consisting of curious metallic plates covered with hieroglyphical characters. Professor Raffinesque, in his Asiatic Journal for 1832, describes similar plates found by him in Mexico, being written from top to bottom like the Chinese language, or from side to side, indifferently, like the Egyptian and Demotic Libyan.   A number of these remains were found in Pike County, Illinois, a few years ago, described as six plates of brass of a bell shape, each having a hole near the small end, with a ring through all of them, and clasped with two clasps. The plates at first seemed to be of copper, and had the appearance of being covered with characters. A cleansing by sulphuric acid brought out the characters distinctly."

Rigdon was of a speculative turn of mind — was possessed of some little scientific ability, and had lectured upon antiquarian and philosophical subjects in the Western States, where he probably picked up a set of these glyphs or plates.   It is certainly more reasonable to assume this than to believe that eleven of Smith's followers made affidavits to a deliberate falsehood when they testified that they had seen " plates having the appearance of gold " in possession of the Prophet.   Three men, Cowdery, David Whitmer, and Martin Harris, affirmed that an angel from heaven came down from God and laid the plates before their eyes, and that they saw the engravings thereon.   This was undoubtedly false as to the angel, but eight others — all Smiths and Whitmers, to be sure, except one — testified that Joseph Smith, Jr., had " shown them the plates and the engravings thereon, that they had handled and ' hefted ' the same, and that they know of a surety that said Smith had the plates in his possession from which the translation was made."   For the credit of human character it is best to assume that Rigdon had furnished Joe with a set of the glyphs which have been described.

The manuscript tale, which was the other corner stone of the Mormon structure, was written by the Reverend Solomon Spalding, about the year 1810 or 1811.   Who he was may be learned from the subjoined statements of his brother and partner, which explain themselves:

" Solomon Spalding was born in Ashford, Conn., in 1761, and in early life contracted a taste for literary pursuits.   After he left school he entered Plainfield Academy, where he made great proficiency in study, and excelled most of his class-mates. He next commenced the study of law, in Windham County, in which he made little progress, having in the meantime turned his attention to religious subjects. He soon entered Dartmouth College, with the intention of qualifying himself for the ministry, where he obtained the degree of A. M., and was afterward regularly ordained. After preaching three or four years, he gave it up, removed to Cherry Valley, New York, and commenced the mercantile business in company with his brother Josiah. In a few years he failed in business, and in the year 1809 removed to Conneaut, in Ohio. The year following I removed to Ohio, and found him engaged in building a forge. I made him a visit in about three years after, and found that he had failed, and was considerably involved in debt. He then told me he had been writing a book, which he intended to have printed, the avails of which he thought would enable him to pay all his debts. The book was entitled, the ' Manuscript Found,' of which he read to me many passages. It was an historical romance of the first settlers of America — endeavoring to show that the American Indians are the descendants of the Jews, or the lost tribes. It gave a detailed account of their journey from Jerusalem, by land and sea, till they arrived in America, under the command of NEPHI and LEHI. They afterward had quarrels and contentions, and separated into two distinct nations, one of which he denominated Nephites and the other Lamanites. Cruel and bloody wars ensued, in which great multitudes were slain. They buried their dead in large heaps, which caused the mounds so common in this country. Their arts, sciences, and civilization were brought into view, in order to account for all the curious antiquities found in various parts of North and South America. I have recently read the book of Mormon, and, to my great surprise, I find nearly the same historical matter, names, etc., as they were in my brother's writings. I well remember that he wrote in the old style, and commenced about every sentence with, ' And it came to pass,' or ' Now it came to pass,' the same as in the Book of Mormon, and, according to the best of my recollection and belief, it is the same as my brother Solomon wrote, with the exception of the religious matter. By what means it has fallen into the hands of Joseph Smith, Jr., I am unable to determine.   JOHN SPALDING."

JOSEPH SMITH

" CONNEAUT, ASHTABULA COUNTY, OHIO, Sept., 1833.

" I left the State of New York, late in the year 1810, and arrived at this place about the first of January following. Soon after my arrival, I formed a partnership with Solomon Spalding, for the purpose of rebuilding a forge which he had commenced a year or two before. He very frequently read to me from a manuscript which he was writing, which he entitled, the ' Manuscript Found,' and which he represented as being found in this town. I spent many hours in hearing him read said writings, and became well acquainted with their contents. He wished me to assist him in getting his production printed, alleging that a book of that kind would meet with a rapid sale. I designed doing so, but the forge not meeting our anticipations, we failed in business, when I declined having anything to do with the publication of the book. This book represented the American Indians as the descendants of the lost tribes — gave an account of their leaving Jerusalem, their contentions and wars, which were many and great. One time, when he was reading to me the tragic account of Laban, I pointed out to him what I considered an inconsistency, which he promised to correct; but by referring to the Book of Mormon, I find, to my surprise, that it stands there just as he read it to me then. Some months ago I borrowed the Golden Bible, put it into my pocket, carried it home, and thought no more of it. About a week after, my wife found the book in my coat pocket, as it hung up, and commenced reading it aloud as I lay upon the bed. She had not read twenty minutes till I was astonished to find the same passages in it that Spalding had read to me more than twenty years before, from his ' Manuscript Found.' Since that, I have more fully examined the said Golden Bible, and have no hesitation in saying, that the historical part of it is principally, if not wholly, taken from the ' Manuscript Found.' I well recollect telling Mr. Spalding that the so frequent use of the words, ' And it came to pass,' ' Now it came to pass,' rendered it ridiculous. Spalding left here in 1812, and I furnished him the means to carry him to Pittsburg, where he said he would get the book printed, and pay me. But I never heard any more from him or his writings, till I saw them in the Book of Mormon.

" HENRY LAKE."

Aaron Wright, Oliver Smith, and Nahum Howard, of Conneaut, make confirmatory statements. Evidence to an unlimited extent might — if necessary — be adduced, showing the substantial identity between Spalding's tale and Smith and Rigdon's revelation. Rigdon's possession of the manuscript is easily explained: It will be seen that Spalding after having failed in business removed to Pittsburg, Pa., where he expected to recoup his fortunes by the publication of his book. He there submitted his manuscript to a firm of printers, Messrs. Patterson & Lambdin, with a view to its issue on joint account, but the proposal was not carried out. What became of the manuscript is now the question? Spalding's widow supposed it to be in a trunk with other writings of her husband which she had removed to Otsego County, New York, after his decease, but upon search it was not to be found. She remembered that while they lived in Pittsburg her husband had taken it to the office of Patterson & Lambdin, but whether it was ever returned she was unable to say. The probability is that it remained with other lumber cn the printers' shelves until it was discovered and appropriated by Rigdon about 1823 or 1824. He at this period resided in Pittsburg and was intimate with Lambdin, the survivor of the printing firm — Patterson having joined the majority. Rigdon remained in Pittsburg nearly three years, and, according to his own statement, abandoned preaching and lived in seclusion for the purpose of studying the Bible. Though it cannot be established by positive proof, there is little doubt that he obtained the Spalding manuscript from Lambdin, and that during his seclusion, instead of studying the Bible he was paving the way for a substitute for it, which he and Smith afterward issued as the Book of Mormon. After the death of Lambdin, Rigdon removed to Geauga County, Ohio, where he began preaching new points of doctrine, which were found — after its publication — to be inculcated in the Mormon Bible. The death of Lambdin left Rigdon sole proprietor of the work which was probably to be issued by them jointly. The latter was now free to bring it out in such manner as he thought best calculated to insure its success. He knew very well that no publisher would touch it on its literary merit, and therefore concluded to announce it to the world as a new revelation from on high. Who more likely to assist in thus exploiting it than the famous money-digger? His juggling feats had been heralded far and wide, and had lost nothing in their telling. His delving schemes had been transferred to Pennsylvania after becoming dishonored in his own country, and faith in the miraculous stone was much stronger abroad than at home. It was undoubtedly with a view to utilizing Joe and his stone that Rigdon paid his first visit to the Smiths. Enveloped in mystery and seclusion, the two worthies plotted and planned, until the whole miserable fraud was formulated, and the new revelation ready to be announced. So many different stories were told by Joe in regard to finding the golden plates that it is impossible to say which was least mendacious. It may be he had never heard of the adage that liars should have good memories. The gist of his tales may be summed up about as follows: A message from heaven disclosed to him the fact that certain golden plates, on both sides of which were engraved finely drawn characters resembling Egyptian hieroglyphics, were lying buried in a hill near his residence. The leaves or plates were said to be about the thickness of tin. On the top of the chest containing the plates were two crystals set in the rims of a bow in the form of spectacles of enormous size. These he denominated the Urim and Thummim,* and only by their aid could the engraving on the plates be understood and translated. The mystic record contained a new revelation from God to man, which was to supersede all that had gone before.

The hill where these plates were buried is located about two miles south of Palmyra, on a farm now owned by George Sampson. There is nothing very remarkable about this hill except its steepness, which makes it difficult to cultivate. When I saw it last, a flock of sheep were grazing on its barren-looking and precipitous sides, unconscious of the fact that they were treading upon ground held by the Mormon Church to be holy, and apparently deriving very little material sustenance from the soil which had yielded such grand results in a spiritual way. It is known to the Mormon Saints as the hill of Camorah, and is visited and gazed at with awe and reverence by numbers of them every year. The exact locality on the hillside where the plates lay buried was indicated to Joe by his magic stone, but that marvelous article was thenceforward to be superseded by the Urim and Thummim. Not long after Rigdon's first

---

* Butterworth's concordance says: "There are various conjectures about the Urim and Thummim, but whether they were stones in the High Priest's breastplate, or something distinct from them is not known. It is evident that the Urim and Thummim were used in making inquiry of the Deity on momentous occasions."

visit, Smith began to assume the role of Prophet, Seer, and Revelator.   He pretended that while engaged in secret prayer in the wilderness an angel of the Lord had appeared to him and announced that "all the religious denominations were believing false doctrines, and, in consequence, none of them were accepted of God as of his Church and Kingdom."   The angel also promised Joseph that the true doctrine and fullness of the gospel should be revealed through him.   From this time forward Joe had revelations whenever he wanted them.   Very soon another angel " commanded " him to go secretly and alone to a certain spot which would be indicated by his celestial guide and there take from the earth a metallic book of sacred origin and of immortal importance to mankind — the power to translate which should be given only to him as the chosen servant of the Most High.   At an appointed hour and under guidance of the angel, Joe repaired to the spot where the sacred records lay buried, which was on the east side of the hill already described. He told a frightful story of the difficulties encountered before he possessed himself of the holy volume.   Ten thousand devils were gathered around the spot and menaced him with sulphurous smoke and flame to deter him from his purpose, but the angel appearing as his protector he soon laid his hands upon the immortal records, together with the Urim and Thummim, and bore them in safety to his humble abode.   Reminding his family of the fact that the angel had said that no human being but himself could look upon the golden plates and live, he laid them away in a napkin like another unprofitable servant that has been mentioned. His claim to their possession was soon noised abroad, and the story of the demons who encompassed him round about, of the smoke, brimstone, and flame through which the angel of the Lord safely conducted him and his treasure, lost nothing as it went from ear to ear.   Curiosity to see the heavenly records ran high, but the death penalty denounced against the mortal who should gaze upon them was sufficient to hold the great majority of his neighbors in check.   Two of the Prophet's intimate acquaintances, Azel Vandruver and William T. Hussey, not having the fear of death before their eyes, begged him for a peep at the " golden plates," and offered to take upon themselves all risk of the penalty denounced.   They were of course denied, but were permitted to see where they were, and observe their shape and size, as they lay concealed under a thick canvas.   Hussey lightly pushed the Prophet aside, exclaiming as he did so, "Egad! I'll see them dead or alive," and whipped off the cover. He was rewarded by a sight of some tile brick. Joe was equal to the emergency. He told his visitors that knowing the deadly penalty of a sight of the real plates he had provided something of about the same size and weight to meet such an emergency as had just arisen. Kind-hearted man! he had saved the life of his friend! Did the Smiths, the Whitmers, Cowdery, Harris, and Page — eleven of them in all — bear false witness in testifying that they had seen the plates, and did Joe not possess even the glyphs that have been described?

With intent to tell the plain truth only about Smith and his coworkers, it is not easy to comply. How can anyone take the conflicting stories of the Prophet and his followers — some of them confederates and some of them dupes — and say how much fact and how much fable they contain? Joe said that no one could see the golden plates and live, yet eleven of his followers testify to having seen them. Rather than believe that these men committed perjury, I have assumed that the Prophet had in his possession plates "having the appearance of gold," which the eleven saw and "hefted." But if he had such plates, they were not under the canvas which Hussey and Vandruver removed. When he found it necessary to have proof of their existence, a revelation from heaven remitted the death penalty so far as eleven of his followers were concerned, for which remission see the eleventh chapter of the second book of Nephi. And thereafter, whenever he became badly tangled in a network of falsehood, a revelation straightened everything out up to date.

Let us now look for a moment at the tales the Prophet himself told his neighbors about his find.

Peter Ingersol, a neighbor, who shared his confidence if anyone did, testifies as follows:

"One day he came and greeted me with a joyful countenance. Upon asking the cause of his unusual happiness, he replied in the following language: 'As I was passing, yesterday, across the woods, after a heavy shower of rain, I found in a hollow, some beautiful white sand that had been washed up by the water. I took off my frock, and tied up several quarts of it, and then went home. On my entering the house, I found the family at the table eating dinner. They were all anxious to know the contents of my frock. At that moment I happened to think of what I had heard about a history found in Canada, called the Golden Bible; so I very gravely told them it was the Golden Bible. To my surprise, they were credulous enough to believe what I said. Accordingly, I told them that I had received a commandment to let no one see it, for, says I, no man can see it with the naked eye and live.   However, I offered to take out the book and show it to them, but they refused to see it, and left the room.   Now,' said Joe, ' I have got the damned fools fixed, and will carry out the fun.'   Notwithstanding he told me he had no such book, and believed there never was any such book, yet he told me that he actually went to Willard Chase, to get him to make a chest in which he might deposit his Golden Bible.   But, as Chase would not do it, he made a box himself of clapboards, and put it into a pillow-case, and allowed people only to lift it, and feel of it through the case."

Mr. Willard Chase makes the subjoined statement:

" In the forepart of September (I believe), 1827, the Prophet requested me to make him a chest, informing me that he designed to move back to Pennsylvania, and expecting soon to get his gold book, he wanted a chest to lock it up, giving me to understand, at the same time, that if I would make the chest he would give me a share in the book.   I told him my business was such that I could not make it; but if he would bring the book to me I would lock it up for him.   He said that would not do, as he was commanded to keep it two years, without letting it come to the eye of anyone but himself.   This commandment, however, he did not keep, for in less than two years twelve men said they had seen it.   I told him to get it and convince me of its existence, and I would make him a chest; but he said that would not do, as he must have a chest to lock the book in as soon as he took it out of the ground.   I saw him a few days after, when he told me that I must make the chest.   I told him plainly that I could not, upon which he told me that I could have no share in the book.

" A few weeks after this conversation, he came to my house, and related the following story:—That on the 22d of September he arose early in the morning, and took a one-horse wagon, of someone that had stayed over night at their house, without leave or license; and, together with his wife, repaired to the hill which contained the book.   He left his wife in the wagon, by the road, and went alone to the hill, a distance of thirty or forty rods from

the road; he said he then took the book out of the ground and hid
it in a tree-top, and returned home.   He then went to the town
of Macedon to work.   After about ten days, it having been suggested that some one had got his book, his wife went after him;
he hired a horse, and went home in the afternoon, stayed long
enough to drink one cup of tea, and then went for his book,
found it safe, took off his frock, wrapt it round it, put it under
his arm, and run all the way home, a distance of about two miles.
He said he should think it would weigh sixty pounds, and was
sure it would weigh forty.   On his return home he said he was
attacked by two men in the woods, and knocked them both down
and made his escape, arrived safe, and secured his treasure.   He
then observed that if it had not been for that stone (which he acknowledged belonged to me) he would not have obtained the book.
A few days afterward, he told one of my neighbors that he had
not got any such book, and never had; but that he had told the
story to deceive the d—d fool (meaning me), to get him to make
a chest.   His neighbors having become disgusted with his foolish
stories, he determined to go back to Pennsylvania, to avoid what
he called persecution.   His wits were now put to the task to
contrive how he should get money to bear his expenses.   He met
one day, in the streets of Palmyra, a rich man, whose name was
Martin Harris, and addressed him thus: — ' I have a commandment from God to ask the first man I meet in the street to give
me fifty dollars, to assist me in doing the work of the Lord, by
translating the Golden Bible.'   Martin, being naturally a credulous man, handed Joseph the money.   In the spring, 1829,
Harris went to Pennsylvania, and on his return to Palmyra, reported that the Prophet's wife, in the month of June following,
would be delivered of a male child that would be able, when two
years old, to translate the Gold Bible.   Then, said he, you will
see Joseph Smith, Jr., walking through the streets of Palmyra,
with a Gold Bible under his arm, and having a gold breastplate
on, and a gold sword hanging by his side.   This, however, by the
bye, proved false.

" In April, 1830, I again asked Hiram for the stone which he
had borrowed of me; he told me I should not have it, for Joseph
made use of it in translating his Bible.   I reminded him of his
promise, and that he had pledged his honor to return it; but he
gave me the lie, saying the stone was not mine, nor never was.
Harris at the same time flew in a rage, took me by the collar and

said I was a liar, and he could prove it by twelve witnesses. After I had extricated myself from him, Hiram, in a rage, shook his fist at me, and abused me in a most scandalous manner. Thus I might proceed in describing the character of these high priests, by relating one transaction after another, which would all tend to set them in the same light in which they were regarded by their neighbors, viz., as a pest to society. I have regarded Joseph Smith, Jr., from the time I first became acquainted with him until he left this part of the country, as a man whose word could not be depended upon. Hiram's character was but very little better. What I have said respecting the characters of these men will apply to the whole family. What I have stated relative to the characters of these individuals, thus far, is wholly true. After they became thorough Mormons, their conduct was more disgraceful than before. They did not hesitate to abuse any man, no matter how fair his character, provided he did not embrace their creed. Their tongues were continually employed in spreading scandal and abuse. Although they left this part of the country without paying their just debts, yet their creditors were glad to have them do so, rather than to have them stay, disturbing the neighborhood.

" Signed,   WILLARD CHASE."

" On the 11th of December, 1833, the said Willard Chase appeared before me, and made oath that the foregoing statement, to which he has subscribed his name, is true, according to his best recollection and belief.   FREDERICK SMITH,
" Justice of the Peace of Wayne County."

Parley Chase affirms as follows: — " I was acquainted with the family of Joseph Smith, Sen., both before and since they became Mormons, and feel free to state that not one of the male members of the Smith family were entitled to any credit whatsoever. They were lazy, intemperate, and worthless men — very much addicted to lying. In this they frequently boasted of their skill. Digging for money was their principal employment. In regard to their Gold Bible speculation, they scarcely ever told two stories alike."

Abigail Harris made the following affirmation, which is sustained by a similar one from Lucy, the wife of Martin Harris:

PALMYRA, WAYNE Co., N. Y., 11th mo. 28, 1833.

" In the early part of the winter in 1828 I made a visit to Martin Harris's, and was joined in company by Joseph Smith, Sen., and his wife. The Gold Bible business, so called, was the topic of conversation, to which I paid particular attention, that I might learn the truth of the whole matter. They told me that the report that Joseph, Jr., had found golden plates was true, and that he was in Harmony, Pa., translating them. The old lady said, also, that after the book was translated, the plates were to be publicly exhibited — admittance twenty-five cents. She calculated it would bring in annually an enormous sum of money — that money would then be very plenty, and the book would also sell for a great price, as it was something entirely new — that they had been commanded to obtain all the money they could borrow for present necessity, and to repay with gold. The remainder was to be kept in store for the benefit of their family and children. This and the like conversation detained me till about 11 o'clock. Early the next morning, the mystery of the Spirit (being myself one of the order called Friends), was revealed by the following circumstance: — The old lady took me into another room, and after closing the door, she said, ' Have you four or five dollars in money that you can lend until our business is brought to a close? the Spirit has said you shall receive four-fold.' I told her that when I gave, I did it not expecting to receive again; as for money, I had none to lend. I then asked her what her particular want of money was; to which she replied, ' Joseph wants to take the stage and come home from Pennsylvania to see what we are all about.' To which I replied, he might look in his stone and save his time and money. The old lady seemed confused, and left the room, and thus ended the visit.

" In the second month following, Martin Harris and his wife were at my house. In conversation about Mormonites, she observed that she wished her husband would quit them, as she believed it was all false and a delusion. To which I heard Mr. Harris reply, ' What if it is a lie; if you will let me alone I will make money out of it! ' I was both an eye and an ear witness of what has been stated above, which is now fresh in my memory, and I give it to the world for the good of mankind. I speak the truth and lie not, God bearing me witness.

" ABIGAIL HARRIS."

Isaac Hale, of Harmony, Pa., with whose daughter the Prophet eloped, did not, as will be seen by what follows, hold his son-in-law in very high esteem.   Joseph seems also not to have made a favorable impression either upon his brother-in-law, Alva Hale, or upon a number of others whose statements are appended:

HARMONY, PA., March 20, 1834.

" I first became acquainted with Joseph Smith, Jr., in November, 1825.   He was at that time in the employ of a set of men who were called ' money-diggers '; and his occupation was that of seeing, or pretending to see by means of a stone placed in his hat, and his hat closed over his face.   In this way he pretended to discover minerals and hidden treasure.

" About this time, young Smith made several visits at my house, and at length asked my consent to his marrying my daughter Emma.   This I refused, and gave my reasons for so doing; some of which were, that he was a stranger, and followed a business that I could not approve; he then left the place.   Not long after this he returned, and, while I was absent from home, carried off my daughter into the State of New York, where they were married without my approbation or consent.

" Soon after this I was informed they had brought a wonderful book of plates down with them.   I was shown a box in which it was said they were contained, which had, to all appearance, been used as a glass box of the common window glass.   I was allowed to feel the weight of the box, and they gave me to understand that the book of plates was then in the box — into which, however, I was not allowed to look.

" I inquired of Joseph Smith, Jr., who was to be the first who would be allowed to see the book of plates.   He said it was a young child.   After this I became dissatisfied, and informed him that if there was anything in my house of that description, which I could not be allowed to see, he must take it away; if he did not, I was determined to see it.   After that the plates were said to be hid in the woods.

" About this time Martin Harris made his appearance upon the stage; and Smith began to interpret the characters, or hieroglyphics which he said were engraven upon the plates, while Harris wrote down the interpretation.   It was said that Harris wrote down one hundred and sixteen pages, and lost them.*

---

* They were stolen by his wife while he was sleeping, and burned.

Soon after this happened, Martin Harris informed me that he must have a greater witness, and said that he had talked with Joseph about it — Joseph informed him that he could not, or durst not show him the plates, but that he (Joseph) would go into the woods where the book of plates was, and that after he came back Harris should follow his track in the snow, and find the book, and examine it for himself. Harris informed me that he followed Smith's directions and could not find the plates, and was still dissatisfied.

"The next day after this happened, I went to the house where Joseph Smith, Jr., lived, and where he and Harris were engaged in their translation of the book. Each of them had a written piece of paper which they were comparing, and some of the words were, 'My servant seeketh a greater witness, but no greater witness can be given him.' There was also something said about 'three that were to see the thing' — meaning, I supposed, the book of plates, and that 'if the three did not go exactly according to the orders, the thing would be taken from them.' I inquired whose words they were, and was informed by Joseph or Emma (I rather think it was the former) that they were the words of Jesus Christ. I told them that I considered the whole of it a delusion, and advised them to abandon it. The manner in which he pretended to read and interpret was the same as when he looked for the money-diggers, with the stone in his hat, and his hat over his face, while the book was at the same time hid in the woods.

"After this, Martin Harris went away, and Oliver Cowdery came and wrote for Smith, while he interpreted, as above described. This is the same Oliver Cowdery whose name may be found in the Book of Mormon. Cowdery continued a scribe for Smith until the Book of Mormon was completed, as I supposed and understood.

"Joseph Smith, Jr., resided near me for some time after this, and I had a good opportunity of becoming acquainted with him, and somewhat acquainted with his associates, and I conscientiously believe, from the facts I have detailed, and from many other circumstances, which I do not deem it necessary to relate, that the whole 'Book of Mormon' (so called) is a silly fabrication of falsehood and wickedness, got up for speculation, and with a design to dupe the credulous and unwary — and in order that its fabricators may live upon the spoils of those who swallow the deception.

" ISAAC HALE."

" Affirmed to and subscribed before me, March 20, 1834.

" CHARLES DIMON,
" Justice of the Peace."

" Alva Hale, son of Isaac Hale, states that Joseph Smith, Jr., told him that his (Smith's) gift in seeing with a stone and hat, ' was a gift from God,' but also states ' that Smith told him, at another time, that this peeping was all d — d nonsense. He (Smith) was deceived himself, but did not intend to deceive others; that he intended to quit the business (of peeping) and labor for his livelihood.' That afterward Smith told him he should see the plates from which he translated the Book of Mormon, and accordingly, at the time specified by Smith, he (Hale) called to see the plates, but Smith did not show them, but appeared angry. He further states that he knows Joseph Smith, Jr., to be an impostor and a liar, and knows Martin Harris to be a liar likewise.

" Levi Lewis states, that he has been acquainted with Joseph Smith, Jr., and Martin Harris, and that he has heard them both say adultery was no crime. Harris said he did not blame Smith for his (Smith's) attempt to seduce E. W., etc. Mr. Lewis says that he knows Smith to be a liar; — that he saw him (Smith) intoxicated at three different times while he was composing the Book of Mormon, and also that he has heard Smith, when driving oxen, use language of the greatest profanity. Mr. Lewis also testifies, that he heard Smith say he (Smith) was as good as Jesus Christ; — that it was as bad to injure him as it was to injure Jesus Christ. With regard to the plates, Smith said God had deceived him — which was the reason he (Smith) did not show them.

" Sophia Lewis certifies, that she heard a conversation between Joseph Smith, Jr., and the Rev. James B. Roach, in which Smith called Mr. R. a d — d fool. Smith also said in the same conversation, that he (Smith) was as good as Jesus Christ; and that she has frequently heard Smith use profane language. She states that she heard Smith say the book of plates could not be opened under penalty of death, by any other person but his (Smith's) first-born, which was to be a male. She says she was present at the birth of this child, and that it was still-born and very much deformed."

The manuscript of the Book of Mormon was at last completed; somewhere, somehow, either in New York or Pennsylvania, and with or without the assistance of Martin Harris. With its completion arose the question of printing and publishing. Harris was enthusiastically in favor of giving the new revelation to the world. As he was expected to furnish means to pay the printer, and as he was, perhaps, the only genuine believer in the doctrines to be promulgated, his wishes were seconded by Smith, Rigdon, and Cowdery. But cupidity was about as strong an element in his composition as credulity, and so the honest and benevolent, but money-loving farmer, proposed to avail himself of the wisdom of others before embarking in the publication scheme. He first consulted his wife, a Quakeress, with a mind of her own, from whom he got, as men usually do from similar sources, the very best kind of counsel and admonition. She denounced the whole scheme as silly and impious, and told him he was being imposed upon, and likely to be defrauded. Burns has told us

"How many lengthened, sage advices,
The husband frae the wife despises."

Harris called her a fool and a woman (she could pardon the first designation, but not the last), and he said: " What if it is a fraud, so long as I make money out of it? " Like most persons who seek advice, he only wanted such as comported with his own preconceived notions.

Discarding the counsel of his faithful wife, he determined to avail himself of the " wisdom of learned men " relative to the genuineness of the plates and the revelation inscribed thereon. He first consulted the village jeweler and silversmith, describing to him gold leaves of a certain size, thickness, and weight, and asked what they would be worth if genuine. The computation was made, but seems not to have been wholly satisfactory. To make assurance doubly sure, he obtained from Smith several pages of antique characters or hieroglyphics purporting to be exact copies from the golden plates, together with the translation thereof, and with them repaired to New York where he solicited the scrutiny of a number of gentlemen whose repute as biblical scholars was so current as to have reached the crafty backwoodsman.   Believing the farmer, though otherwise, apparently, a man of sound judgment, to be a religious monomaniac, they scouted the whole thing as too absurd for serious consideration, and commiserated him as a victim of fanaticism and fraud. Harris, however, stood firmly by his belief, and returned their commiseration four-fold, declaring them to be " a stiff-necked and rebellious generation," and quoting against them one of his favorite texts, that " God hath chosen the foolish things of the world to confound the wise."   What one of the scholars applied to by Harris thought of Joseph's golden phylacteries and the hieroglyphics thereon is plainly set forth in the following letter:

" NEW YORK, Feb. 17, 1834.

" The whole story about my having pronounced the Mormonite inscription to be ' reformed Egyptian hieroglyphics ' is perfectly false.   Some years ago, a plain, and, apparently, simple-hearted farmer, called upon me, with a note from Dr. Mitchell, of our city, now deceased, requesting me to decipher, if possible, a paper which the farmer would hand me, and which Dr. M. confessed he had been unable to understand.   Upon examining the paper in question, I soon came to the conclusion that it was all a trick, perhaps a hoax.   When I asked the person who brought it how he obtained the writing, he gave me, as far as I can now recollect, the following account: — A ' gold book,' consisting of a number of plates of gold, fastened together in the shape of a book by wires of the same metal, had been dug up in the northern part of the State of New York, and, along with the book, an enormous pair of ' gold spectacles! '   These spectacles were so large, that if a person attempted to look through them his two eyes would have to be turned toward one of the glasses, merely, the spectacles in question being altogether too large for the breadth of the human face.   Whoever examined the plates through the spectacles was enabled not only to read them, but fully to understand their meaning.   All this knowledge, however, was confined at that time to a young man who had the trunk containing the book and spectacles in his sole possession.   This young man was placed behind a curtain, in the garret of a farm house, and, being thus concealed from view, put on the spectacles occasionally, or rather looked through one of the glasses, deciphered the characters in the book, and having committed some of them to paper, handed copies from behind the curtain to those who stood on the outside. Not a word, however, was said about the plates having been deciphered 'by the gift of God.' Everything, in this way, was effected by the large pair of spectacles. The farmer added, that he had been requested to contribute a sum of money toward the publication of the ' golden book,' the contents of which would, as he had been assured, produce an entire change in the world, and save it from ruin. So urgent had been these solicitations, that he intended selling his farm and handing over the amount received to those who wished to publish the plates. As a last precautionary step, however; he had resolved to come to New York and obtain the opinion of the learned about the meaning of the paper which he brought with him, and which had been given him as a part of the contents of the book, although no translation had been furnished at the time by the young man with the spectacles. On hearing this odd story, I changed my opinion about the paper, and instead of viewing it any longer as a hoax upon the learned, I began to regard it as part of a scheme to cheat the farmer of his money, and I communicated my suspicions to him, warning him to beware of rogues. He requested an opinion from me in writing, which, of course, I declined giving, and he then took his leave, carrying the paper with him. This paper was, in fact, a singular scrawl. It consisted of all kinds of crooked characters, disposed in columns, and had evidently been prepared by some person who had before him, at the time, a book containing various alphabets. Greek and Hebrew letters, crosses and flourishes, Roman letters inverted or placed sideways, were arranged in perpendicular columns, and the whole ended in a rude delineation of a circle divided into various compartments, decked with various strange marks, and evidently copied after the Mexican calendar, given by Humboldt, but copied in such a way as not to betray the source whence it was derived. I am thus particular, as to the contents of the paper, inasmuch as I have frequently conversed with my friends on the subject since the Mormonite excitement began, and well remember that the paper contained anything else but ' Egyptian hieroglyphics.' Some time after, the farmer paid me a second visit. He brought with him the ' golden book ' in print, and offered it to me for sale. I declined purchasing. He then asked permission to leave the book with me for examination. I declined receiving it, although his manner was strangely urgent.

I adverted once more to the roguery which had been, in my opinion, practised upon him, and asked him what had become of the
gold plates. He informed me that they were in a trunk with
the large pair of spectacles. I advised him to go to a magistrate and have the trunk examined. He said the 'curse of
God' would come upon him should he do this. On my pressing
him, however, to pursue the course which I had recommended,
he told me that he would open the trunk if I would take the
'curse of God' upon myself. I replied that I would do so with
the greatest willingness, and would incur every risk of that
nature, provided I could only extricate him from the grasp of
rogues. He then left me.

"I have thus given you a full statement of all that I know
respecting the origin of Mormonism, and must beg you, as a
personal favor, to publish this letter immediately, should you
find my name mentioned again by these wretched fanatics.

"Yours respectfully,   CHARLES ANTHON."

The plain talk of Professor Anthon availed nothing with the
farmer. He returned to Palmyra more intent than ever upon
spreading abroad the good tidings which he firmly believed were
contained in the Book of Mormon. But for his faith and
fanaticism, the golden legend might never have been given to
mankind, for he was the only person of means and credit who
had embraced the new doctrine. Accordingly, with a view to
printing and publication, Joseph Smith, his brother Hyrum,
Oliver Cowdery, and Harris, paid a visit early in the summer of
1829 to Egbert Grandin, at that time a printer in Palmyra, and
publisher of the *Wayne Sentinel*, and asked his price for printing and binding one edition of three thousand copies of the work.
Harris would guarantee payment if a satisfactory bargain
could be struck. Mr. Grandin declined positively to entertain
the proposal, and in the presence of the Smiths and Cowdery,
advised Harris, who was his friend, to have nothing to do with
the inchoate revelation. His admonition was kindly received
but stubbornly dismissed by Harris, and resented with pious indignation by the Smiths and Cowdery. A number of the friends
and neighbors of Harris tried to dissuade him from his purpose, and for a time he seemed to waver in his confidence regarding the legend, but the Prophet was a spell-binder, and his arts
were crowned with ultimate success.

Mr. Grandin having refused to reconsider his determination, though earnestly entreated to do so, application was next made to Thurlow Weed, then editor and publisher of an Anti-Masonic paper in Rochester, and several sheets of the manuscript were submitted to him, with a statement of the whole number required to be printed and bound. What Mr. Weed thought of the scheme is here given in his own words. He says: " After reading a few chapters, it seemed such a jumble of unintelligible absurdities that we refused the work, advising Harris not to mortgage his farm and beggar his family." Mr. E. F. Marshall, of Rochester, was then applied to, and gave terms for printing and binding the book, agreeing to accept Harris as security for payment. With this estimate, Smith and his companions returned to Palmyra, and assuring Mr. Grandin that the work would be printed by Marshall if he further declined it begged him to reconsider his determination, and save them much inconvenience and cost of travel, by doing it near their homes, as the manuscript was to be delivered at the office in the morning and after examination of proof taken away daily; they holding it to be sacred, and not to be left in worldly hands. Upon this statement of their case, Mr. Grandin, after advising with a number of his discrete and fair-minded townsmen, agreed to print and bind five thousand copies of the Book of Mormon for the sum of three thousand dollars, taking a bond and mortgage on the farm of Harris as security for payment. The contract was carried out to the satisfaction of all parties, and the complete edition was delivered early in the summer of 1830.

A difficulty was encountered during the progress of the work which worried the Saints not a little. In endeavoring to convince his wife of the desirability of assisting in " the work of the Lord," Harris had taken to his house and shown her one hundred and sixteen pages of the manuscript, probably that portion which he had helped to copy. The gentle dame, acting in what she believed to be — and really was — her own and her husband's interest, crept softly out of bed " in the dead watch and middle of the night," whilst Martin Harris " in holy matrimony snored away," and reduced the writing to ashes. This she kept a profound secret until after the book was published. Tricksters are the first to suspect trickery. Smith and Harris believed the manuscript to have been stolen by wicked and designing men, intent upon bringing God's will to naught, and suspected Mrs. Harris of being their accomplice. In the endeavor to extort a confession from her by Harris, a quarrel arose, and their relations as husband and wife were sundered, never to be renewed. This incident clearly establishes the fact that the Book of Mormon was not a translation from golden or any other plates in the possession of the Prophet. Had it been, they would simply have been obliged to supply the missing pages by a retranslation. But fearing these were still in existence and might be brought forward to show that their work was not a translation of the revealed will of the Most High, but the craft of knaves, they simply ignored that portion of it altogether. Had they undertaken to rewrite it from memory, comparisons might have shown the odious fact that the Supreme Will was changeable.

The Book of Mormon was launched, but was not favored by prospering gales. To transfer the simile to terra firma, the seed fell upon a rocky and barren soil. The godly regarded it as little less than impious; as a travesty (which, in fact, it was) of the book they revered; and the unregenerate scoffed. The result was that outside of the Saints, who numbered less than a score, and perhaps another score whose curiosity led them to buy it, it was dead lumber on the printer's shelves. Harris' fine farm, about two miles from Palmyra village, was sold — by private sale, not by foreclosure — to pay the printer. The historian is pleased to state that Mrs. Harris declined to join in the mortgage, and that upon her separation from her husband, eighty acres of land, with comfortable buildings, were set off for her personal use and behoof. It may be mentioned that, while unalterably hostile to her husband's fanatical action, she held Mr. Grandin fully justified, under the circumstances, in undertaking the printing contract. The maid with the milking pail has many prototypes of the sterner sex in the business world. This is the way Harris counted his unhatched chickens: 5,000 books at $1.25 per copy, is $6,250; cost of printing and binding, $3,000; net profit $3,250, or more than 100 per cent.; how the thing resulted has already been shown. It may be added that when the Smiths were overtaken — as they often were — by those dire necessities known as food and raiment, they bartered the sacred volumes to supply those needs, and in some cases at a considerable discount from the trade price, although Harris had been promised a monopoly of the sales until he was reimbursed, and the penalty of instant death had been denounced against anyone who should sell the work for less than a dollar and a quarter. But though despised and rejected by the friends and neighbors of the Prophet, the Book of Mormon has since gone through many editions, and has been translated into a number of foreign languages. Truly, " a prophet is not without honor save in his own country, and in his own house." The title page is as follows:

" THE

" BOOK OF MORMON;

" AN ACCOUNT WRITTEN BY THE HAND·OF MORMON, UPON PLATES TAKEN FROM THE PLATES OF NEPHI.

" Wherefore it is an abridgment of the Record of the people of Nephi; and also of the Lamanites; written to the Lamanites, which are a remnant of the House of Israel; and also to Jew and Gentile; written by way of commandment, and also by the spirit of prophecy and of Revelation. Written, and sealed up, and hid up unto the Lord, that they might not be destroyed; to come forth by the gift and power of God unto the interpretation thereof; sealed by the hand of Moroni, and hid up unto the Lord, to come forth in due time by the way of Gentile; the interpretation thereof by the gift of God: an abridgment taken from the Book of Ether.

" Also, which is a Record of the People of Jared, which were scattered at the time the Lord confounded the language of the people when they were building a tower to get to Heaven; which is to show unto the remnant of the House of Israel how great things the Lord hath done for their fathers; and that they may know the covenants of the Lord, that they are not cast off forever; and also to the convincing of the Jew and Gentile that Jesus is the Christ, the External God, manifesting himself unto all nations. And now if there be fault, it be the mistake of men; wherefore condemn not the things of God, that ye may be found spotless at the judgment seat of Christ.

" By JOSEPH SMITH, Junior,
" Author and Proprietor.

" Palmyra:

" Printed by E. B. Grandin, for the Author.

" 1830."

The absurdity of calling Smith the author of a Divine revelation was omitted in revised editions printed at Nauvoo and Salt Lake. The first edition contained the following cautionary notice, having reference to the manuscript burned by Mrs. Harris:

" *To the Reader* —

"As many false reports have been circulated respecting the following work, and also many unlawful measures taken by evil-designing persons to destroy me, and also the work, I would inform you that I translated, by the gift and power of God, and caused to be written, one hundred and sixteen pages, the which I took from the Book of Lehi, which was an account abridged from the plates of Lehi, by the hand of Mormon; which said account some person or persons have stolen and kept from me, notwithstanding my utmost exertions to recover it again — and being commanded of the Lord that I should not translate the same over again, for Satan had put it into their hearts to tempt the Lord their God, by altering the words, that they did read contrary from that which I translated and caused to be written; and if I should bring forth the same words again, or, in other words, if I should translate the same over again, they would publish that which they had stolen, and Satan would stir up the hearts of this generation, that they might not receive this work: but behold, the Lord said unto me, I will not suffer that Satan shall accomplish his evil design in this thing; therefore thou shalt translate from the plates of Nephi, until ye come to that which ye have translated, which ye have retained, and behold, ye shall publish it as the record of Nephi; and thus I will confound those who have altered my words. I will not suffer that they shall destroy my work; yea, I will show unto them that my wisdom is greater than the cunning of the devil. Wherefore, to be obedient unto the commandments of God, I have, through His grace and mercy, accomplished that which He hath commanded me respecting this thing. I would also inform you that the plates of which hath been spoken, were found in the township of Manchester, Ontario County, New York.

THE AUTHOR.

CONTENTS OF THE BOOK OF MORMON.

The corner stone of the Church of the Latter-Day Saints may be said to have been laid by the publication of the Gold Bible, but the superstructure was not raised in the Genesee Country. A few meetings were held in the log cabin of the Prophet, at which neither singing, prayer, or preaching were attempted, the exercises being limited to readings from the new bible, with interpretations and comments by Joseph. The Rev. Sidney Rigdon preached one sermon in Palmyra, in the hall of the Young Men's Association. Martin Harris vainly endeavored to secure a church for this performance. Christian people regarded the Mormons as blasphemers, and their services as little short of rank impiety. Pomeroy Tucker, who listened to the sermon, thus describes his impressions: " Altogether, though evidencing some talent and ingenuity in its matter and manner, and delivered with startling boldness and seeming sincerity, the performance was, in the main, an unintelligible jumble of quotations, assertions, and obscurities, which was received by the audience as shockingly blasphemous as it was painful to hear. The manifestations of disfavor were so unequivocal that Harris assented to the suggestion of his " Gentile " friends, that no further request be made for the use of the hall, and regular preaching on the Mormon plan was never again attempted in

Palmyra by Rigdon or any other man, according to my recollection." *

The reception of the new doctrine was not at all satisfactory to the Saints. Financially, it was a failure, and Joe's assertion that he had invented a scheme by which he could live without work seemed likely to prove fallacious. The seed indeed fell upon stony ground. The majority of Smith's neighbors were orthodox, devout, God-fearing men, to whom the new doctrine seemed sacrilegious. The remainder was composed of those who, finding it hard to believe the myths, miracles, and fables of the Scriptures, yet preserved a reverent attitude toward all honestly entertained beliefs, and those occasional agnostics who, rejecting all revelation, and especially the last one, maintained toward Smith and his followers an attitude of jeering but not ill-natured hostility. A community so composed did not furnish material for successful proselytizing. Not more than thirty heads of families had embraced the faith up to the time a removal westward had been resolved on. But among the converts was a man of signal influence and ability, the Rev. Parley P. Pratt, of Loraine County, Ohio, who debarked from a canal boat at Palmyra long enough to espouse the new faith, and remained for many years one of the pillars of the Morman hierarchy. Rigdon and Pratt " Prepared the way of the Lord " by preaching the new doctrine at Mentor and Kirtland, Ohio, where it was more favorably received than in the neighborhood of its origin. In the later part of the year 1830, the Smiths, Cowdery, Harris, the Whitmers, and other original Latter-Day Saints, shaking the dust from their shoes as a testimony against the Gentiles of the Genesee, prepared for their *hegira* to Ohio.

Just at this juncture it became evident that an unmarried sister of the Prophet would before very long make a contribution to the census of that year. Joe immediately had a revelation from on high that the conception was immaculate, and that the Gentile world was to be astonished by the birth of a new Prophet, Priest, and King. Martin Harris and the others loudly inquired, " Why not? " A question much easier to ask than to answer. If this thing could happen in the first century, why not in the nineteenth? " The power of the Highest shall overshadow thee," might as well be spoken to a Gentile maiden in Western New

---

* This reminds me of the low comedian who said he had played King Lear, but never twice in the same city.

York as to a Jewish one in Nazareth!   To gainsay this is to deny to the Deity the first and greatest of his attributes — omnipotence.   No one believing in the first advent could deny the possibility of a second, and the probabilities in either case seem about evenly balanced.   But there were people ungenerous enough to allude to the fact that the Rev. Sidney Rigdon had been an inmate of the Smith family at various times for more than a year.   Proceeding from scoffers and the unregenerate, such allusions were held by the Saints to be no reproach.   However begotten, the child was a female, and lived but a few hours. The Prophet satisfied Harris and the others by telling them that Divine wrath had, in this way, punished some act of Mormon disobedience.

Reinforced by the arrivals from Wayne and Ontario counties, and by the active labors of Smith, Harris, Cowdery, and the others, the ministrations of Pratt and Rigdon were blessed by the ingathering of more than a hundred converts to the new revelation, and Kirtland, for a time became the chief seat of the Mormon colony, and it was here that their Church was thoroughly organized and established.   Here Brigham Young, the great ruler and organizer, the man who, after the death of the Prophet, swayed with autocratic power the destinies of the hierarchy, was converted and joined the society in 1832.   The State of Vermont has the honor, if any it be, of being the birthplace of the founder of the Mormon faith, and of his much abler successor.   Brigham's early training was on his father's farm, among the green hills.   On his removal to the State of New York, he followed the trade of a painter and glazier, which was his occupation when he joined the Mormons at Kirtland, in 1832. A born leader, with an intuitive knowledge of human character, capable of swaying masses of men by the power of an electric will, Young, from the start, was an influential and prominent man in Mormon affairs.   When the High Council of the Church, consisting of twelve high priests, was organized, Young was ordained one of the number, and soon after was elected president of the Council.   Had his ambition led him to supersede Smith, there is little doubt that he could have done so, but Mormonism was yet an experiment, and he bided his time.   And here at Kirtland the Church was strengthened by the admission to membership of two of its ablest advocates and defenders, Orson Pratt and Orson Hyde.

The Church being now organized and established, the next move of the Prophet was to secure funds for its endowment and support, and here the system of tithing was adopted, which, enlarged and strengthened by Young, has been continued up to the present time. Ex-Governor Harding, of Utah, says: " Everything is subject to this system, from the tenth egg to the tenth ox, from the tenth cent to the tenth dollar; the poor girl who works out by the week and the rich farmer and money-lender being alike subject to this indiscriminate levy ' in the Lord's name.' " The revelations to Joseph on this head were numerous and to the point. Here is one of them: " In answer to the question, ' O, Lord, show unto thy servants how much thou requirest of the properties for a tithing? ' verily thus saith the Lord: ' I require all the surplus property to be put into the hands of the bishop of my Church of Zion, for the building of mine house, and for the priesthood, and for the debts of the presidency of my Church, and this shall be the beginning of the yearly tithing of my people,' et cetera." No circumlocution about that. Another revelation directs " That all the monies which can be spared, it mattereth not whether it be little or much, be sent up to the land of Zion, unto those whom I have appointed to receive; " and another declares that " Those which shall not observe this law [of tithing] shall not be found worthy to abide among you." Still another commands the faithful to " Build a house in which my servant Joseph shall live and translate, and to furnish and support the same, it being my will that my servant shall live without labor." Joe had at last solved the problem how to escape the penalty denounced against Adam. And not this alone: stimulated by revelations which his dupes sincerely believed to be Divine emanations they erected at Kirtland a temple which cost, in money and freely contributed labor and materials, over fifty thousand dollars. A dwelling for the Prophet was built and furnished, and money and valuable personal property flowed in from the system of tithes. He established a bank, built a flouring mill, and opened a store.

Notwithstanding these appearances of prosperity and permanency, it soon became evident that Kirtland was not to be the abiding place of the Saints. They did not live upon good terms with their neighbors. The orthodoxy of Northern Ohio execrated and spat upon the Mormon creed, and scorned the impostors who originated it. Aside from questions of belief, the

Saints were accused of immoral and criminal practices, contrary
to good order and good neighborhood.   The demeanor of the
leaders was exasperating and defiant.   As in the case of an Irish
coachman who had helped to disperse a parade of Orangemen and
returned to his duties bearing upon his person visible signs of
the encounter, and who was asked by his employer why the love
of God made him hate his neighbor, and why he could not con-
cede to others what he demanded for himself — freedom of opinion?   " ' Dade, sor," was the reply, " it was not their religion at
all, at all, that roused me passion, it was the irritatin' music; "
the band was playing the " Battle of the Boyne " as they passed
by.— And so it was, perhaps, the " irritatin' " bearing of the
Saints, rather than their teachings, which, at Kirtland and elsewhere during their long career, made them objects of popular
opprobrium.

Whatever may have been their reasons for removal, the community, after a sojourn of less than two years in Ohio, decided
that the promised land was nearer the setting sun, and determined upon a change of locality.   Rigdon and Cowdery were
sent forth as explorers, and on their return from an extended
tour, reported in favor of the State of Missouri as the future
home and Zion of the faithful.   The Prophet having visited and
approved of the locality selected, a revelation to his followers
commanded them to " Remove unto the land appointed and consecrated for the gathering of the Saints, wherefore this is the
land of promise, and the place for the City of Zion.   Behold,
the place now called Independence is in the center, and the spot
for the temple is lying westward upon a lot not far from the
Court House; wherefore, it is wisdom that the land should be
purchased by my people, and also my tract lying westward, even
unto the line running between the Lamanite and Gentile, and also
my tract bordering by the prairies, inasmuch as my disciples are
enabled to buy land."   They are further directed to " send up
treasures " and are promised " an inheritance in this world,"
and that " their works shall follow them."   Need it be told that
a large tract of land was selected and purchased, a town site
laid out which the energy and self-sacrificing industry of these
people soon built up, and early in 1834 a majority of the brethren had become residents of the flourishing town of Independence, Jackson County, Missouri.   A few, however, chiefly those
with families and material interests, remained at Kirtland to

work farms, dispose of them and other property, and better pre-
pare for removal to the new colony. Among those who tarried
in Ohio were Pratt and Young. After seeing the new settlement well under way, Smith returned and joined them, for the
purpose, he said, of "making money for the benefit of the
Church." Having a commodious, well-furnished dwelling, a
bank, a mill, and a store, he was in no hurry to part with them,
evidently thinking they were the result of his own business
capacity, and not what they really were, the creation of revelations and tithes. The outcome was soon reached. His bank
exploded, his mill stopped, and the shutters were put up at his
store and not taken down. Secularly he was a failure. Without a hundred credulous fools to pour into his lap one-tenth of
all their earnings he would have starved in the streets or have
gone back to fishing, fortune-telling, and trapping for a living.
Popular indignation rose high at Kirtland against him and his
religious pretensions. Hastily collecting his portable effects,
and disposing to the best advantage of those which could not be
removed, he departed for the promised land in Missouri. Young
fled with him. This was in 1835. The panic of 1836-37 struck
Joseph a year in advance. In 1838, he and Rigdon, being at
Kirtland together, were arrested on charges of swindling in
connection with their wild-cat bank and other fraudulent schemes.
They escaped from the sheriff at night and made their way to
Missouri on horseback. Smith's account of the affair, as published in the Mormon newspaper at Independence, was to the
effect that they "left Kirtland to escape mob violence, with
which they were threatened under color of legal process, and were
followed more than two hundred miles by hellhounds armed with
knives and pistols."

The Saints' rest was not found in Missouri. Their neighbors
in that State were, to a great extent, a different people from
those left behind in Western New York and Northern Ohio. The
Missourians of that period can hardly be called an orthodox
and law-abiding people. The rougher elements of border civilization were prominent if not predominant, and with these the
Saints were soon in collision. It requires no prophet to foretell
the result. After a few years of almost continuous warfare
with the citizens and public authorities of the State, in which
blood was shed on both sides, the Mormons were banished. There
is little doubt that they were badly treated. Missouri had no

right to interfere with their form of worship, and if her statutes were broken or disregarded, punishment should have been meeted out under the forms of law and not by mob violence.   But the Mormons had to go, and did go, and on this occasion they went east instead of west.   Before tracing them to their new homes in Illinois, let us hear some of the reasons given for their expulsion from Missouri.   General Clark, commander of the State militia, in a dispatch to Gov. Baggs, dated November 10, 1838, said: " There is no crime from treason down to petit larceny, but these people, or a majority of them, have been guilty of — all, too, under the counsel of Joseph Smith, Jr., their Prophet. They have committed treason, murder, arson, burglary, robbery, larceny, and perjury.   They have formed societies to circumvent the laws and put them at defiance, and to plunder, burn, and murder and divide the spoils for the use of their Church."   A formidable indictment, truly, and drawn with genuine Southwestern luridity!   Let us further hear from the Governor on this subject.   In a special communication to the Legislature, after the Mormons had been assisted over the border, he says: " These people had violated the laws of the land by open force and avowed resistance to them; they had undertaken, without the aid of the civil authority, to redress their real or fancied grievances; they had instituted among themselves a government of their own, independent of and in opposition to the government of this State, that had, at an inclement season of the year, driven the inhabitants of an entire county from their homes, ravaged their crops and destroyed their dwellings.*   Under these circumstances it became the imperious (?) duty of the Executive to interfere and exercise the powers with which he was (?) invested, to protect the lives and property of our citizens, to restore order and tranquillity to the country, and maintain the supremacy of the laws."   And let us also hear what an unprejudiced historian has to say anent these troubles: " By enlightened people the Mormons were regarded as the victims of misguided vengeance in Missouri.   The ruffianly violence they met at the hands of lawless mobs, in several instances resulting in deliberate murder, finds no extenuation in any real provocation.   Due process of law afforded adequate redress for any criminalities of which they might be found guilty after

* What were the ancestors of the James and Younger boys doing all this time?

legal trial."* But they had to go. Time was not even given them to settle up their affairs. So determined were the people of Missouri to be rid of them, that commissioners were appointed by the Governor to sell their property, pay their debts, and aid them in getting away. The Legislature appropriated two thousand dollars for this purpose, and liberal contributions to hasten their exodus were made by individuals.

By the end of 1839, the Saints had established themselves at a point on the Mississippi River, in Hancock County, Illinois, which they named Nauvoo. As usually happens, persecution seemed to replenish their ranks, and inflame their zeal. Revelations fell thick and fast from the pen of the Prophet, and money, material, and labor flowed in abundantly. In less than two years a handsome town was built on the banks of the great river, and its inhabitants were generally well received by the people of the surrounding country. In 1842 a liberal city charter was granted to Nauvoo by the Legislature of Illinois. The privilege of organizing a strong military force was among the extraordinary powers conceded by this charter. An armed force of over 4,000 men was enrolled by the Prophet, who took command with the title of General. He evidently did not intend to be again driven forth by hostile neighbors. The church militant was henceforth to be the church triumphant. Mormonism now flourished as never before. Accessions poured in from all quarters at home and from abroad. Pratt and Young had been sent to Europe to proselytize and spread the new gospel. In the spring of 1841, Young embarked at Liverpool with 769 of the faithful for the promised land, and additions from that source continue up to the present. The number of Saints in Nauvoo at this time was estimated to be from 12,000 to 15,000. The Nauvoo house was built, " where the weary traveler may find rest and health therein." Suites of well-furnished rooms were appropriated to the use of the Prophet and his family, free of all expense. He was now Commander of the Legion, Mayor of the City, and High Priest of the Theocracy. His fortune swelled him** to such an extent that he proposed to become a candidate for the presidency, and gravely opened a correspondence with Messrs. Clay and Calhoun in regard to the policy he ought to

* Pomeroy Tucker's " History of Mormonism."

** " His fortune swells him—its rank he's married," says Sir Giles Overreach in the play. Joe was very much married.

pursue if elected. Describing his position at this time, Mr. Tucker says: " From the vagabondish, taciturn ' Joe Smith ' at the inception of the Mormon scheme, he had become the rubicund, genial, affluent, autocrat Prophet of 220 pounds avoirdupois, with forty wives, all told."*   The same season that saw the completion of the Nauvoo house witnessed the laying of the corner stone of a temple which cost, when finished, a million dollars. How the money was raised for these structures may be learned from the following revelations to the people through their Prophet. Though alleged to proceed from on high, they are not couched in either good or grammatical language, but are very much to the point in their chief object— the raising of money :

" And again, verily I say unto you, my servant George Miller is without guile, he may be trusted because of the integrity of his heart ; and for the love which he has to my testimony ; I the Lord loveth him.   I therefore say unto you, I seal upon his head the office of a bishopric, like unto my servant Edward Partridge, that he may receive the consecrations of mine house, that he may administer blessings upon the heads of the poor of my people, saith the Lord. Let no man despise my servant George, for he shall honor me.   Let my servant George, and my servant Lyman, and my servant John Snider, and others, build a house unto my name, such a one as my servant Joseph shall show unto them, upon the place which he shall show unto them also.   And it shall be for a house of boarding, a house that strangers may come from afar to lodge therein — therefore let it be a good house, worthy of all acceptation, that the weary traveler may find health and safety, while he shall contemplate the word of the Lord, and the corner stone I have appointed for Zion.   This house shall be a healthy habitation, if it be built unto my name, and if the governor which shall be appointed unto it shall not suffer any pollution to come upon it.   It shall be holy, or the Lord your God will not dwell therein."

" And again, verily I say unto you, I command you again to build a house to my name, even in this place, that ye may prove yourselves unto me, that ye are faithful in all things whatsoever I command you, that I may bless you, and crown you with honor, immortality, and eternal life.

---

* Tho revelation permitting spiritual wives was given to the Prophet at Nauvoo, in 1843, but polygamy did not become a tenet of the church until after the removal to Utah.

" And now, I say unto you, as pertaining to my boarding-house, which I have commanded you to build for the boarding of strangers, let it be built unto my name, and let my name be named upon it, and let my servant Joseph and his house have place therein from generation to generation. For this anointing have I put upon his head, that his blessing shall also be put upon the heads of his posterity after him, and as I said unto Abraham, concerning the kindreds of the earth, even so, I say unto my servant Joseph, in thee, and in thy seed, shall the kindreds of the earth be blessed.

" Therefore, let my servant Joseph, and his seed after him, have place in that house from generation to generation for ever and ever, saith the Lord, and let the name of that house be called the Nauvoo House, and let it be a delightful habitation for man, and a resting place for the weary traveler, that he may contemplate the glory of Zion, and the glory of this the corner stone thereof; that he may receive, also, the counsel from those whom I have sent to be as plants of renown, and as watchmen upon her walls.

" Behold! verily I say unto you, let my servant George Miller, and my servant Lyman Wright, and my servant John Snider, and my servant Peter Hawes, organize themselves, and appoint one of them to be a president over their quorum for the purpose of building that house.

" And again, verily I say unto you, if my servant George Miller, and my servant Lyman Wright, and my servant John Snider, and my servant Peter Hawes, receive any stock into their hands, in monies, or in properties wherein they receive the real value of monies, they shall not appropriate any portion of that stock to any other purpose, only in that house; and if they do appropriate any portion of that stock anywhere else, only in that house, without the consent of the stockholders, and do not repay four-fold, they shall be accursed, and shall be removed out of their place saith the Lord God, for I the Lord am God, and cannot be mocked in any of these things.

" Let my servant Vinson Knight lift up his voice long and loud in the midst of the people, to plead the cause of the poor and needy, and let him not fail, neither let his heart faint, and I will accept of his offerings, for they shall not be unto me as the offerings of Cain, for he shall be mine, saith the Lord. Let his family rejoice and turn away their hearts from affliction, for I have chosen and anointed him, and he shall be honored in the midst of his house, for I will forgive all his sins, saith the Lord. Amen.

" Let my servant Isaac Galland put stock in that house, for I the Lord God loveth him for the work he hath done, and will forgive all his sins, therefore let him be remembered for an interest in that house from generation to generation. Let my servant Isaac Galland be appointed among you, and be ordained by my servant William Marks, and be blessed of him, to go with my servant Hyrum to accomplish the work that my servant Joseph shall point out to them, and they shall be greatly blessed.

" Let my servant William Law pay stock in that house for himself and his seed after him, from generation to generation. If he will do my will let him not take his family unto the eastern lands, even unto Kirtland; nevertheless I the Lord will build up Kirtland, but I the Lord have a scourge prepared for the inhabitants thereof. Let no man go from this place who has come here assaying to keep my commandments. If they live here, let them live unto me, and if they die, let them die unto me; for they shall rest from all their labors here, and shall continue their works. Therefore, let my servant William put his trust in me, and cease to fear concerning his family, because of the sickness of the land. If ye love me, keep my commandments, and the sickness of the land shall redound to your glory."

The Prophet was now surrounded by all the evidences of material and spiritual growth and permanency, and if he and his followers had shown a decent respect for the opinions of mankind they might to this day have remained in undisturbed possession of their new Zion. The revelation from heaven given to Joseph in 1843, permitting a plurality of wives, was for a long time withheld from the mass of his followers, and was imparted as a secret only to the dignitaries of the Church. By the statutes of Illinois bigamy was a crime. The bishops, priests, and elders forming the High Council of the hierarchy, alone availed themselves of the permission given by revelation, and endeavored to " keep on the windy side o' the law " by being " sealed " spiritually to their additional helpmeets, instead of being married according to usual forms. The people of Illinois were not to be hoodwinked by any such euphemistic nonsense as this. They held a wife to be a wife, whether spiritual or temporal, whether " sealed " or " asked on the banns." The leaders of the Church adopted polygamy, or what was its equivalent, with many misgivings. They felt it to be a bold and probably a hazardous doctrine. It was a plain infraction of the teachings of the Mormon Bible; that authority says: " Wherefore my brethren, hearken unto the word of the Lord: there shall not any man among you have, save it be but one wife, and concubines he shall have none." A few of the leaders stood by this doctrine and opposed the new revelation as heretical and dangerous. The Prophet professed great concern of mind, and went through the farce of fleeing from the city to avoid being the promulgator of the repugnant command. He soon returned with the awful tale that he was met by an angel with a flaming sword, who denounced against him the penalty of instant death if he did not return and set forth the new revelation. There is no limit to human credulity. This story satisfied all Mormondom. But it did not satisfy the people of Illinois, and thenceforward there was no peace for those who believed and practised the polygamous doctrine until they were driven, root and branch, from the soil of the State.

In previous contests between the Saints and their Gentile neighbors, the former had been charged with every crime except bigamy, and now that was added, and was the principal cause of the riot and bloodshed at Carthage. While it will not be pretended that either of the parties to the quarrel was wholly right or wrong, let us see how far the accusations against the followers of the Prophet may be justified by Mormon testimony. Expulsions from the society and published proscriptions began at Kirtland. Martin Harris, whose money had laid the foundation of the whole miserable fraud, but who was now a squeezed orange, was expelled from the Church and, in company with others, was posted in the Elders' Journal by Smith as follows: " There are negroes who wear white skins as well as black ones: Granus Parish, and others who acted as lackeys, such as Martin Harris; but they are so far beneath contempt that a notice of them would be too great a sacrifice for a gentleman to make." Yet as long as he had money Harris was prominent in Mormon affairs, and was certainly a zealous defender of the faith, as the following predictions will show:

" Within four years from September, 1832, there will not be one wicked person left in the United States; that the righteous will be gathered to Zion [Missouri], and that there will be no president over these United States after that time.

" MARTIN HARRIS."

" I do hereby assert and declare, that in four years from the date hereof every sectarian and religious denomination in the United States shall be broken down, and every Christian shall be gathered unto the Mormonites, and the rest of the human race shall perish. If these things do not take place, I will hereby consent to have my hand separated from my body.

" MARTIN HARRIS."

While the Mormons were in Missouri, a paper was drafted by Sidney Rigdon, and signed by eighty-four Mormons, the object of which was to drive away the dissenters. It was addressed to Oliver Cowdery, David Whitmer, John Whitmer, William W. Phelps, and Lyman E. Johnson. Of these Oliver Cowdery and David Whitmer were two of the three witnesses that testified to the truth of the Book of Mormon. This paper charges these dissenters, viz., Oliver Cowdery, David Whitmer, etc., with monstrous vices and crimes. It states that Cowdery was arrested for stealing, and the stolen property was found in the house of William W. Phelps, Cowdery having stolen and conveyed it there; that they had endeavored to destroy the character of Smith and Rigdon by every artifice they could invent, not even excepting the basest lying; that they had disturbed the Mormon meetings of worship by a mob of blacklegs; that Oliver Cowdery and David Whitmer united with a gang of counterfeiters, thieves, liars, and blacklegs of the deepest die, to deceive, cheat, and defraud the Mormons out of their property, by every art and stratagem which wickedness could invent; using the influence of the vilest persecutions to bring vexations and law suits, villainous prosecutions, and even stealing not excepted; that Cowdery attempted to sell notes on which he had received pay; that he and David Whitmer swore falsely, stole, cheated, lied, sold bogus money (base coin), and also stones and sand for bogus; that letters in the post-office had been opened, read and destroyed; and that those same men were concerned with a gang of counterfeiters, coiners, and blacklegs."

Taking their own account of themselves, were the Mormons desirable neighbors or good citizens?

That the Prophet himself was not an estimable or law-abiding person may be gathered from the following affidavit: " James C. Owens testifies that Smith said he cared nothing about the Missouri troops, nor the laws; that they were a d—d set, and God should d—n them, so help him Jesus Christ; that he meant to go on as he had begun, and take his own course, and kill and destroy; and he told the men to fight like angels; that heretofore he had told them to fight like devils, but now he told them to fight like angels — that angels could whip devils; that God would send two angels where they lacked one man. He said they might think he was swearing; but that God Almighty would not take notice of him in cursing such a d—d set as those were. He said they pretended to come out as militia, but that they were all a d—d set of mobs. He stated, at one time, that as they had commenced consecrating in Davies County, he intended to have the surrounding counties consecrated to him; that the time had come when the riches of the Gentiles should be consecrated to the Saints."

John Cleminson, clerk of the Caldwell circuit court, testifies that the Danites were taught to support the presidency in all their designs, right or wrong, and to obey them in all things; and whoever opposed them in what they said or desired to have preformed should be expelled from the county, or put to death. They were further taught that if any one betrayed the secret designs of the Danite society he should be killed and laid aside, and nothing should be said about it. When process was filed against Smith and others, in witness's office, for trespass, Smith told him not to issue a writ; that he did not intend to submit to it; that he would not suffer it to be issued, etc.; insomuch that witness, knowing the regulation of the Danite band, felt himself intimidated and in danger in case he should issue it. The object of the Mormon expedition to Davies was to drive out all the citizens of the county, and get possession of their property. It was frequently observed, among the Mormon troops, that the time had come when the riches of the Gentiles should be consecrated to the Saints. It was a generally prevailing understanding among them " that they would oppose either militia or mob, should they come out against them; for they considered them all mob at heart."

In reference to the Mormon dissenters, Dr. Avard, the Danite teacher, said: " I will tell you how I will do them; when I meet one damning the presidency, I can damn them as well as he; and if he wants to drink, I can get a bowl of brandy, and get him half drunk; and taking him by the arm, lead him to the woods or brush, and be into his guts in a minute, and put him under the sod."

Rigdon, in a sermon, said he would assist in erecting a gallows on the square, and hang all the dissenters. Smith was present, and followed Rigdon. He spoke of the fate of Judas, and said that Peter had hung him; and that he himself approved of Mr. Rigdon's sermon, and considered it a good one. Little did Mr. Rigdon think, when breathing forth threatenings and slaughter against dissenters, that he himself would, in a short time, be expelled from the Church, and " delivered over to the buffetings of Satan." Yet so it was.

Affairs now rapidly drifted toward their fatal termination. Smith was charged by a seceding member of the Church with alienating the affections of his wife, and "sealing " her unto himself, and a suit for damages as well as for the crime of bigamy was brought against him by the injured husband. Similar charges were also brought against other dignitaries of the Church. Attempts to arrest them were resisted by the military power under command of the Prophet. The mistake of authorizing him to enroll, arm, and equip the Nauvoo Legion was now apparent. State troops were called out to enforce obedience to law. The situation was critical. Religious fanaticism was in hostile array against legal authority, and the worst of all wars was impending. Anxious to avoid a collision, the Governor proposed to Joseph and Hyrum Smith their surrender to the sheriff, and the disbandment of their armed followers, as the only means of saving their own lives and their city from destruction. If this was done, he promised them protection on their way to prison, and during their confinement, and an unbiased legal investigation of the matters in dispute between them and their neighbors, pro and con. The Smiths assented and were conveyed to the county jail at Carthage, which was placed under a strong military guard. Most of the men composing it were at bitter enemity with the Saints, and in a few days the greater part of the detail had deserted. On the afternoon of the 27th day of June, 1844, the remnant of the command was overpowered by a mob of about two hundred armed and disguised men, who broke opened the prison doors and murdered Joseph and Hyrum Smith.

There is little doubt that deserters from the Governor's guard led the attack. His Excellency hastened to the scene, and was greatly affected by the brutal assassination that had taken place, and intensely indignant that his pledge of safe conduct and custody had been violated. He hastily sent word to the Mormons at Nauvoo, to defend themselves, if necessary, in any possible way, until he could afford them protection. He at once issued a statement in which, among other things, he says: " The pledge of security to the Smiths was not given upon my individual responsibility alone. Before I gave it I obtained a pledge of honor, by a unanimous vote of the officers and men under my command, to sustain me in performing it. If the assassination of the Smiths was committed by any of these, they have added treachery to murder, and have done all they could to disgrace the State and sully the public honor." These murders were not alone a great crime — they were a great blunder as well.   A strong tide of public sympathy flowed in toward the Mormons, and the foundations of their Church were laid upon broader lines, and strengthened and cemented by the blood of the martyrs. The Prophet was lauded, lamented, and canonized by his people. What others thought of him may be learned, in part, from the following characterization which appeared in a religious journal of the time:

" Various are the opinions concerning this singular personage; but whatever may be thought in reference to his principles, objects, or moral character, all agree that he was a most remarkable man.   Born in the very lowest walks of life, reared in poverty, educated in vice, having no claims to even common intelligence, coarse and vulgar in deportment, Smith succeeded in establishing a religious creed, the tenets of which have been taught throughout America; the Prophet's virtues have been rehearsed in Europe; the ministers of Nauvoo have found a welcome in Asia; Africa has listened to the grave sayings of the seer of Palmyra; the standard of the Latter-Day Saints has been reared on the banks of the Nile; and even the Holy Land has been entered by the emissaries of the impostor. He founded a city in one of the most beautiful situations in the world, in a beautiful curve of the ' Father of Waters,' of no mean pretensions, and in and about it he had collected a population of 25,000, from every part of the world. The acts of his life exhibit a character as incongruous as it is remarkable. If we can credit his own words,

and the testimony of eye-witnesses, he was at the same time the
vicegerent of God and a tavern-keeper — a prophet and a base
libertine — a minister of peace and a lieutenant-general — a
ruler of tens of thousands and a slave to all his own base passions — a preacher of righteousness and a profane swearer — a
worshiper of Bacchus, mayor of a city, and a miserable bar-room
fiddler — a judge on the judicial bench and an invader of the
civil, social, and moral relations of men — and, notwithstanding
these inconsistencies of character, there are not wanting thousands
willing to stake their soul's eternal salvation on his veracity."

When the consternation and excitement following the death
of the head of the Church had in part subsided, the question of
electing his successor began to be agitated.   Mr. Rigdon seems
to have assumed the Prophet's functions after his taking off, apparently little doubting that his assumption would be ratified
by his associate Elders, whenever consideration of the succession
should engage their attention.   He had been from the first the
trusted friend and counselor of the Prophet.   Co-equally with
him he was the " author and proprietor " of the Book of Mormon.
But for his possession of the Spalding manuscript, and his
ability to transpose, transcribe, and travesty the Scriptures, the
golden revelation would, in all probability, never have been given
to mankind.   By priority of membership, and of service in the
Church, he was surely entitled to the mantle of his predecessor.
But he was not a man of real ability.   He was showy rather than
solid, and was estimated at his true value by most of his brethren.
Opposed to him, as a candidate for the presidency of the Church,
was Brigham Young.   Few political priests from Thomas a
Becket to Richelieu have been " entirely great " ; Young was one
of the few.   He was Strafford and Laud combined.   He estimated at its proper value the prize for which he was contending.
He had seen the people over whom he aspired to rule build cities
and temples, and pour their wealth ungrudgingly into the lap of
the head of the Church, at whose hands no reckoning was required.
The future gave him promise of dictatorship over half a million
unquestioning and obedient subjects.   Could he succeed, supreme
power and " the potentiality of growing rich beyond the dreams
of avarice " would be his.   Possibilities such as these were not to
be surrendered to another without making an effort to grasp them.
The effort was successful; Young was unanimously chosen to
fill the place left vacant by the death of Joseph Smith, Jr.

After his expulsion from the Church, Rigdon returned to the Genesee Country and passed the evening of his days in Friendship, Allegany County, New York; but his lips forever remained sealed in regard to his connection with the origin of Mormonism. Many attempts to break his silence were made, but none ever succeeded. The following letter from the postmaster at Friendship, reveals the fact that his children have inherited their father's reticence:

" DEAR SIR:

" Mr. Rigdon never gave any information, either oral or written, in regard to Mormonism, although frequently solicited to do so; and although he has children living here and elsewhere, it would avail nothing to attempt to get any information from them.   Respectfully,

" R. A. SCOTT, P. M."

As has been shown, a majority of the pioneer Mormons either seceded or were expelled from the Church. Martin Harris was proffered a restoration to fellowship, but declined it. He revisited the scene of his delusion, in 1858, a very poor man, and is understood to have passed away some years later, at Kirtland. Parley P. Pratt was killed in Arkansas in 1857, by an irate husband whose wife had been converted and sealed by the proselyting elder. There are some communities where lives, not lawsuits, are the penalty of breaking up the domestic fireside. A communication in the *New York Times* of February 25, 1888, announced the death at Richmond, Missouri, on the 25th of January of that year, of David Whitmer. He was one of the three original witnesses who testified " that an angel of God came down from Heaven and brought the plates and laid them before our eyes, that we saw and beheld them, and the engravings thereon " — with much more to the same effect. The *Times'* correspondent says: " Subsequently all of these three men renounced Mormonism and declared their testimony false." Having taken some pains to investigate the origin and early history of Smith's revelation, the writer can find nothing confirmatory of the latter portion of this statement.*   It is too im-

---

* The following letters effectually dispose of it:
    CLIFTON SPRINGS, N. Y., Sept. 15, 1889.
    DEAR SIR :—Referring to the enclosed cutting from the *New York Times*, of February 25, 1888, I beg to ask whether Mr. Whitmer ever declared his

portant, if true, to have escaped all previous and subsequent investigation. One of the strangest of the many strange features of Mormon history is the fact that though a number of the pioneer professors withdrew or were expelled from the Church no one of them ever attacked its doctrines, or denounced the fraud in which they are supposed to have been participants. The *Times* states that " Mr. Whitmer at the time of his death had in his possession the original manuscripts of the Book of Mormon in a state of perfect preservation." All this proves nothing; it neither establishes nor overthrows the Solomon Spalding theory, and sheds no new light upon the question of the authorship of the golden revelation. The statement that the manuscript of Spalding's work, which had long been lost, was discovered in the Sandwich Islands in 1885, and is now in the library of Hiram College, Ohio, adds nothing to the stock of knowledge we now possess. It had previously been compared with the Book of Mormon, and their similarity established. Unless Mr. Rigdon left with his heirs a statement regarding it, we are probably in possession of all the facts concerning the authorship of the Golden Bible which will ever be made known.

Here this narrative, which has already been carried far beyond the boundaries of the Genesee Country, must end. In his interesting, eloquent, and learned review of " Ranke's History of the Popes," Macaulay tells us, " There is not and there never was on this earth, a work of human policy so well deserving of examination as the Roman Catholic Church." If the Church of the

---

testimony in regard to having seen the golden plates to be false? After being expelled from the Church, Cowdery was reinstated and resumed his functions as an Elder and preacher. Do you know when and where he died, and whether he renounced Mormonism a second time, or died in the faith? Are any of Mr. Whitmer's family still residents in your vicinity, and if so will you kindly give me the name and address of some one of them? Be good enough to re-inclose the cutting with your reply and oblige

Your obedient servant,
E. W. VANDERHOOF.

To the Postmaster at Richmond, Mo.

REPLY.

RICHMOND, MO., Sept. 18th, '89.

DEAR SIR:—David Whitmer never renounced Mormonism. He never declared that his testimony in regard to plates was false. He was regarded by everybody as an honest man. By this writer who knew him intimately for many years, and was his family physician, he was regarded as an honest but misguided or deceived man. His son, David J. Whitmer, and his grandson, George W. Schemich, reside here; also his nephew, Jno. C. Whitmer, who is an Elder in the Mormon Church. Oliver died here. He never renounced Mormonism that I ever heard of. Respectfully,
S. T. BASSETT, M. D., P. M.

Latter-Day Saints was equally deserving, the writer is not the proper person to make the examination. Born within a few miles of the Hill of Camorah, at about the period when the new revelation was given to the world, he was taught by orthodox parents that it was an impudent and impious fraud. Written by him, the history of the Mormon Church would not be impartial. But he may show how unprejudiced writers have regarded it. Professor Renan, in " The Apostles," tells us that " our own age has witnessed religious movements quite as extraordinary as those of former times: movements attended with as much enthusiasm, which have already had, in proportion, more martyrs, and the future of which is still undetermined. I do not refer to the Mormons, a sect in some respects so degraded and absurd that one hesitates to seriously consider it. There is much to suggest reflection, however, in seeing thousands of men of our own race living in the miraculous in the middle of the nineteenth century, and blindly believing in the wonders which they profess to have seen and touched. A literature has already arisen pretending to reconcile Mormonism and science. But what is of more importance, this religion, founded upon silly impostures, has inspired prodigies of patience and self-denial. Five hundred years hence, learned professors will seek to prove its divine origin by the miracle of its establishment."

The introduction to the Book of Mormon, published by Wright & Co., of New York, about the time of the movement to Utah, says:

" That a single man, in the midst of the enlightenment of this century, should have been able to throw the lines of mysticism so thoroughly over the minds of hundreds and thousands of men and women, is not more wonderful than the earnest and self-denying faith with which his devotees have sustained an unbroken unity, under circumstances of remarkable privation and peril. Nor is it less surprising that the assumption of a power very nearly absolute, by one man, who is regarded as the legitimate successor of the original Prophet, has come to be accepted by this people as a divine ordination, and that to one guiding spirit alone is yielded the homage and obedience which insure the autocratic sway of Brigham Young. Considered in all their relations — religious, political, moral, or social — the Mormons are a curious people. Occupying for their headquarters a portion of the American continent which is far removed from the influences of civilization, and indeed is for many months in the year totally inaccessible — cooped up among overhanging mountains — destitute of the refinements of ordinary social life — bent beneath the sway of an unscrupulous hierarchy — holding to practices which, elsewhere than in their own territory, would subject them to the penalties of the law ; and, withal, noted for a spirit of zeal, industry, and perseverance which has enabled them to convert the wildest moods of nature into servants of their will — the Mormons have earned an enduring reputation for sincerity, and energy, and capacity. When the secrets of their origin, and progress, and government shall have been added to the published record of their religious belief, this people will rank among the most extraordinary of all the sects that have sprung into life as the world has run its course."

But there are signs which lead us to believe that the end of Mormonism is approaching. Civilization spans the continent, and there is no further retreat within our jurisdiction where the Saints can, for any length of time, find solitude. Brigham Young left no successor at all his equal in boldness and ability. The chief-priests of the hierarchy no longer bid defiance to a Government which expresses the will of sixty-five millions* of people, and have ceased to laugh at its courts and trample with impunity upon its laws. Utah, freed from polygamy, will soon join the sisterhood of States, and Mormonism, surrounded by enlightenment, liberty, and law, must " die amid its worshipers."

---

* The population of the United States in 1887.

MORGAN AND ANTI-MASONRY

"Perhaps thou wert a Mason and forbidden,
By oath, to tell the secrets of thy trade."
— Address to the Mummy.

WHAT is known to-day under the name of Free-masonry had its origin in the mechanical art of cutting, joining, and setting stones. It dates back to the middle ages, but enthusiastic members of the order claim to have traced it to the days of Solomon's Temple, and the Tower of Babel. In what may be called cathedral-building times, hundreds of masons, — aside from those resident in the locality where the erection was going forward, — were employed in building church edifices. As these itinerants moved from place to place, it occurred to some of the more active minds among them that an organization of their craft, by means of which a skilled workman could make himself known through certain grips and passwords, would facilitate their employment on new work, and do away with the necessity of showing their skill by actual handicraft. These grips, pass-words, and other symbols, the initiated were bound to keep secret, thus laying the foundation stone upon which the Order of Free and Accepted Masons rests to-day. They were denominated "Free" because exempted by various Papal bulls from the operation of laws governing and regulating common labor. Being thus under the patronage of the Popes, and mainly employed in church building, masons were bound by their rules to observe certain pious duties, and though no obligation of that kind exists to-day, yet modern masonry is founded in the "prac-tice of the moral and social virtues," and the salient features of its creed are charity and brotherly love. It has flourished in England since the tenth century, and on its roll of membership have been inscribed the names of Kings and Princes from the days of Henry VII., who was grand master of the English lodges, down to the Prince of Wales, who stands high among his fellow craftsmen to-day. Though masonry has perhaps taken stronger root amongst English-speaking people than elsewhere, yet it flourishes in a greater or less degree in France, Russia, Prussia, Holland, and Denmark, and has obtained some footing in British India. It has existed in Spain and Italy, though generally under control of the government, and sometimes, in the former country under ban of the Inquisition. It has, however, usually been permitted to flourish without governmental interference, and in an act of parliament passed in 1799 for the suppression of secret societies, Freemasonry was specially excepted. In the more liberal and enlightened times in which we live, so far from it being thought necessary to regulate the craft by statute, it is regarded as beneficent and worthy by a great majority even of those who have not lifted the veil which hides its harmless mysteries, though it has not wholly escaped hostility and bitter opposition in this country, and in the blazing light of the nineteenth century. More than sixty years ago it received a blow in Western New York from which it reeled and staggered, and though it has now almost wholly recovered from the storm of denunciation and obloquy rained upon it at that time, yet on the minds of a number of worthy people the events of 1826 have stamped an ineradicable hostility to secret societies of every name and nature.

On the 11th day of September, 1826, William Morgan was arrested in Batavia on a warrant sworn out by Nicholas G. Chesebro, master of a Masonic lodge at Canandaigua, and was conveyed to the latter place and arraigned before the justice issuing the warrant — Jeffrey Chipman, Esq., — the charge against him being that he had stolen a shirt and cravat which he had borrowed from E. C. Kingsley. Chesebro and two or three other Masons who had accompanied Morgan from Batavia appeared as his accusers, but failed to substantiate their charge and he was discharged by the justice who had issued the warrant. He was at once rearrested on a small debt due, or claimed to be due, for a tavern bill which had been assigned to Chesebro by Aaron Ashley. Judgment was rendered against him for two dollars by the justice, and upon the oath of Chesebro an execution was issued on the spot, and Morgan was thrown into Canandaigua jail. Both charges were trumped-up affairs, manufactured, as it afterwards appeared, for the purpose of getting possession of his person and compelling him by intimidation and threats to give up to his accusers a manuscript he had written revealing the secrets of masonry. About 9 o'clock on the even-

ing of the 12th, the day succeeding his incarceration, Chesebro and his fellow conspirators appeared at the jail with an
order for Morgan's release signed by the convenient justice who
had acted in the case.   The equally convenient jailer was absent,
and the prisoner was clandestinely taken from the jail by a
number of Masons, bound, gagged, hurried into a covered carriage, and rapidly driven in the direction of Rochester.   It is
now known that many persons were cognizant of these movements, and that in fact a majority of the active lodge attending
members of the Masonic fraternity in the counties of Ontario,
Monroe, Genesee, Orleans, and Niagara approved of and numbers of them aided in this outrage upon personal liberty.   Re-
lays of horses were ready on the route over which the prisoner
passed, and a perfectly organized plan of proceedings had evidently been adopted in regard to the abduction.   It was not
until they were made the subject of a searching legal investigation, assisted by expert detectives specially employed by the authorities, that these things were brought to light, and for a long
time even the route taken by the abductors remained a mystery.
It is now known that the carriage passed through Rochester
and thence on the ridge road westerly towards Lockport, where
a cell in the jail had been prepared for Morgan's reception.   At
a place called Wright's Corners the programme was changed and
he was driven to Lewiston, and thence to Fort Niagara, where he
was confined in the magazine.   Colonel Ezekiel Jewett was in
command of the fort, and during Morgan's detention there he
was in the custody of the Commandant, of Colonel King of
Niagara County, and of Elisha Adams.   He had in fact been
passed from one set of custodians to another three or four times
in going from Canandaigua to the fort.   During his confinement every effort was made to force him to reveal the hiding
place of his manuscript, but without avail.   He maintained a defiant atttude, and vehemently demanded to be released.   When
all hope of liberation had vanished, he partially lost fortitude
and begged to see his wife and children.   But not even a promise that they should be brought to him could induce him to disclose the place of concealment of his manuscript.   Meantime a
council of the members of the Masonic fraternity met at the fort
and deliberated upon his case.   It is said that three propositions
were discussed.   The first was to give him a sum of money and
settle him on a farm in Canada, provided he would pledge him-

self to destroy his revelations; second, to deliver him to the
Masonic commander of a British Man-of-War at Montreal or
Quebec; or third, to drown him in Niagara River. The last
proposal met with strong opposition. High words and a quarrel ensued among the deliberators, and when William Morgan
disappeared from the fort, sometime between the 19th and 29th
days of September, 1826, he became as utterly lost to human
ken as though he had never existed.

Who was William Morgan? Although scores of men are
still living in Western New York who had reached their majority
at the time of this abduction, and probably half a score survive
who knew him personally and saw him go to and fro to his daily
vocations, yet his personal history is wrapped in obscurity,
and it is almost impossible to say with accuracy who and what
he was. Judge Hammond in his " Political History of New
York " says he was a native of Virginia, a printer by trade, and
a Mason of the royal arch degree. Chancellor Whittlesey in the
same work in an article on Political Anti-Masonry, contributed at
the request of Hammond, says that Morgan's book pretended to
reveal a few of the first degrees of masonry, and leaves the
inference that its author was a Mason who had attained those
degrees though he does not distinctly say so. Another account
says that he was a bricklayer and stone mason, and a native of
Massachusetts.* Morgan in his book gives no account of himself, but iterates and reiterates in the most positive language
the statement that he was not then and had never been a member
of the Masonic fraternity, and that in publishing his revelations
he violated no Masonic oath, for he had never taken one. How,
then, could he reveal the mysteries of the Masonic Craft? Simply
by having them revealed to him by some one who was a Mason,
and such an one was his coadjutor, David C. Miller, of Batavia,
who was to print his books and share his profits. There is no
absolutely certainty that Morgan wrote the revelations that were
published in his name, but if he did, he was not a Mason, unless
his solemn assertions on that point are false. Regarding his

---

* Morgan was a Virginian and a mason by trade. Having accumulated a
little money in that occupation he removed to Richmond and began merchan-
dizing in a retail way. From there he went to Canada where he engaged in
brewing. A fire destroying his brewery he was left penniless, and resumed
his mechanical work, at first in Rochester, and later in Batavia. He married in
Virginia a Miss Pendleton who at the time of his abduction was only four and
twenty, and was left penniless, with a child in arms and one about two years
of age, dependent on her for support.

trade or profession it is safe to conclude that he was not a printer, for had he been he could have put his " copy " into type himself, and destroyed his manuscript as he went along. I assume, therefore, the truth of the statement that he was a stone-mason, and might have been a member of the original craft, had he lived in the days of Hiram Abbiff and King Solomon's Temple. But whatever was his vocation, it seems reasonably certain that up to the time when he threatened to reveal Masonic secrets he had not been successful in life, and that his pamphlet was to be published with a view to pecuniary profit. His ambition to better his fortune was shared by his partner, Miller, who, neither before nor after the Anti-Masonic excitement, was a man who stood well in the community where he lived. But if Miller was to share the pecuniary rewards of his partner he also had to share his persecutions. Members of the Masonic order learning that he was about to publish a book revealing the secrets of their craft took active measures to suppress it, and made a number of attempts to obtain possession of the " copy." In fact, Miller was the first though not the greater martyr. Very much the same tactics were resorted to in his case as were afterward employed against Morgan. In August, 1826, he was arrested in a civil action, but obtained bail. His bondsman after a few days had elapsed surrendered him to the sheriff, and on a Saturday afternoon he was lodged in jail.   Be it remembered that in those days imprisonment for debt was the law of the land. The object of his incarceration seems to have been to get him out of the way, while his lodgings and the premises where the revelations were to be printed could be searched. His perse-cutors were not rewarded by a discovery of the objectionable manuscript, and in their disappointment fired the building sup-posed to contain it. The incendiary attempt was discovered in time to be frustrated. On the 12th of September, Miller was arrested on a warrant issued by a justice of the peace of the village of LeRoy, and in charge of a constable started for the office of the magistrate issuing the process. The annoyances, threats, and arrests to which he had already been subjected, had aroused his friends and neighbors, and a number of them followed him to see that he met with no foul play. At Stafford, a town on the road, he was taken from the carriage in which he was being driven, to a Masonic lodge, and an effort was made to so far intimidate him as to obtain the embryo revelations. A large party of his friends gathered in front of the lodge and demanded his release. He was brought out, saw counsel, and learned for the first time what was the nature of the charge against him. It was a civil action for debt, but all bail was refused. Both parties then set out for LeRoy, and on arrival he demanded that his case should be heard at once. His friends were so numerous and determined, that his demand was acceded to, and discharge at once followed, as no evidence was found against him. He hastened his return to Batavia, his friends foiling an attempt to rearrest him. In September, 1827, three of the parties engaged in this outrage upon personal liberty and private rights were tried for false imprisonment, riot, and assault and battery, and were convicted and sentenced to different terms of imprisonment in the county jail.

It may be very well imagined that such transactions as these produced a powerful sensation in the communities where they occurred, but the fire that glowed with such fervent heat at a later period burnt slowly at first, principally because of the difficulties thrown in the way of everyone attempting an investigation, and because of the truth of the adage that " what is everybody's business is nobody's." Another reason grew out of the fact that a gubernatorial election was going forward, and as both candidates were Masons there was no opportunity for connecting these events with politics. Anti-Masonry at this time had hardly spread beyond the villages of Batavia, LeRoy, Canandaigua, Rochester, and Lockport. East of Cayuga Bridge a majority of the voters, whether Clintonians or Bucktails, went to the polls in blissful ignorance of the false imprisonment of Miller or of the abduction of Morgan. Railroads and electric telegraphs had not yet been introduced, and the hebdomadal stage coach was not an active disseminator of news. DeWitt Clinton was elected governor. He was a Mason, holding the highest degree then conferred by the order. Had his opponent, Judge Rochester, not been a member of the fraternity, there is little doubt that the western counties would at that early period have given him a sufficient number of votes to have made him governor. But he and his competitor were tarred with the same stick, though not in the same degree.

In endeavoring to give some account of the excitement which followed in the wake of these events and, for more than five years, absorbed the public mind to the exclusion of almost every other subject, I wish it to be understood that, in speaking of one of the parties to the controversy as "the people" the designation includes not that large class alone which is opposed to all secret societies, but also the larger class of law-abiding citizens, who, caring not one straw whether their neighbors were or were not members of the Masonic order, were commendably indignant against the hot-headed, active, and criminally-zealous members of the fraternity, who had bid defiance to the laws of the State, and the authority of its courts, and had constituted themselves judges, jurors, and executioners of an American citizen against whom no offense punishable by our statutes had been proven or even alleged. And, on the other hand, there were many Masons of that class which took no active part in lodge matters, and had not in fact attended a lodge meeting for years, who disapproved of any criminal offense against the laws on the part of their impulsive brethren. But this class to a very great extent was forced into an attitude of defense if not hostility by the intemperate denunciation of Anti-Masons, who charged the Masonic order, and every individual member of it, with being guilty of the crime which had been committed by zealous, impulsive, and wrong-headed lodge-going members.

The gubernatorial election being settled, the people who were cognizant of the fact that Morgan, after being discharged from the custody of the law, had been illegally and violently seized, and had disappeared no one knew whither, began to investigate the matter with a view to solving the mystery surrounding the affair, and ascertaining whether a crime had been committed, and if so, by whom. A public meeting having these objects in view was called at Batavia and a committee was appointed which at once proceeded to Canandaigua and began a searching inquiry after Morgan. The facts ascertained by the committee have already been stated. When made public they produced a powerful impression in the community, and meetings were called in other places, particularly in those towns through which the prisoner had been conducted, with a view of ascertaining the fate he had met at the hands of his captors. No definite conclusion was reached, but the facts elicited pointed to the commission of a flagrant crime, and aroused the suspicion that it was attended by the sacrifice of human life. These public meetings, and the investigating committees appointed by them, were composed of citizens of all creeds and all shades of political

WILLIAM MORGAN

opinion, and in many places Masons were invited to attend them
and assist in the investigations, and were urged, in order to avoid
a stigma upon their institution, to assist in upholding the violated
majesty of the law. Very little encouragement was met with
from Masonic sources, and with scarce an exception no Mason
aided the early attempts to uncover the mystery connected with
Morgan's abduction and disappearance. On the contrary,
Masons as a body cast ridicule upon these meetings and the committees appointed by them, and justified openly and publicly
whatever acts had been committed by their brethren in punishment of Morgan for the attempt they believed he was about to
make to reveal the secrets of their order. The committees were
told that the governor, the judges, jurors, sheriffs, and witnesses were all Masons, and were openly defied and taunted with
their inability to bring punishment upon any one connected
with their high-handed violation of the laws of the State and
the liberty and safety of one of its citizens. It need hardly be
said that this tone was met and repelled by one equally bitter and
galling. Masons were denounced to their faces as murderers
and justifiers of murder, as cutthroats and outlaws, and the
Masonic institution was charged with being, by its constitution,
rules, and oaths, inimical to the laws of the land, and the obligations of good citizenship and good neighborhood. Its existence
was denounced as dangerous to the common weal, and its absolute
suppression by statute was strongly demanded.

Stimulated by mutual accusation and retort the excitement
rose to fever heat and it is a marvel that internecine strife was
avoided. Chancellor Whittelsey has well said " that the public
feeling was lashed into such a state of intense fury that under
almost any other government the outbreak would have culminated in horror and bloodshed, and must have done so here but for
the safety valve provided by our institutions, the ballot box."
When the committees or caucuses met in a number of the western
counties in the spring of 1827 to nominate candidates for town
officers, it was pretty generally resolved and carried that no Free-
mason should be supported, as they " were unfit to be voted for
by freemen, or to hold any office of trust in the community."
In this way the ballot box was introduced into the controversy,
and political Anti-Masonry had its origin.

In January, 1827, Loton Lawson, Nicholas G. Chesebro, John
Sheldon, and Edward Sawyer were arraigned at Canandaigua

before Judge Enos T. Throop, afterward governor of the State, charged with " conspiracy to abduct." Developments were expected which would unravel the mystery surrounding the fate of Morgan, and the disappointment was very great when the inculpated parties pleaded guilty, and thus avoided any probing of the affair by the counsel for the prosecution. In sentencing the prisoners Judge Throop addressed them as follows: " Your conduct has created in the people of this section of the country a strong feeling of virtuous indignation. The court rejoices to witness it,—to be made certain that a citizen's person cannot be invaded by lawless violence without its being felt by every individual in the community. It is a blessed spirit, and we do hope that it will not subside; that it will be accompanied by a ceaseless vigilance and untiring activity, until every actor in this profligate conspiracy is hunted from his hiding place and brought before the tribunals of his country to receive the punishment merited by his crime. We think we see in this public sensation the spirit which brought us into existence as a nation, and a pledge that our rights and liberties are destined to endure." Three years later this judge, acting as governor, in his message to the legislature, spoke of the Anti-Masonic excitement as " originating in an honest zeal overflowing its proper boundaries, misdirected in its efforts, and carrying into public affairs matters properly belonging to social discipline." And this same judge, acting as governor, refused to turn over to John C. Spencer, the attorney specially appointed by the State to untangle the web of what the governor, acting as judge, had denounced as "this profligate conspiracy," the reward of two thousand dollars which Governor Clinton had offered for the very purpose to which Mr. Spencer wished to apply it. And furthermore, Mr. Spencer in his letter of resignation following the refusal of acting Governor Throop, complained that even his confidential communications to the governor in relation to the conspiracy had been disclosed to the counsel for the conspirators. Judge Throop had become governor by the appointment of Martin Van Buren to a seat in General Jackson's cabinet. He wished to become governor by a vote of the people, and probably thought the " eftest way " to accomplish his desire would be to throw cold water in 1830 on the " righteous spirit of virtuous indignation " which as judge he so strongly commended in 1827. Very honest judges sometimes make very shrewd politicians.

The result of this trial served only to increase the Anti-Masonic excitement. It was alleged, and with apparent reason, that by pleading guilty and thus preventing the introduction of evidence, the Masons had tacitly admitted that their acts would not stand the test of judicial investigation, and the demand for a searching legal inquiry became so powerful that acting governor Pitcher (he became governor by the death while in office of DeWitt Clinton) recommended to the legislature the passage of a law appointing a special attorney to take charge, on behalf of the State, of all legal proceedings connected with Morgan's fate. The recommendation became a law, although unasked for, and even opposed by the Anti-Masons, and Daniel Moseley, a distinguished member of the Onondaga bar, received the appointment. He had hardly formed his plan for the prosecution of these cases when he was made a judge of one of the circuits of the State, and accepted the position. Governor Van Buren, who had succeeded acting Governor Pitcher, promptly appointed John C. Spencer of Canandaigua Mr. Moseley's successor. Mr. Van Buren showed his usual acumen in selecting a political opponent as public prosecutor. The position required not only a man of high legal attainments but of great moral and physical courage, as the sequel will show. If Mr. Spencer succeeded, he was sure to bring upon himself the wrath of the entire Masonic fraternity; if he failed, he was equally certain to be denounced by the Anti-Masons. Success would bring credit to the governor making the appointment, while failure would damage a formidable political opponent. Mr. Van Buren certainly earned the designation of The Fox of Kinderhook. But whatever may have been the governor's motive in making it, the appointment gave entire satisfaction to even the most rabid leaders of the Anti-Masonic movement. Mr. Spencer was thoroughly imbued with the idea that a horrible crime had been committed; not so much by individuals, who were merely its agents, as by a secret society, bound together by oaths of horrid import; and he believed with all the earnestness of his strong and austere nature that the existence of such a society, capable not only of performing deeds of violence and murder but bound in certain cases by the terms of its organization to perform them, was a menace to the individual, to society, and to the State. He entered upon the discharge of his duties with characteristic zeal and determination, and his profound ability and wide and varied experience as a lawyer encouraged the hope, and warranted the expectation, that the perpetrators of this bold crime would be unmasked and brought to justice. Keen and experienced detectives were employed to lay it bare, and every scheme promising success was pushed with renewed vigor by Mr. Spencer. Of course, all this brought upon him a storm of hostile criticism from the Masonic fraternity, and provoked the bitter enmity of all who were in any way connected with the fate of Morgan. Mr. Spencer's friends became seriously fearful for his safety. They represented to him that if, as he believed, assassins had abducted and made way with Morgan, they were quite capable of an attempt upon himself. But in spite of the fears of his family and friends, and of a number of anonymous letters containing most fearful threats, he continued to perform his duties as public prosecutor with unflinching vigor and determination. Two of these letters read as follows:

" To John C. Spencer: Sir —
"As you are seeking the blood of those who never injured you, remember that your own blood will run quite as easily and as red as theirs. Therefore Beware! Beware !!

Revenge."

" To Hon. John C. Spencer :
" Dear Sir — Your life is in danger ! Assassins are upon your track! Do not regard this warning lightly, but look to yourself, for you are watched by secret foes!

A Friend."

To these and other anonymous communications, whether from blustering foes or pretending friends, Mr. Spencer gave little heed. But the rule that the writer of an anonymous letter is *prima facie* a coward, and that anyone seriously intending to do bodily harm to another in a stealthy manner will never advertise the intention, did not hold good in this case. Two attempts upon his life were made within a short time of each other, but both were fortunately unsuccessful. On his way from his office to his residence, on a dark night, a desperate thrust was made at him by a man armed with a short, straight sword drawn from a

JOHN C. SPENCER

cane. The lunge would probably have proved fatal, had not the assassin stumbled over a stone as he sprang towards Mr. Spencer, thereby causing his weapon to err in its aim. Before he could recover himself and repeat the attempt, the assailant was disarmed and arrested, but, with what was thought by many to be misplaced leniency, Mr. Spencer refused to prosecute him, and he was discharged.

Shortly after this, while returning alone from a professional visit to an adjoining town, night overtook him while yet a number of miles from home. The weather was balmy, the road good, and he permitted his horse to move slowly along, when, suddenly, a bullet whistled past his head, and the sharp crack of a rifle rang in his ears. Putting spurs to his horse he reached home in safety, escaping the assassin's bullet as he had his dagger.

It was most fortunate that neither of these attempts succeeded. The public mind was not in a state to bear additional excitement, and it is not pleasant, and perhaps not wise, to think of the consequences that might have followed the assassination of the special prosecuting officer employed by the State to examine into the offence committed, and if possible to unearth and bring to justice those who had committed it. One of the least harmful of these consequences would have been the election of an Anti-Masonic governor and legislature, and the enactment of laws hostile if not fatal to the existence of the Masonic order in our State.

Of course, members of the order said, and still say, that there was no intention to take the life of Mr. Spenecr; that these attempts were made for the purpose of intimidating him only; but whatever may have been the intent of the erring marksman, there is little doubt that the party with the sword-cane was in dead earnest, and was only prevented from executing his purpose by the stumble which misdirected his aim.

But whether meant or not, the threatening letters, and attempts upon him with dagger and bullet, had no effect to turn Mr. Spencer from the performance of the duties entrusted to him by the government of the State. He laid the iron hand of the law upon all whom he believed to be concerned in the dark deed against Morgan. Many prominent persons were arrested and indicted, and a number of them pleaded guilty to the charge of conspiring to abduct the man who had so mysteriously disappeared from human vision.

Among the more important trials that took place were the People against Mather, and the People aganist Jewett. Being regarded as test cases, these trials excited intense interest, and were watched by crowds of eager partisans, both of the accused and accusers. The case of Mather was heard at the Orleans circuit before Judge Addison Gardiner. He was fully aware of the heated state of the public mind, and of the demands of public clamor, but casting away all such considerations he stood firmly for justice as interpreted by the law, believing it to be the " end of government, and of civil society." His decision during the progress of the trial that a witness — one William Daniels — need not answer a question put by the public prosecutor on the ground that a direct answer would criminate him, and tend toward his infamy and disgrace, was fatal to the case of the People, the jury after a protracted cousultation bringing in a verdict of not guilty. The result disappointed and irritated Mr. Spencer, as he believed Mather to be guilty, and he at once moved for a new trial on the grounds of misdirection by Judge Gardiner in the case of this particular witness, and of errors in various other rulings. The appeal was heard before the general term of the Supreme Court in September, 1830, Hon. William L. Marcy presiding. In contending for a new trial, Mr. Spencer brought all his remarkable powers of mind and all his vast resources as a lawyer to bear upon the court, but a majority of the judges were against him, and with their decision the case rested forever. Its trial however elicited facts and unfolded circumstances strongly inculpating others, and led to the trial of the other case mentioned — the People against Jewett.

The acquittal of Mather served rather to intensify than to allay the Anti-Masonic excitement. It was contended with great bitterness and acrimony that his escape was due to legal technicalities and quibbles, and that if the public prosecutor had not been prevented by the court from proving his case, conviction and not acquittal must have been the verdict.

It is not, then, to be wondered at that the town of Lockport, where the trial of Jewett took place, was thronged by a crowd of vehement and turbulent persons, a majority of whom were Anti-Masons. In this case Hon. William L. Marcy presided, and controlled with quiet but firm dignity, and unswerving impartiality, the participants in the trial and the excited spectators of the scene. The accused, Colonel Ezekiel Jewett, was the most prominent person yet brought before the courts for complicity in the mysterious taking off of Morgan. He was commander of Fort Niagara, where the abductors had confined their prisoner, and from whence he had disappeared, as it proved, forever. This time conviction seemed certain. The strong hand of the law held the prisoner firmly in its grasp, and Mr. Spencer, who had labored with untiring zeal, and had devoted every resource of his strong intellect and profound legal attainments to the task of unmasking the great offence, now believed that the hour of triumph had come.

There was one man who knew, or was believed to know, all about the guilt or innocence of the accused. This man was Orsamus Turner. He took the witness stand amid a silence that was almost audible and a hushed expectation almost painful. The audience that crowded the court room believed that the fate of William Morgan was now to be revealed. The preliminary questions were put by Mr. Spencer in a tone and manner that indicated the importance of the testimony he expected to elicit. These questions were answered with self-possession and in a firm tone by the witness, but when the vital point was reached, and the question was put, the answer to which was expected to show conclusively the guilt of the accused, a paleness overspread Turner's face, his mouth closed with rigid firmness, a look of determined obstinacy flashed from his eyes, but no answer came from his defiant lips. It is useless to attempt any description of the intense and painful interest which pervaded the vast audience, and almost suspended the respiration of those composing it, while awaiting the answer of the witness and during the first few moments after it was seen that none could be expected. The deep voice of William L. Marcy broke the almost smothering silence. In a tone that conveyed every emotion excited by the scene he said: " Witness, are you aware of the consequences of your refusal to answer? " " I am," was the firm reply. In authoritative, dignified, and most impressive language, Judge Marcy depicted to Turner the evil consequences to himself and to society that would flow from his obstinacy, and said " the court still gives you an opportunity to avoid the punishment which will surely follow your rash contumacy; answer the counsel's question." The question was repeated by Mr. Spencer. A faint flush succeeding his pallor was the only indication given by the witness that he had heard it. Another profound silence, of sufficient duration to indicate that no answer could be elicited, was broken by the judge who said,— " Sheriff, convey the witness to the common jail, and keep him in solitary confinement until you are directed to release him by the court." Turner was taken by the Sheriff and a number of assistants to Lockport jail. But long and weary as was his incarceration it served only to increase his obstinacy, and so far as the fate of Morgan is concerned his lips remained forever sealed.*

Although Mr. Spencer was again thwarted in his attempt to convict one of the conspirators in what he thought was a dark crime, his efforts to bring it to the light were not abated, and his faith in ultimate success remained unshaken. The secret detectives employed by the State revealed to him the names of other implicated parties, whose prosecution he determined upon, but in order to proceed with a reasonable chance of success he asked of the State that the sum of two thousand dollars — the amount of the reward offered by Gov. Clinton — be turned over to his use. He thought this moderate amount was necessary to procure the attendance of witnesses, pay for further detective service, and carry out other plans he had made for successfully performing the duties devolving upon him as public prosecutor by the State authorities.   Greatly to his surprise acting Governor Throop refused to accede to his demand.   Mr. Spencer at once tendered his resignation, and retired from a contest which had so long enlisted his earnest sympathies as a man, his eminent ability as a lawyer, and his splendid powers as an advocate. He retired from the field with full confidence that victory was within his grasp.

With his withdrawal interest in the legal aspects of the case began to abate.   The statute of limitation intervened to prevent further prosecution for anything except murder, and no charge for that crime could be maintained without producing the body

---

* Orsamus Turner was a printer by trade, and wrote a history of the Phelps and Gorham and of the Holland Purchase. Together with Eli Bruce and Jared Darrow he was indicted for a conspiracy to kidnap and carry away William Morgan, and was tried at the Ontario County General Sessions in August, 1828.   Bruce was convicted.   A verdict of *not guilty* was returned in favor of Turner and Darrow.   Turner remained in jail until all further prosecution of the abductors of Morgan was abandoned.   When set at liberty he was received by a large body of Masons mounted on horseback, and was escorted through the principal streets of Lockport to his home.

FRANCIS GRANGER

of the victim, and demonstrating by evidence that it had been foully dealt by. The corpus delicti was wanting; and the saying, " that it is easy enough to kill a man but very hard to get rid of the body," once more proves that there is no rule without an exception, and the fate of Morgan remains forever shrouded in the mystery which from the first has surrounded it.

But though it seemed impossible to procure testimony that would convict the presumed slayers of Morgan, interest in his fate, and acrimonious and heated discussions concerning it, by no means ceased. In the case of Mather Judge Gardiner had decided that a witness need not answer an incriminating question ; and on appeal had been sustained by a majority of the full bench. If this provoked indignation and hostile criticism from Anti-Masons, it may well be imagined that their tongues and pens were not silent over the refusal of Turner to reply to a vital interrogatory, though commanded by the law, and its minister Judge Marcy, to do so. It was vehemently and logically asserted that a truthful answer to Mr. Spencer's question must have revealed the secret of Morgan's murder and convicted Jewett of guilty participation in it. Turner had only to open his lips falsely, and the accused would have walked out of court free and exonerated. But he was a man of too much honor to violate the oath he had taken by telling a falsehood, and of too much loyalty to his friend to utter the words that would have brought upon him a felon's fate ; he therefore maintained an absolute and inflexible silence and accepted its consequences. All this and much more was bitterly urged by the opponents of Masonry. Its defenders could only say in reply that the evidence of Turner if given would have been unimportant, and that his obstinacy in refusing to testify was as much a surprise to them as to any one.

Sometime previous to these trials the last of the Anti-Masonic meetings that were non-political in character was held at Lewiston. It was made up chiefly of the investigating committees appointed by some half dozen previous assemblages in various towns who had met to compare notes, and make public such results as they had arrived at. Their conclusions when published, some time afterwards, showed to their own satisfaction, and the satisfaction of those who reposed confidence in them, that Morgan had been abducted and forcibly carried with but little delay from Canandaigua to Fort Niagara, had been confined in the magazine of the fort for a period not exceeding ten days, and had been taken thence, and there, or near there, had been put to death. There seems to have been no better reason for arriving at this latter conclusion than that given by Lord Byron, in Beppo:

"If a man wont let us know
That he's alive, he's dead, or should be so."

It is not my design to give an extended account of political Anti-Masonry, but a few of the prominent events connected with it will be glanced at. The first political convention of Anti-Masons was held in LeRoy in the spring of 1828. Its main object seems to have been to direct the public mind to the dangerous tendencies of Freemasonry, and invoke action against the order. No party resolution was passed, except one which asserted that Freemasonry and free government could not coexist. It recommended the calling of a State convention at Utica in the following August, and appointed Samuel Works, Henry Ely, Frederick F. Bachus, Frederick Whittlesey, and Thurlow Weed a general central committee; and these gentlemen, with the addition of Bates Cook and Timothy Fitch, constituted such committee so long as Anti-Masonry remained a political issue.

The Utica convention met according to appointment. It " resolved as a measure necessary to counteract the influence and destroy the existence of Masonic societies, that it is expedient for this convention, in pursuit of the good objects to be accomplished, wholly to disregard the two great political parties that at this time distract the State and nation, in the choice of candidates for office, and to nominate Anti-Masonic candidates for governor and lieutenant governor;" and the convention accordingly named Francis Granger of Ontario and John Crary of Washington County for these positions. Mr. Granger had already been put in nomination for the office of lieutenant governor by the National Republican party on a ticket headed by Judge Smith Thompson for governor. This party supported Mr. Adams for president, and Mr. Granger had to choose between his political convictions, which were anti-Jackson, and his social and moral opinions which were opposed to Masonry. He accepted the nomination for lieutenant governor tendered by the National Republicans, and was roundly abused by the Anti-Masons for so doing. Almost every event of consequence at this time seemed to stimulate the Anti-Masonic excitement. The people denounced Mr. Granger and determined, come weal come woe, to have candidates for governor and lieutenant governor who represented the Anti-Masonic sentiment. In their hot-headed and intemperate zeal they went off half-cock and filled out their ticket by nominating for governor in place of Mr. Granger, Solomon Southwick of Albany. Mr. Crary remained on the ticket although he had positively promised his neighbor Samuel Stevens (who was specially commissioned to see him re-garding the matter) to write a letter of declination as soon as possible after Mr. Granger's should be made public. Mr. South-wick was editor of a newspaper in Albany, but was what practical, clear-headed men call a scatterbrain and blatherskite, was vision-ary, pompous, and self-assertive, and, through these and other de-fects of character, had become bankrupt in pecuniary resources and political reputation. He had been a Mason, but had re-nounced his associations with that organization, and had acted in concert with recalcitrant Masons in the western counties in pre-paring for publication a general renunciation and exposition of Masonry. Many Anti-Masons of the better class refused to sup-port him, and a number of county conventions declined to concur in his nomination. Messrs. Van Buren and Throop were elected by a minority vote, receiving 136,794 ballots as against 106,444 for Thompson and Granger, and 33,345 for Southwick and Crary. This defeat by no means disheartened the Anti-Masonic party, and in 1829 they elected Albert H. Tracy senator from the eighth district by a majority of 8,000 votes, and carried the counties of Erie, Niagara, Orleans, Genesee, Livingston, Monroe, Allegany, Cattaraugus, Chautauqua, Steuben, Seneca, and Washington, polling, as was computed, about 67,000 votes.

An Anti-Masonic convention was held at Albany in February, 1829, and another in the same month in 1830. The latter as-semblage after passage of the usual resolutions denunciatory of Masonry, and providing for calling a State convention to nom-inate a candidate for governor, brought forward specific charges against the grand chapter of the State for furnishing funds to aid the abductors of Morgan in escaping from justice, and peti-tioned the legislature, then in session, to appoint a committee with authority to summon witnesses, and send for persons and papers, to the end that the action of the grand chapter in interfering with the administration of the laws might be thoroughly sifted and investigated.   By referring the whole matter to the attorney general the legislature in effect refused the committee, and the majority of that body were charged with being hostile to any inquiry into the misdeeds of Masonry.

A State convention of Anti-Masons was held at Utica in August, 1830.   The party had forgotten its denunciation of Mr. Granger for refusing to accept its first nomination, and placed him at the head of its ticket with Samuel Stevens of New York for lieutenant governor.   The National Republicans generally concurred in these nominations.   The election was warmly contested, and resulted in the election of Governor Throop by a little more than 8,000 majority.   An Anti-Masonic national convention met in Baltimore in 1832 and nominated William Wirt for president.   He was defeated by Andrew Jackson.   A New York convention in the same year again nominated Francis Granger for governor and Samuel Stevens for lieutenant governor.   They were defeated by William L. Marcy by nearly 10,000 votes.   This practically ended political Anti-Masonry. It was thenceforward merged in the whig party which came into power by the election of Mr. Seward as governor in 1838.

In looking back over these events it seems a marvel that Anti-Masonry should have become so great and vital a power; dominating, as it did for more than four years, the politics of the State west of Cayuga Bridge, and twice coming within a few thousand votes of obtaining mastery from Long Island to Lake Erie.   Much as we value human life the fate of no one individual could have been the sole cause of kindling and keeping alive for years the fiery indignation of the people against the institution of Masonry.   Above and beyond all thought of Morgan and his fate was the settled conviction in the minds of law-abiding men that Masonry required of its adherents such oaths, and the performance toward each other of such obligations, as unfitted them for the duties of good citizenship in any community where questions of life, liberty, and property might arise between those who were Masons and those who were not.   There was the apparently well-founded belief that Masons regarded the secrets of their craft as more inviolable than the laws of the land, more sacred than human life, and that the one might be trampled under foot, and the other sacrificed, to prevent the proceedings within a Masonic lodge from becoming known to anyone outside its walls.   And in thus exalting the laws of the

lodge above the law of the land, Masons brought upon themselves
a storm of fiery opposition that practically annihilated their
order in Western New York, seriously threatened its existence
throughout the State, and rendered it for a long time unpopular
throughout the length and breadth of the land.

I shall venture no opinion as to the fate of William Morgan.
Members of the Masonic fraternity have always asserted in the
most positive way that his life was not taken by anyone connected
with their order. The following letter addressed to Mr. Spencer
during his connection with the Anti-Masonic trials gives the current Masonic view of his disappearance:

" Sir —

" It is useless for you to attempt to convict any person for
killing Morgan, for he is still alive. He was taken to Canada,
the Canada lodges refused to receive him. He was offered a
large sum of money to leave the country forever and to leave
immediately. If he refused, death would follow sure and certain.
As he published his book for money he was willing to banish
himself for a price. He is now in a foreign country under an
assumed name, and he will never be heard from again. ' Murder
will out,' they say, but as Morgan was never murdered there is
in this case no murder to come out. Time will pass on, you will
go to the grave, and so shall I, and so will all that now live, but
it will never turn out that Morgan was murdered.

" Invisible, But True."

It will occur to most people that if the statements in this
letter are true Morgan was a more mercenary and heartless
wretch than even his detractors have charged him with being.
To abandon home, and country, and wife and children, for the
traitorous silver of Judas, was an act of sordid cruelty almost
beyond belief.

Judge Hammond in his " Political History " says: I assume
as a historical truth, and I regret that I am compelled to do so,
that William Morgan was, with a view of preventing the dis-
closure of the mysteries of Masonry, murdered in cold blood
by men holding a respectable rank and standing in society."

Hon. William Marcy who wrote the opinion of the full bench
in the case of the People against Mather, and who presided at the
trial of Jewett, was probably more familiar with the legal aspects

of the Anti-Masonic cases than any other person except Mr. Spencer. His opinion was summarized as follows: " The mysterious obscurity which hangs over this affair justifies a well-founded suspicion that Morgan came to an untimely end."

The opinion of one more person, himself an actor in a subordinate way in this dark drama, will be quoted. A wealthy stage proprietor by the name of Ganson was indicted for being concerned in the abduction of Morgan. It was shown that one of his coaches was used in the conveyance of Morgan over a part of the route traversed by his captors. The driver of the coach was placed upon the witness stand.

" Who gave you the waybill that night?" asked the public prosecutor.

" I don't remember."

" Who was in the coach when you started from Batavia? "

" I think there was three men; one of them I think was Morgan."

" Who shut the coach door? "

" I can't tell."

" Did you receive directions from any person? "

" Yes; somebody told me to drive like hell, for there was a man inside who was bound for that place."

" Did you obey orders? "

" I think one of the men went through," was the reply.

What goes on within the precincts of a Masonic lodge is matter of concern to members of the fraternity only. Having made this statement, I shall contravene it by saying that my Masonic friends (I have scores of them, and esteem them highly) go through performances that to an outsider look like a combination of mummery, superstition, horseplay, and burlesque. But this opinion is based upon the supposition that the so-called mysteries were correctly revealed by Morgan. If they were and are true in every detail, I see no reason why any level-headed Mason should object to their publication. It is one of the marvels of the 19th century that a proposal to print and circulate them should have created such a frenzy of opposition in Masonic circles, and led to such high-handed and illegal proceedings as were taken against the work and its author. No Mason with half a grain of sense would to-day give himself the least trouble to prevent their publication. A more absolutely inconsequential mess of rubbish was never printed and bound.

Any person who should commit the entire book to memory, and practice every word, look, nod, grip, motion, and genuflection, until he had reached what he believed to be complete mastery of every detail, and should by such means gain admission to a lodge, would be detected and exposed before he had been there half an hour, and whatever punishment is merited by a sneak and blackguard ought to be administered to him on the spot. And this leads me to say, in conclusion, that Morgan and his codajutor in the publication of his revelations were not men of high tone and standing in the community where they lived, and that their pamphlet, published for pecuniary gain, was the work of sneaks and perjurers, who were hardly entitled to sympathy. In saying this it is not meant to excuse Masonic violations of the law, much less to justify Masons in taking human life. But whatever may be individual opinion concerning his fate, it is only just to say that there is no legal proof that William Morgan was put to death by members of the Masonic fraternity.

THE FOX SISTERS AND ROCHESTER KNOCKINGS.

"Knock, knock, knock: Who's there?
i' the name of Belzebub?"

"The earth hath bubbles,as the water has,
And these are of them."
—MACBETH.

A NUMBER of new faiths, beliefs, religious, or discoveries relating to the spiritual world have found in the Genesee Country a home and origin, if not a permanent abiding place. It was here that Jemima Wilkinson planted her colony of followers, believing herself and them to be so far removed from prying neighbors and from the temptations abounding in the haunts of men that they could never again be surrounded by them — an error in itself sufficient to throw discredit upon the assumption that her nature was spiritual and the future to her an open book.

Here, too, Joseph Smith, junior, found, or pretended to have found, the golden plates, with the wonderful hieroglyphics engraved thereon, from which was translated the Mormon Bible. Joseph seems to have been the corollary of Jemima — the inference derived from a preceding proposition. He lived for fifteen years within a score of miles from her settlement, which was well known to all the country around, — saw her surrounded with all the comforts of life, and as many of its luxuries as were current at that period; the mistress of thousands of broad acres, with houses, barns, horses, carriages, purple and fine linen — all without labor, money, or price — the free gifts of her devoted adherents ;— is it any wnoder, then, seeing all this, that Joseph, who from his youth up had been miserably poor and constitutionally averse to work, should have concluded that the business of founding a new faith was rather a good one (for the founder) and one in which he would at once engage? He had the requisite capital — low cunning and an adamantine front. He saw clearly the weak point in Jemima's creed — her prohibition of marriage — and went rather to the other extreme, for what is the good of a religion without followers? And here, too, the youthful daughters of a country blacksmith originated modern spiritualism.

The humble abode in which a faith numbering more than two million adherents had its birth is located on the farm of Artemas W. Hyde, Esquire, about two and a half miles in a northeasterly direction from the village of Newark in the County of Wayne. Intended for the occupancy of a mechanic or farm laborer, it was never a structure of much pretension, and the wear and tear of nearly three-quarters of a century has added nothing to its appearance. A renewal of the siding some years ago and a coat of pea-green paint have given it rather a smart exterior, but inside it is low-studded, shabby, and tumble-down. There are three rooms on the ground floor, but if there are any above they must be directly under the ridge-pole, as the house is but one story in height.

The faith, belief, doctrine, or whatever other name may be given to the discovery of these young ladies, is too nearly contemporaneous to have a prominent place in pioneer history; and as it has been absolutely repudiated by them, and the means by which the so-called spiritual manifestations were produced fully and publicly exposed, I shall attempt only an outline of its origin and early progress.

In December, 1847, the family of Mr. John D. Fox moved from Rochester into the little tenement which has been described. It consisted at the time of the father, mother, and two daughters named Margaretta and Catharine, aged respectively about fifteen and twelve years. An elder sister, Ann, was the wife of Mr. Fish of Rochester, and a son David lived on a farm near the house in which the spirits first manifested themselves in an auricular way. The family of Mr. Fox moved into Mr. Hyde's tenement, as has been stated, in December, 1847, and, at Mr. Hyde's earnest request, moved out in May, 1848, returning whence they came; therefore the thumping, by means of which communication between the spiritual and material worlds was carried on, got the name of " Rochester Knockings." These knockings were first heard one evening in the latter part of March, 1848. After the Fox family had retired for the night, but before all were asleep, a noise which appeared to proceed from the bedroom in which the young ladies slept, and which sounded as though some one was knocking lightly on the floor, was heard. The entire household got up and searched the premises thoroughly, but could discover no cause for the sounds. It was said that a perceptible jar was felt by placing the hands on bedposts and chairs and also while standing on the floor. Nothing strange, so far as the jarring is concerned. The old house was so shaky that the movement of a child across the floor would cause it, and everything standing on it, to vibrate. The sounds were continued as long as anyone was awake, or, rather, as long as the young ladies were awake, for, by their own confession and public demonstration, it has been shown that they produced the raps that were supposed to emanate from the spirit world. Next evening the noises were heard again, and on the following night the neighbors were called in. On the last evening of March, 1848, after Mr. Hyde had retired for the night, a hurried rap on his door summoned him from his slumbers. A neighbor, so much excited as to be hardly intelligible, informed him that a murder had been committed in the little tenement of which he was the owner, and that his immediate presence there was desired. On the way over, Mr. Hyde, much to his relief, learned that the homicide was not a recent one, but had been committed some years before, and that spirits were revealing it by means of raps which could be heard distinctly. Being a level-headed, shrewd, well-educated, and wealthy man, he at once concluded that his neighbor had been sent on a fool's errand, and has never changed his mind. He has often said that if he had next day built a high fence around his tenant house and charged one dollar admission to the premises he would probably have strangled modern spiritualism in its cradle.

The country for miles around was in a state of feverish excitement over the supernatural revelations. The story that a murder had been committed flew on the wings of the wind and gathered detail on its way. People were all the more ready to believe it, because the ghostly victim revealed from the spirit world the

"Deep damnation of his taking off."

Evidence that in the court of a country justice would not have been sufficient to convict an American citizen of African descent of stealing a pullet was thought by an excited populace to be strong as proofs from Holy Writ that some one had done foul murder. The residents of the neighboring villages of Newark, Palmyra, and Lyons swarmed upon Mr. Hyde's premises. The

rural population of two counties hitched their horses along his
fences on each Sabbath day, and listened with open-mouthed wonder to the revelations said to have been made by the spirit of the
victim.   He was a peddler.   His name, age, and birthplace were
learned by means of raps, as will be hereafter explained.   In the
same way it was ascertained that he had been married, was the
father of five children and had been murdered by a former resident of the house and his body buried in the cellar.   Excavations were at once begun, the volunteer grave-diggers little
doubting that the gashed and gory body of the peddler would
soon be unearthed.   It is needless to say that no sign or trace of
a dead body was found, and the ghastly farce of looking for one
was soon discontinued.   When it became evident that no remains
were buried in the cellar, the spirits changed their tale and said
the bones of the defunct had been exhumed by the murderer,
placed in a piece of old stove pipe and thrown into Mud Creek,
a deep and sluggish stream not far from the house; but a thorough raking of the creek failed to bring them to light.   At this
day the only mystery about the whole business is, how two girls
of twelve and fifteen could at that period of their lives have so
effectually humbugged an intelligent community.   Annoyed and
incommoded by the crowds attracted to his premises, and fully
persuaded of the fraudulent nature of the so-called revelations,
though not able at the time to account for them, Mr. Hyde besought his tenants to find other quarters, and they accordingly
returned to Rochester.   As it is not my intention to trace the
faith which the Fox young ladies founded beyond the little village of Hydesville, we will go back and note its progress up to
the time they left the premises where it originated.   It is not
believed by those acquainted with Mr. and Mrs. Fox that they
had part or lot in originating the rappings, or knew until some
time afterward that their daughters had the power of producing
them.   He had passed middle life, was a blacksmith by trade, and
bore the reputation of being an honest, industrious mechanic.
His wife, a woman of ordinary intelligence and blameless life,
had never been noted for mental vagaries of any sort.   If the
daughters were prompted at all it must have been by their elder
sister, Mrs. Fish, but evidence of her complicity during the residence of the family in Hydesville is wholly wanting.   The following statement by Mrs. Fox was made soon after the rappings
were first heard, and seems ingenuous enough.   She says, in part:

" On Friday night, we concluded to go to bed early and not let it disturb us; if it came, we thought we would not mind it, but try and get a good night's rest. My husband was here on all these occasions, heard the noise, and helped search. It was very early when we went to bed on this night; hardly dark. We went to bed so early, because we had been broken so much of our rest that I was almost sick.

" My husband had not gone to bed when we first heard the noise on this evening. I had just laid down. It commenced as usual. I knew it from all other noises I had ever heard in the house. The girls, who slept in the other bed in the room, heard the noise, and tried to make a similar noise by snapping their fingers. The youngest girl is about twelve years old; she is the one who made her hand go. As fast as she made the noise with her hands or fingers, the sound was followed up in the room. It did not sound any different at that time, only it made the same number of noises that the girl did. When she stopped, the sound itself stopped for a short time.

" The other girl who is in her fifteenth year, then spoke in sport, and said, ' Now, do just as I do. Count one, two, three four,' etc., striking one hand in the other at the same time. The blows which she made were repeated as before. It appeared to answer her by repeating every blow that she made. She only did so once. She then began to be startled and then I spoke and said to the noise, ' Count ten,' and it made ten strokes or noises. Then I asked the ages of my different children successively, and it gave a number of raps, corresponding to the ages of my children.

" I then asked if it was a human being that was making the noise; and if it was, to manifest it by the same noise. There was no noise. I then asked if it was a spirit; and if it was, to manifest it by two sounds; I heard two sounds as soon as the words were spoken. I then asked, if it was an injured spirit, to give me the sound, and I heard the rapping distinctly. I then asked if it was injured in this house; and it manifested it by the noise. If the person was living that injured it; and got the same answer. I then ascertained by the same method that its remains were buried under the dwelling, and how old it was. When I asked how many years old it was; it rapped thirty-one times; that it was a male; that it had left a family of five children; that it had two sons and three daughters, all living. I

asked if it left a wife; and it rapped. If its wife was then living; no rapping. If she was dead; and the rapping was distinctly heard. How long it had been dead; and it rapped twice."

Mrs. Fox asked if the noises would continue if she called in
the neighbors that they might hear it. There was rapping the
same as when it was supposed affirmative answers were given.
Mrs. Redfield, the nearest neighbor, was first called. The children had informed her previously, that strange noises were heard
in the house, and she went, thinking to have some sport with the
family. She found the girls very much agitated. Mrs. Fox
said, "Mrs. Redfield, what shall we do? We have heard the
noise for some time, and now it answers all our questions, and we
cannot account for it."

Mrs. R. heard the sounds, and commenced asking questions,
which were answered correctly, greatly to her astonishment.
She says the girls continued to be much frightened, and she told
them not to be afraid; if it was a revelation from the spirit
world, it was not to injure them. One of the girls said with
much feeling, — "We are innocent; how good it is to have a
clear conscience!"

Messrs. Redfield, Duesler, Hyde, Jewell, and their wives were
subsequently called during the same evening. They asked many
questions, and received answers. Questions relating to the age,
number of children, etc., of the persons present, are said to
have been answered correctly. Mr. Fox and Mr. Redfield remained in the house during the night. Mrs. Fox and her daughters spent the night at the house of one of the neighbors.

The following is a portion of a statement made by a neighbor who attempted, without success, to unravel the mysteries of
the Fox dwelling, and unearth the murdered peddler:

"I went over again on Sunday, between one and two o'clock,
P. M. I went into the cellar with several others, and had them
all leave the house over our heads; and then I asked, if there
had been a man buried in that cellar, to manifest it by rapping
or any other noise or sign. The moment I asked the question,
there was a sound like the falling of a stick, about a foot long
and half an inch through, on the floor in the bedroom over our
heads. It did not seem to bound at all; there was but one sound.
I then told Stephen Smith to go right up and examine the room,
and see if he could discover the cause of the noise. He came

back and said he could discover nothing, — that there was no one in the room, or in that part of the house. I then asked two more questions, and it rapped in the usual way. We all then went upstairs, and made a thorough search around the rooms, but could find nothing.

"I then got a knife and fork and tried to see if I could make the same noise by dropping them, but I could not. This was all I heard on Sunday. There is only one floor, or partition, or thickness between the bedroom and cellar — no place where anything could be secreted to make the noise. When the noise was heard in the bedroom, I could feel a slight tremulous motion or jar.

"There was some digging in the cellar on Saturday night. They dug until they came to water, and then gave it up. The question had been previously asked, whether it was right that they should dig on that night; and there was no rapping. Then whether it was wrong; and the rapping was heard. Whether they should dig on Sunday; no rapping. On Monday; and the rapping commenced again. However, some insisted on digging at this time, and dug accordingly, but with no success.

"On Monday night heard this noise again, and asked the same questions I did before, and got the same answers. This is the last time I have heard the rapping. I can in no way account for this singular noise, which I and others have heard. It is a mystery to me, which I am wholly unable to solve. I am willing to testify under oath that I did not make the noises or rapping which I and others heard; that I do not know of any person who did or could have made them; that I have spent considerable time since then, in order to satisfy myself as to the cause of it, but cannot account for it on any other ground than that it is supernatural. I lived in the same house about seven years ago, and at that time never heard any noises of the kind in and about the premises. * * *

"I never believed in haunted houses, or heard or saw anything but what I could account for before; but this I cannot account for.

　　　　　"(Signed)　　　　　　　　　Wm. Duesler.
"April 12, 1848."

Before the removal of the family to Rochester, Mrs. Fox and her daughters, including Mrs. Fish, had established a code of

signals with the spirits.   One rap meant no; two, yes; three or
four, undecided; and five in quick succession, that the question
could not be answered by yes or no, but recourse must be had to
the alphabet.   The manner in which the letters were used may
be learned from the following brief statement signed by several
members of the family:

" During the first inquiries to learn the name of the person
who was represented as the injured spirit, it was asked if it would
rap at the initials of his name.   It rapped in the affirmative,
and on calling over the letters, it rapped at the letters C, R; and
at a subsequent period, David Fox, one of the family, spent
several hours in communication with it, and learned the whole
name; and afterwards Mrs. A. S. Fish learned that five succes-
sive raps were an indication, or signal, to repeat the alphabet,
when questions were asked, to which a simple negative or affirmative would not be a correct reply without qualification.

" It is thus that directions are now given in answer to questions; and often it voluntarily calls by the signal for the
alphabet, and communicates entire sentences, many of them interesting, and of considerable length.

" Mrs. Ann L. Fish,
" Mrs. Margaret Fox,
" C. R. Brown,
" David S. Fox.

" Rochester, March 6, 1850."

As will be seen by the statements, the family had for some
time been residents of Rochester.   The young ladies had upon
their arrival in that city been taken in charge by their eldest
sister, Mrs. Fish, under whose chaperonage spiritual " seances "
began, and were continued until more ambitious aspirants for
spiritual honors outbid the original mediums and supplanted
them in popular favor.   The Fox sisters stopped at rapping
and table tipping, the public appetite for which was soon ap-
peased.   Then came LaRoy Sunderland, the Eddy Brothers,
Foster, Hume, Cora Hatch, the Davenport Brothers, and last,
but by no means least, Madam Dis Debar.   Scattered amongst
these greater lights was a crowd of mediums and clairvoyants
who exhibited for a consideration their powers in dingy and
awe-inspiring apartments in all the great cities of the country.

The spirits no longer deigned to communicate by means of vulgar thumps, but betook themselves to a very legible kind of writing, to painting works of art, to interpreting the thoughts of their patrons, to viva voce colloquies, in which the tone of voice and manner of speaking were a curious and sometimes rather startling imitation of the original when on earth. No one well acquainted with the late Mr. Lawrence Jerome ever thought him a man who could be easily awed or humbugged, but after a spiritual interview with his old friend Richard Schell he said to me, " It was Uncle Dick's voice exactly and had his peculiarities of pronunciation and expression. If you don't want to believe in this thing, don't go near it."

In Professor Sinnett's work on Esoteric Buddhism an attempt is made to explain the phenomena which puzzled Mr. Jerome: Premising that the Professor is a believer in all sorts of occult manifestations, including spiritual mediumship, I quote: " It is possible, however, for yet living persons to have visions of Devachan,* though such visions are rare, and only one-sided, the entities in Devachan sighted by the earthly clairvoyant being quite unconscious themselves of undergoing such observation. The spirit of the clairvoyant ascends into the condition of Devachan in such rare visions, and thus becomes subject to the vivid delusions of that existence. It is under the impression that the spirits, with which it is in Devachan bonds of sympathy, have come down to visit earth and itself, while the converse operation has really taken place. The clairvoyant's spirit has been raised toward those in Devachan. Thus many of the subjective spiritual communications — most of them when the sensitives are pure minded — are real, though it is most difficult for the uninitiated medium to fix in his mind the true and correct pictures of what he sees and hears. In the same way some of the phenomena called psychography — though more rarely — are also real. The spirit of the sensitive, getting odylized, so to say, by the aura of the spirit in the Devachan, becomes for a few minutes that departed personality, and writes in the handwriting of the latter, in his language and in his thoughts, as they were during his lifetime. The two spirits become blended in one, and the preponderance of one over the other during such phenomena determines the preponderance of personality in the characteristics exhibited. Thus, it may be incidentally observed,

---

* He defines Devachan as a " state or condition — not a locality."

what is called rapport, is, in plain fact, an identity of molecular vibration between the astral part of the incarnate medium and the astral part of the disincarnate personality."
There is much more of the same sort, though by no means so clear as what has been quoted.

> "He who understands it would be able
> To add a story to the Tower of Babel."

One of the first attempts by scientific men to account for the rappings was made during a visit of the Fox sisters to Buffalo by Doctors Austin Flint, Charles A. Lee, and C. B. Coventry of the University of that city. These gentlemen being, of course, aware of the fact well known to all surgeons, that dislocated bones return to their place with an audible snap, conducted their investigations with a view to ascertaining whether the sisters produced the sounds heard, by means of their toe, ankle, or knee joints, and became thoroughly convinced that they did so. The result of a number of examinations of Mrs. Fish and her sister Margaretta, was published in the *Buffalo Medical Journal*, March, 1851. In it the professional gentlemen before named say : " Having traced the knockings to their source, explained the mechanism of their production, and thus divested them of their supernatural character, and of all mystery, we turn to another aspect presented by the field of inquiry," et cetera. The exposures made by the Fox sisters at the Academy of Music in New York, in 1888, fully demonstrated that Messrs. Flint, Lee, and Coventry made a correct diagnosis thirty-seven years before. In a personal letter to the *New York Tribune*, dated February 28, 1851, Doctor Charles A. Lee, one of the three medical gentlemen named, gives a full account of a private " seance " with Mrs. Fish and Miss Fox, at which a few friends of both parties were present, the object of which was to show on the part of the ladies that they had no agency in producing the raps, and on the part of the doctor that they had. The result showed most conclusively that when proper precautions were taken to prevent the ladies from snapping their joints, no sounds were heard, thereby establishing the fact that the rappings were physical and not spiritual. Unrestrained, the ladies produced the sounds at will. A writer in the *New York Express*, over the signature of Shadrack Barnes, exposed the science of toeology, and in private seances demonstrated his ability to rap loudly, and though all were looking at his feet no motion of them could be discovered.

But this did not stop the progress of the Fox girls. They visited nearly every large town and city in the Union, holding crowded seances at one dollar per head admission, and had they not been superseded by more inventive and expert performers would doubtless have amassed considerable money. Exposure, however, went hand in hand with the new schemes brought forward to astonish and awe the credulous, and draw money from the curious. Examination showed the Eddy Brothers to be impostors, whose house in Vermont was strung with wires by means of which their wonders were performed. These wires were concealed between the sheathing and plastering. Any of the skillful prestidigitators now before the public can outdo the Davenport Brothers at their own mysterious cabinet trick, and can produce spiritual writing or painting equal to that of Foster or Madam Dis Debar.

Although an inscription over the door of the little house in Wayne County states that spiritualism originated there, the announcement is hardly correct. The idea of spiritualistic communication is not modern. Swift satirized it nearly two centuries ago. In his voyage to Glubbdubdrib, that veracious traveler, Lemuel Gulliver, tells us that he found the island inhabited by spirits — its name signifying the land of sorcerers and magicians. He says: " I soon grew so familiarized to the sight of spirits that after the third or fourth time they gave me no emotion at all, or, if I had any apprehensions left, my curiosity prevailed over them. For his Highness the Governor ordered me to call up (were they all below?) whatever persons I would choose to name from the beginning of the world up to the present time, and command them to answer any questions I should think fit to ask. I accordingly demanded Alexander the Great, who assured me that he was not poisoned, but died of a bad fever by excessive drinking. I next called up Hannibal who told me he had never a drop of vinegar in his camp. Cæsar, Brutus, and Pompey were next brought forward. I found the first two in very good accord; Cæsar freely confessing that the greatest actions of his life were not equal by many degrees to the glory of taking it away." Socrates, Epaminondas, Cato, Homer, and Aristotle were successively interviewed, and furnished shafts for some of Swift's keenest satire. He traced the ancestry of

great families, showing their mental, moral, and physical de-
terioration, and says: " Neither could I wonder at all this,
when I saw such an interruption of lineages by pages, lackeys,
coachmen, valets, gamesters, players, captains, and pickpockets."
Thus it will be seen that the idea of communication with those
who have gone before is not new.   It existed in Swift's mind,
and has never had any other existence with him or his successors.
But while with Swift it was a figment of imagination and a vehicle
for satire, it has appealed to many acute intellects with all the
power of faith supported by the sanctions of reason.   Men of
cultivated minds and strong will power have in all ages been
carried away by spiritualism or its equivalent under some other
designation.   Keen intellects are quite as ready as dull ones to
attribute to supernatural agencies those things which they are
unable to comprehend, and men whose incredulity in regard to
matters of fact outside of their observation and experience
amounts almost to a disease are ready enough to believe in spirits,
ghosts, vampires, and other " insubstantial pageants."   Doctor
Samuel Johnson may be quoted as a conspicuous example of this
class.   He knew very little of the world outside of London, and
beyond the circle of his daily ramble from the Rainbow Tavern,
Fleet Street, to Charing Cross, he knew very little of that.
Macaulay says that " he talked of remote countries and past
times with wild and ignorant presumption, and could discern
clearly enough the folly and meanness of all bigotry except his own."   And, having seen nothing of mankind and of
the world, he believed nothing he had not seen.   He browbeat
into silence a gentleman who was giving a truthful account of
hurricanes in the West Indies, and almost gave the lie direct to
a modest Quaker who told him that red-hot balls were fired at the
siege of Gibraltar.   " Never tell that story again," said the
bumptious old Doctor, " you cannot think how poor a figure you
make, relating anything so improbable."   Yet he believed in
ghosts — if located in London — and went to hunt one in Cock
Lane.   One whole compartment of Sir Walter Scott's library
at Abbotsford was full of volumes having reference to the ghosts,
spirits, witches, and other supernatural agencies with which his
poetry and romance abound.   And if these distinguished men
had lived in Rochester or New York in the middle of the nineteenth century it is highly probable that Judge Edmonds, Louis
Napoleon, Commodore Vanderbilt, and Luther R. Marsh would

not have been most conspicuous among the believers in spiritualism. For there is no doubt that faith in the unseen, unknown, and unknowable is one of the strongest elements of man's nature, whether he be prince or peasant, learned or unlettered; for such faith is the foundation upon which all creeds from Bramah and Buddha to Joanna Southcote and Joe Smith have been built. Men will admit that they may be mistaken regarding occurrences which took place yesterday before their very eyes, but faith implies something beyond the world of fact and demonstration, something that can neither be proved or disproved, and therefore they cling to it with a firmness which the axe and the fagot have no power to shake. The Mormon believes that Joseph Smith had direct revelations from the Most High: It is impossible to prove that he did not. Men of intelligence and cultivated minds bought Joanna's " Seals," believing them to possess a mysterious power for good in the affairs of this life and of the life to come. The Fox sisters claimed communication with the spirit world, and the falsity of this claim was never quite satisfactorily established until they themselves did it. Even their confession has not shaken the faith of one in a hundred of the believers in spiritualism. Although they originated the latter-day manifestations, they are regarded as apostates, whose assertions were good enough to found a faith but are not good enough to overthrow it. And here the question naturally propounds itself: Did the Fox sisters found a faith? Is spiritualism entitled to be called a religious belief? An article in the *Baptist Quarterly* for April, 1888, by the Rev. Stanley McKay, of Canandaigua, giving a sketch of the origin of Mormonism and Spiritualism styles them " Two American Religions." So far as Mormonism is concerned it is doubtless entitled to the appellation. It has a church polity and government, a doctrine and covenants; has built houses and temples of worship, and maintained in them all customary religious forms and observances. Whatever may be its future, it has for nearly sixty years been an aggressive, concentrative, and defiant faith. Spiritualism has accomplished none of these things. It is diffusive, and is scattered over the earth, each one of its adherents a law unto himself or herself. At one period the believers in spiritualism hired a hall and listened on the Sabbath to the mild rhapsodies of Cora Hatch, or the transcendental rubbish of a long-haired advocate of the other sex, but even this is no longer

the vogue. Without local habitation, creed, or doctrine, spiritualism drifts hither and thither upon the shifting waves of speculation, each individual believing and teaching whatever at the
moment is uppermost in his own disordered mind. It has formulated no dogmas, and fulminated no anathemas. It does not
undertake to bind the consciences or direct the footsteps of its
followers. Agnosticism and infidelity are no bar to its fold,
which seems to be the natural refuge of free thinking. The Fox
sisters make a public exposition of the humbug of the knockings
and the world looks on and jeers. But if Joseph Smith, Junior,
were alive to-day, as he might easily be, and should make a clear
exposure of the frauds upon which the Mormon creed is based,
his life would not be worth eight-and-forty hours' purchase.
The Danites, the Destroying Angels, and the Avengers of Blood,
tolerate no apostasy, high or low. Good or bad, the doctrine
taught in the church founded by Smith, and strengthened and
broadened by the power and ability of Brigham Young, may
fairly be called an American religion; but the slack-twisted,
scatter-brained theories of individual spiritualists are entitled
to no such distinction. But by whatever names the two systems
may be known, it is evident that their decay is rapidly progress-
ing, and within a near period they seem destined to a common
oblivion. The gentile rules in Salt Lake City. The head of
the church proclaimed not long ago that there were to be no more
revelations, notwithstanding which a recent interview between
the Most High and Elder Woodruff has resulted in an announcement to the faithful that they must henceforward obey the laws
of the land rather than the laws of the hierarchy. This strangles
the other twin relic — polygamy.

Spiritualism culminated within fifteen years after the Fox
sisters reproduced it. It probably reached its height in the
decade following its new birth. In the period from 1850 to 1860
it had a startling growth. Every neighborhood had its mediums, and half the families in the land essayed table-tipping, if
nothing beyond. In the Kremlin, the Tuilleries, and Bucking-
ham Palace there were believers if not experts. Residents
in the gilded homes of New York, Boston, and Philadelphia, and
in the bark cabins located in the gulches and canyons of Cali-
fornia alike essayed to get a peep behind the veil. Divinity,
law, medicine, and literature furnished recruits — bright and
shining ones — to the spiritualistic ranks. Louis Napoleon and

Mr. Hume were on a most intimate footing. It is hard to decide even now which was the greater juggler.

Perhaps no better illustration of the spread of spiritualism can be given than the following from Hawthorne's Italian Note Book, under date Florence, June 9, 1858. He was visiting the Brownings, and says: "There was no very noteworthy conversation; the most interesting topic being that disagreeable and now wearisome one of spiritual communications, as regards which Mrs. Browning is a believer and her husband an infidel. Browning and his wife had both been present at a spiritual session held by Mr. Hume and had seen and felt the unearthly hands, one of which had placed a laurel wreath on Mrs. Browning's head. Browning, however, avowed his belief that these hands were affixed to the feet of Mr. Hume who lay extended in his chair with his legs stretched far under the table. The marvelousness of the fact melted strangely away in Browning's hearty gripe, and at the sharp touch of his logic; while his wife ever and anon put in a litle word of gentle expostulation." It is easy to pardon in Mrs. Browning the vanity which was ready to defend the hand which had placed a laurel wreath upon her brow.

The sculptor Powers and his wife were firm believers in the marvels of Mr. Hume, although the latter was unquestionably a knave. But he and his ilk are no longer permitted to rob the credulous with impunity as Madam Dis Debar has recently discovered.

The offspring of falsehood and deceit, Mormonism and Spiritualism, were born in the same neighborhood, though a period of twenty years separates their natal days. It is possible that some individual life which antedates theirs will see them pass away as active and aggressive forces, and become a byword and a memory in the land of their origin.

The story of the Cock Lane Ghost bears such a striking resemblance to the early history of spiritualism as herein related, that I give it at length, as told in a work entitled Memoirs of Extraordinary Delusions, by Charles Mackay:

"At the commencement of the year 1760, there resided in Cock Lane, near West Smithfield, in the house of one Parsons, the parish clerk of St. Sepulchre's, a stockbroker, named Kent. The wife of this gentleman had died in childbed during the previous year, and his sister-in-law, Miss Fanny, had arrived from Norfolk to keep his house for him. They soon conceived a mutual affection, and each of them made a will in the other's favor. They lived some months in the house of Parsons, who, being a needy man, borrowed money of his lodger. Some difference arose betwixt them, and Mr. Kent left the house and instituted legal proceedings against the parish clerk for the recovery of his money.

" While this matter was yet pending, Miss Fanny was suddenly taken ill of the smallpox; and, notwithstanding every care and attention, she died in a few days, and was buried in a vault under Clerkenwell church. Parsons now began to hint that the poor lady had come unfairly by her death, and that Mr. Kent was accessory to it, from his too great eagerness to enter into possession of the property she had bequeathed to him. Nothing further was said for nearly two years; but it would appear that Parsons was of so revengeful a character, that he had never forgotten or forgiven his differences with Mr. Kent and the indignity of having been sued for the borrowed money. The strong passions of pride and avarice were silently at work during all that interval, hatching schemes of revenge, but dismissing them one after the other as impracticable, until, at last, a notable one suggested itself. About the beginning of the year 1762, the alarm was spread over all the neighborhood of Cock Lane that the house of Parsons was haunted by the ghost of poor Fanny, and that the daughter of Parsons, a girl about twelve years of age, had several times seen and conversed with the spirit, who had moreover, informed her, that she had not died with the smallpox, as was currently reported, but of poison administered by Mr. Kent. Parsons, who originated, took good care to countenance these reports; and, in answer to numerous inquiries, said his house was every night, and had been for two years, in fact, ever since the death of Fanny, troubled by a loud knocking at the doors and in the walls. Having thus prepared the ignorant and credulous neighbors to believe or exaggerate for themselves what he had told them, he sent for a gentleman in a higher class of life to come and witness these extraordinary occurrences. The gentleman came accordingly, and found the daughter of Parsons, to whom the spirit alone appeared, and whom alone it answered, in bed, trembling violently, having just seen the ghost, and been again informed that she had died from poison. A loud knocking was also heard from every part of the chamber, which so mystified the not very clear understanding of the visitor, that he departed, afraid to doubt and ashamed to believe, but with a promise to bring the clergyman of the parish and several other gentlemen on the following day to report upon the mystery.

" On the following night he returned, bringing with him three clergymen and about twenty other persons, including two negroes, when, upon a consultation with Parsons, they resolved to sit up the whole night and await the ghost's arrival.   It was then explained by Parsons, that although the ghost would never render itself visible to anybody but his daughter, it had no objections to answer the questions that might be put to it by any person present, and that it expressed an affirmation by one knock, a negative by two, and its displeasure by a kind of scratching. The child was then put into bed along with her sister, and the clergymen examined the bed and bedclothes, to satisfy themselves that no trick was played, by knocking upon any substance concealed among the clothes.   As on the previous night, the bed was observed to shake violently.

" After some hours, during which they all waited with exemplary patience, the mysterious knocking was heard in the wall, and the child declared she saw the ghost of poor Fanny. The following questions were then gravely put by the clergymen, through the medium of one Mary Frazer, the servant of Parsons, and to whom it was said the deceased lady had been much attached.   The answers were in the usual fashion, by a knock or knocks: —

" ' Do you make this disturbance on account of the ill usage you received from Mr. Kent? '—'Yes.'

" ' Were you brought to an untimely end by poison? ' ' Yes.'

" ' How was the poison administered, in beer or purl? '— ' In purl.'

" 'How long was that before your death? '— ' About three hours.'

" ' Can your former servant, Carrots, give any informantion about the poison? '—' Yes.'

" ' Are you Kent's wife's sister? ' — 'Yes.'

" ' Were you married to Kent after your sister's death? ' — ' No.'

" ' Was anybody else, besides Kent, concerned in your murder? ' — ' No.'

" ' Can you, if you like, appear visibly to anyone? ' —' Yes.'

" ' Will you do so? ' — ' Yes.'

" ' Can you come out of this house? ' — 'Yes.'

" ' Is it your intention to follow this child about everywhere? ' — ' Yes.'

" Are you pleased in being asked these questions? ' — ' Yes.'

" ' Does it ease your troubled soul? ' — ' Yes.'

[Here there was heard a mysterious noise, which some wise-acre present compared to the fluttering of wings.]

" ' How long before your death did you tell your servant, Carrots, that you was poisoned? — An hour? ' — ' Yes.'

[Carrots, who was present, was appealed to; but she stated positively that such was not the fact, as the deceased was quite speechless an hour before her death. This shook the faith of some of the spectators, but the examination was allowed to continue.]

" ' How long did Carrots live with you? ' — ' Three or four days.'

[Carrots was again appealed to, and said this was the case.]

" ' If Mr. Kent is arrested for this murder, will he confess? ' — ' Yes.'

" ' Would your soul be at rest if he were hanged for it? ' — ' Yes.'

" ' Will he be hanged for it? ' — ' Yes.'

" ' How long a time first? ' — ' Three years.'

" ' How many clergymen are there in this room? ' — ' Three.'

" ' How many negroes? ' — ' Two.'

" ' Is this watch (held up by one of the clergymen) white? ' —' No.'

" ' Is it yellow? ' — ' No.'

" ' Is it blue? ' — ' No.'

" ' Is it black? ' — ' Yes.'

[The watch was in a black shagreen case.]

" ' At what time this morning will you take your departure? '

" The answer to this question was four knocks, very distinctly heard by every person present; and accordingly, at four o'clock precisely, the ghost took its departure to the Wheatsheaf public house, close by, where it frightened mine host and his lady almost out of their wits by knocking in the ceiling right above their bed.

" The rumor of these occurrences very soon spread over London, and every day Cock Lane was rendered impassable by the crowd of people who assembled around the house of the parish clerk, in expectation of either seeing the ghost, or of hearing the mysterious knocks.   It was at last found necessary, so clamorous were they for admission within the haunted precinct, to admit those only who would pay a certain fee, an arrangement which was very convenient to the needy and money-loving Mr. Parsons.   Indeed, things had taken a turn greatly to his satisfaction; he not only had his revenge, but he made a profit out of it.   The ghost, in consequence, played its antics every night, to the great amusement of many hundred people and the great perplexity of a still greater number.

" Unhappily, however, for the parish clerk, the ghost was induced to make some promises which were the means of utterly destroying its reputation.   It promised, in answer to the questions of the Reverend Mr. Aldritch of Clerkenwell, that it would not only follow the little Miss Parsons wherever she went, but would also attend him, or any other gentleman, into the vault under St. John's Church, where the body of the murdered woman was deposited, and would there give notice of its presence by a distinct knock upon the coffin.   As a preliminary, the girl was conveyed to the church, where a large party of ladies and gentlemen, eminent for their acquirements,.their rank, or their wealth, had assembled.   About ten o'clock on the night of the first of February, the girl having been brought from Cock Lane in a coach, was put to bed by several ladies in the house of Mr. Aldritch, a strict examination having been previously made that nothing was hidden in the bedclothes.   While the gentlemen, in an adjoining chamber, were deliberating whether they should proceed in a body to the vault, they were summoned into the bedroom by the ladies, who affirmed, in great alarm that the ghost had come, and that they heard knocks and scratches.   The gentlemen entered accordingly, with a determination to suffer no deception.   The little girl, on being asked whether she saw the ghost, replied, ' No; but she felt it on her back like a mouse.' She was then required to put her hands out of the bed, and they being held by some of the ladies, the spirit was summoned in the usual manner to answer, if it were in the room.   The question was several times put with solemnity; but the customary knock was not heard in reply in the walls, neither was there any scratching. The ghost was then asked to render itself visible, but it did not choose to grant the request. It was next solicited to give some token of any sort, or by touching the hand or cheek of any lady or gentleman in the room; but even with this request the ghost would not comply.

" There was now a considerable pause, and one of the clergymen went down stairs to interrogate the father of the girl, who was waiting the result of the experiment. He positively denied that there was any deception, and even went so far as to say that he himself, upon one occasion, had seen and conversed with the awful ghost. This having been communicated to the company, it was unanimously resolved to give the ghost another trial; and the clergyman called out in a loud voice to the supposed spirit that the gentleman to whom it had promised to appear in the vault was about to repair to that place, where he claimed the fulfillment of its promise. At one hour after midnight they all proceeded to the church, and the gentleman in question, with another entered the vault alone, and took their position alongside of the coffin of poor Fanny. The ghost was then summoned to appear, but it appeared not; it was summoned to knock, but it knocked not; it was summoned to scratch, but it scratched not; and the two retired from the vault, with the firm belief that the whole business was a deception practised by Parsons and his daughter. There were others, however, who did not wish to jump so hastily to a conclusion, and who suggested that they were, perhaps, trifling with this awful and supernatural being, which, being offended with them for their presumption, would not condescend to answer them. Again, after a serious consultation, it was agreed on all hands that, if the ghost answered anybody at all, it would answer Mr. Kent, the supposed murderer; and he was accordingly requested to go into the vault. He went with several others, and summoned the ghost to answer whether he had indeed poisoned her. There being no answer, the question was put by Mr. Aldrich, who conjured it, if it were indeed a spirit, to end their doubts — make a sign of its presence, and point out the guilty persons. There being still no answer for the space of half an hour, during which time all these boobies waited with the most praiseworthy perseverance, they returned to the house of Mr. Aldritch, and ordered the girl to get up and dress herself. She was strictly examined, but persisted in her statement that she used no deception, and that the ghost had really appeared to her.

" So many persons had, by their openly expressed belief of the reality of the visitation, identified themselves with it, that Parsons and his family were far from being the only persons interested in the continuance of the delusion. The result of the experiment convinced most people; but these were not to be convinced by any evidence, however positive, and they, therefore, spread abroad the rumor, that the ghost had not appeared in the vault because Mr. Kent had taken care beforehand to have the coffin removed. That gentleman, whose position was a very painful one, immediately procured competent witnesses, in whose presence the vault was entered and the coffin of poor Fanny opened. Their deposition was then published; and Mr. Kent indicted Parsons and his wife, his daughter, Mary Frazer the servant, the Reverend Mr. Moor, and a tradesman, two of the most prominent patrons of the deception, for a conspiracy. The trial came on in the court of King's Bench, on the 10th of July, before Lord Chief Justice Mansfield, when, after an investigation which lasted twelve hours, the whole of the conspirators were found guilty. The Rev. Mr. Moor and his friend were severely reprimanded in open court, and recommended to make some pecuniary compensation to the prosecutor for the aspersions they had been instrumental in throwing upon his character. Parsons was sentenced to stand three times in the pillory, and to be imprisoned for two years; his wife to one year's and his servant to six months' imprisonment in the Bridewell. A printer, who had been employed by them to publish an account of the proceedings for their profit, was also fined fifty pounds, and discharged."

If John Bell, the honest and inoffensive occupant of the little house in Hydesville at the time the peddler was said to have been murdered, had taken measures in imitation of the London stockbroker, and appealed to our courts against the conspirators who were trying to fasten upon him the commission of a capital crime, a result might have been reached which would have stamped out spirit-rapping as effectually as the decision of Lord Mansfield did in 1760.

The last appearance of the Fox sisters was upon a different stage and with surroundings very different from those that witnessed their debut. The tumble-down tenement in Wayne County is exchanged for the crowded and brilliantly-lighted Academy of Music in New York. The girls of twelve and fifteen have become middle-aged ladies. Margaretta — Mrs.

Kane — is upon the stage. Her sister Catherine — Mrs. Jenkins — looks on approvingly from a stage box. A *Tribune* reporter shall tell the rest of the story.

SPIRIT MEDIUMS OUTDONE.

LIVELY RAPPINGS IN THE ACADEMY OF MUSIC.

DR. RICHMOND AND ONE OF THE FOX SISTERS GIVE EXHIBITIONS OF THEIR SKILL BEFORE A REMARK-ABLY RESPONSIVE CROWD — SPIRITUALISM FORMALLY RENOUNCED.

Dr. Cassius M. Richmond has been for some time advertising the death of spiritualism, coupled with the announcement on posters, appropriately bordered in deep black, that he is the new Jack-the-Giant-Killer who will slay it.   He gave it a hard knock in the Academy of Music last night, where an immense audience assembled, most of the people in it. to encourage him, others to hinder him, others to make nuisances of themselves. It was in many respects a rare and remarkable gathering.   One could easily pick out in the crowded seats professional men of all sorts — ministers, physicians, and lawyers, scholarly men and women, men of repute in legitimate scientific research, others notorious in the walks of humbug, women well known by the frequenters of materialization " seances," the distinguished " cranks " who adorn every such occasion, and Sunday-night idlers who came from the same motive from which Artemus Ward's " Uncle Simon, he clum up a tree," namely, to see what they could see.

Well, they got their money's worth in fun as well as in in-struction, for Dr. Richmond's genial, off-hand manner, entirely unpractised, as he never faced such an audience before, soon resolved the meeting into a big, free-and-easy party, where any-body who felt that way could help out the lecturer.   The enter-tainment was a success.   That was to be expected, because Dr. Richmond is not only an exceptionally expert " conjurer," but he had in reserve two of the women whose names were for years sacred to the Spiritualists, Margaret and Katy Fox, now Mrs. Kane and Mrs. Jenkins, who added the new superstition of " spirit rapping " to the terrors of mysticism many years ago.

SPIRITS WROTE HIS INTRODUCTION

Dr. Richmond did not deliver any " set " lecture. He said he had forgotten his manuscript, a failing of his memory that was applauded. But he got the " spirits " to write an introduction for him on an apparently clean slate. When it appeared it read: " Ladies and gentlemen, I am not going to add to the brilliant arguments pro and con that have been crowded in on the subject of spiritualism. I am here simply to use my best efforts to dispel, if possible, the greatest delusion and the most gigantic fraud of the nineteenth century. I am on trial — you are judge and jury. If I do not illustrate what I advocate, condemn me. If I do, to your satisfaction, give me your approbation and support."

A man in the corner of the orchestra, with a pallid face adorned by a deep-black mustache and imperial, got up and asked with a scornful German accent: " Vat has dot got to do mit spiritualism? "

" Put him out! " cried a unanimous gallery.

" No, sir! " yelled the excited Spiritualist, " I'll talk against you and the Fox sisters, too! "   (Cheers and jeers.)

" Now, by your talk you have washed the slate again," said Dr. Richmond quietly, and sure enough the writing had vanished as mysteriously as it came.

Then the Doctor got together a committee of fifteen and proceeded to perform a number of exceedingly pretty tricks.   The audience felt a little bit " out of it " because Dr. Richmond has not yet learned Herrmann's knack of allowing the house to see everything that is going on as well as the committee sees it.   But nearly everybody was patient and good natured, and the fifteen gentlemen grouped on the stage in attitudes painfully suggestive of a mob of citizens at rehearsal, got lots of encouragement, such as: " Move up, supers! " " Break away, there! " " Play ball! "

A MESSAGE FROM A DEAD EMPEROR

Dr. Richmond allowed the committee to choose the name of a dead person. This was written on a slip of paper while the Doctor was off the stage. He returned with a table and a brass rod, and with the aid of these implements and a little brass box ascertained from the " spirits " that the name of the Emperor

Frederick William had been chosen, and got a beautiful slate message from his dead majesty.

Next Dr. Richmond read the number of a bank note held by one of the committee. They drew lots to determine who should do the experiment, using a hatful of papers, all marked but one.

" Fellow that draws the blank paper stuck for the drinks, eh?" asked a wag in the gallery.

The nervous looking young man who drew the blank remained on the stage with the " professor." His companions retired and left him blooming alone. He chose a note. Dr. Richmond scanned his face and wrote on a blackboard, 3,848,355.

" That's not the number of the note," said the young man.

" Oh! The first 3 should be B."

" Right! "

Applause greeted this feat, and it was redoubled when the demonstrator successfully " mind-read " the denomination of it — $5.

The Dis Debar writing-pad trick and spirit-picture trick were reproduced with equal success. Dr. Richmond said that a friend of his in Philadelphia would give $5,000 to any medium who would induce the spirits, in a fair and open way, and in a manner genuine beyond a doubt, to manifest their presence by even a scratch an inch long on a slate.

Then he introduced Margaret Fox Kane, a little, compact woman, dark eyed, and dark haired, and dressed in black, and using eyeglasses with black cord and heavy black rims. Her sister Katy sat in a stage box and was a silent, attentive, and assenting witness of what Margaret said and did.

Mrs. Kane was highly excited, and spoke in a tragic way that made some ill-mannered wit address her as " Jimmy Owen O'Conor," which somewhat detracted from the effect of her solemn public renunciation of spiritualism, declaration of its falsehood, and resolution to tell " the truth, the whole truth, and nothing but the truth, so help me God." This declaration was carefully written out, and Mrs. Kane delivered it in a fragmentary and mirth-provoking style, scanning a sentence by the aid of her eyeglasses, then turning to the audience and slowly repeating it.

SHE DID THE RAPPING WITH HER BIG TOE

After that she sat on a chair, with her feet on a sounding-board, so that the raps might be distinctly heard, and Dr. Richmond explained that the lady did the knocking with her big toe. A committee of physicians, among whom was Dr. Dinsmore, examined her feet, amid titters and blushes in the orchestra and irreverent remarks from the gallery. She had slipped off a shoe to facilitate this scientific investigation, and putting the stockinged foot on the board, the audience heard a series of raps, " rat-tat-tat-tat-tat," increasing in sound from faint to loud, and apparently traveling up the wall and along the roof of the Academy. Then she got down to the orchestra floor and repeated the experiment successfully there. Going back on the stage, she stood upright on the board, adjured the " kind, dear spirits," and there was a rain or rather a hailstorm of responsive knocks.

Of course there was a punster around to suggest that spiritualism " isn't worth a rap any longer." The exposure was certainly thorough and successful, and Dr. Richmond received the congratulations of all his friends on the successful initiation of his anti-humbug crusade. He promised to give a materialization " seance " in the Academy of Music by-and-by, and said it would be so effective and realistic that no medium could excel it.

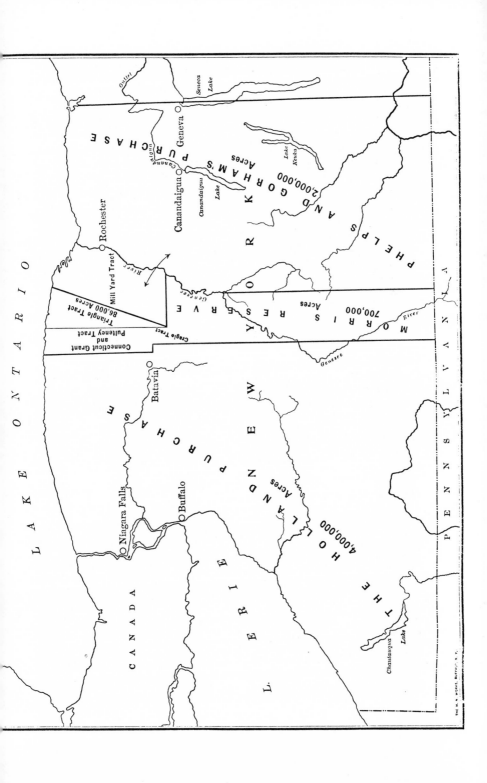